# Concise
# Encyclopedia
# of Information
# Technology

# Concise Encyclopedia of Information Technology

ADRIAN V. STOKES

A SPECTRUM BOOK

Prentice-Hall, Inc., Englewood Cliffs, New Jersey 07632

*Library of Congress Cataloging in Publication Data*

Stokes, Adrian V.
    Concise encyclopedia of information technology.

    British ed. published under title: Concise encyclo-
paedia of information technology. c1982.
    "A Spectrum Book."
    1. Electronic data processing—Dictionaries.
I. Title.
QA76.15.S86  1983        001.64'03'21        82-24115
ISBN 0-13-167213-4
ISBN 0-13-167205-3 (pbk.)

Originally published as *Concise Encyclopaedia of Information Technology*
by Gower Publishing Company Limited, Aldershot, Hants GU11 3HR, England.
© Adrian V. Stokes, 1982.

ISBN 0-13-167213-4

ISBN 0-13-167205-3 {PBK.}

Cover design © 1983 by Jeannette Jacobs
Manufacturing buyer: Pat Mahoney

Prentice-Hall International, Inc., *London*
Prentice-Hall of Australia Pty. Limited, *Sydney*
Prentice-Hall Canada Inc., *Toronto*
Prentice-Hall of India Private Limited, *New Delhi*
Prentice-Hall of Japan, Inc., *Tokyo*
Prentice-Hall of Southeast Asia Pte. Ltd., *Singapore*
Whitehall Books Limited, *Wellington, New Zealand*
Editora Prentice-Hall do Brasil Ltda., *Rio de Janeiro*

# Contents

Introduction     vii

Main Section     1

Appendix A: Acronyms and Abbreviations     253

Appendix B: ASCII Character Set     269

Appendix C: EBCDIC Character Set     271

# Introduction

The term "information technology" is perhaps not too clearly understood and there have been various attempts to define what it means, the most definitive being the UNESCO one.

> The scientific, technological, and engineering disciplines and the management techniques used in information handling and processing; their applications; computers and their interaction with men and machines; and associated social, economic, and cultural matters.

It is difficult to define what "information technology" is accurately. It is even more difficult to understand all the terms used in connection with information technology, especially since so many new ones are being coined. Dictionaries of computer science are often of little use since they may be out of date but, more important, they tend to concentrate on the formal terminology of computer science. While it is important to know what an AVL tree is, it is perhaps more important to understand what is meant by such esoteric terminology as "after the glitch in processing today, we zapped in a patch to cure the bug."

This book is intended to achieve both aims, concisely. It defines a large number of computer terms, both formal and informal, while, at the same time, giving lengthier descriptions of a number of terms of particular importance. It has a number of emphases: first, to define all the important terms used in information technology; secondly, to define all terms used in as concise and meaningful a way as possible; third, in some cases where it is not possible to give a very full description, to give references to other literature where more information can be obtained. Finally, the book has been designed to be as easy to use as possible. For example, each term is defined as briefly as possible and then, if necessary, a more detailed explanation is given. In order to make each definition self-contained, it is sometimes necessary to duplicate definitions but this has been reduced as much as possible. Where one definition refers to another, if this is not obvious, the term referenced is printed in italics. In addition, since there is often confusion about the order in reference books, any terms that include special characters such as "/" are listed as if they were spelled without that character (thus "I/O" is listed as if it were "IO").

This book is intended to be a useful reference book for anyone with an interest in information technology.

# Concise
# Encyclopedia
# of Information
# Technology

# A

**ABACUS:** A mechanical device for performing arithmetic calculations. It operates by sliding beads on parallel wires and the beads are arranged either in groups of ten or five and two. High speeds can be achieved by an expert. The origins of the abacus are in Mesopotamia in about 3000 BC but it is now more often associated with China.

**ABEND:** An acronym for *ABnormal END*. That is, termination of a job following detection of an error.

**ABL:** An acronym for *Atlas Basic Language*, an assembler language (with no operation code mnemonics) on the Atlas computer.

**ABORT:** To terminate prematurely execution of a job (or operation of system) following an error indication. Often in interactive computer systems, the typing of a single character (frequently control-C) allows the user to abort a job.

**ABSCISSA:** The x-axis (horizontal) of a graph. The y-axis is known as the *ordinate*.

**ABSOLUTE ADDRESS:** The actual location in (main) storage of a particular item of data. Also known as *machine address*.

**ABSOLUTE ADDRESSING:** A method of addressing locations in (main) storage using absolute addresses.

**ABSOLUTE ASSEMBLER:** An assembler which produces object programs in which all addresses are absolute addresses and which hence cannot be relocated.

**ABSOLUTE CODE:** Programs written using absolute addresses and absolute operation codes so that they may be entered into a computer memory and executed with no further processing required.

**ABSOLUTE CODING:** Programming using *absolute code*.

**ABSOLUTE ERROR:** The magnitude of an error taking no account of the sign.

**ABSOLUTE OPERATION CODE:** The numeric value of an operation code. Used in *absolute code*.

**ABSOLUTE VALUE:** The value of some number without any regard for its sign.

**AC:** An abbreviation for *accumulator*.

**ACC:** Another abbreviation for *accumulator*.

**ACCEPTANCE TEST:** A test (or set of tests) used to check that a system conforms according to agreed specifications.

**ACCESS (vb):** To obtain data from or place data in storage. The storage may be main or peripheral. The data may, in fact, be an instruction (in which case, it is usually stored in main memory). In this case, the word "access" usually implies executing the instruction as well as retrieving it.

**ACCESS METHOD:** Used to indicate the method of accessing data on backing storage, for example, QSAM — Queued Sequential Access Method.

**ACCESS TIME:** The time between the issuing of a read command and the obtaining of the data to which the command related. It usually refers to the time taken to read data from a peripheral device into main memory.

**ACCUMULATOR:** Part of the arithmetic unit of a computer in which (partial) results are formed (or accumulated). It is nearly always a register and is often referred to implicitly in instructions although, in computers with more than one register, one is often designated the accumulator by convention.

**ACCURACY:** A measure of the exactness of an approximation to the real value. It is often confused with *precision*.

**ACE:** An acronym for *Automatic Computing Engine*, one of the earliest computers. It successor was *DEUCE*.

**ACK:** Acknowledgement. A control character widely used to acknowledge correct receipt of a message. In ASCII, its value is binary 0000110 (control-F).

**ACM:** An abbreviation for *Association for Computing Machinery*, an American professional association which has a large number of SIGs (Special Interest Groups) active in many areas of computer science.

**ACOUSTIC COUPLER:** A device for converting digital signals into acoustic signals enabling data to be transmitted over the PSTN with no electrical connection between the terminal and the line. It is usually not possible to use an acoustic coupler for bandwidths greater than 300 bits/second.

**ACOUSTIC DELAY LINE:** A delay line which stores data using the propagation of sound waves in a suitable medium (often mercury). Now obsolete.

**ACOUSTIC MEMORY:** A storage medium using acoustic delay lines.

**ACRONYM:** In theory, a group of letters formed from the first (or, sometimes, other than the first) letters of a name. However, in practice, the ''acronym'' is often first decided then suitable words selected to fit this. An example of this is BASIC which has now acquired the status of an acronym meaning ''Beginners' All Purpose Symbolic Instruction Code''. A list of acronyms in common usage is given in Appendix A.

**ACTIVITY RATIO:** The ratio of the number of records being updated to the total number of records within that file.

**ACTP:** An acronym for *Advanced Computer Technology Project*, a project funded by the UK Government for research and development by industry into advanced techniques.

**ACU:** An acronym for *automatic call unit*.

**ADA:** In 1975, the US Department of Defense started a program called the ''High Order Language Commonality Program'' to establish a single high-level language for DoD applications. A set of requirements were defined, known as ''Steelman'' and various companies submitted language specifications to fulfil these requirements. The final language, which was called ''Ada'' after Ada Lady Lovelace who was the daughter of Lord Byron and programmed Charles Babbage's first computers, was designed by CII-Honeywell Bull. A preliminary Ada reference manual was published in 1979.

**ADAPTIVE CONTROL SYSTEM:** A control system which adapts it own behaviour to suit the environment in accordance with data from that environment which it obtains by continuous monitoring.

**ADAPTIVE ROUTING:** A technique of routing in a distributed computer network which adapts to changing conditions by adjusting its parameters in accordance with data obtained by continuous monitoring. *ARPANET* uses an adaptive routing system.

**ADC:** An acronym for *analogue to digital converter*.

**ADCCP:** An acronym for *Advanced Data Communication Control Procedure*, a *bit-oriented* line-level protocol.

**ADDEND:** One of the operands in an addition. The addend is added to the augend to produce the sum. In most computer systems, the addend remains unchanged throughout this operation while the augend is replaced by the sum.

**ADDER:** The hardware device in a computer which performs addition. It takes three inputs, the addend, augend and carry and produces two outputs, the sum and a carry.

**ADDITION:** The operation of combining an augend and an addend to form a sum according to the usual rules of arithmetic.

**ADDITION WITHOUT CARRY:** A synonym for *exclusive-or*.

**ADDRESS:** This word, used either as a verb (meaning to give an address) or a noun, means a reference, usually a number, indicating the location of a specified item, usually in main memory or on backing storage. Thus, "the address of variable A is 8000". An address may be given in any one of a large number of ways and these various methods are given under the name of the method (e.g. *absolute addressing*) and under the heading *addressing*. Instructions are also referred to as "n-address instructions" where "n" denotes the number of items addressed by the instruction.

**ADDRESS BUS:** A physical connection between a processor and memory. The processor places an address on the bus and the memory responds by placing the contents of that address back on the bus.

**ADDRESS FORMAT:** The format of the address part of an instruction.

**ADDRESS MODIFICATION:** The altering of an address within an instruction. This can be achieved in two ways, either by the actual changing of the instruction as stored in memory or by the effect of, for example, an *index register* when the *effective address* is formed by modifying the address by the contents of the index register.

**ADDRESS REGISTER:** A register which contains the address of the current instruction.

**ADDRESSING:** The technique of referring to an item by means of an address. There are a large number of methods by which these can be done and they are described individually under the appropriate heading. The ones described herein are as follows:
  * Immediate
  * Direct (or Absolute)
  * Indirect
  * Register
  * Indexed
  * Base/Displacement
  * Stack
  * Relative

**ADP:** An acronym for *automatic data processing*.

**AFIPS:** An acronym for *American Federation of Information Processing Societies*.

**AFNOR:** An acronym for *Association Française de Normalisation*, a French standards body which is a member of ISO.

**AGRIS:** An acronym for *Agricultural Information System*.

**ALGOL:** An acronym for *ALGOrithmic Language*. The first such language, Algol 58, was developed for use by mathematicians to represent algorithms. In 1960, the "Report on the Algorithmic Language ALGOL 60" was published by IFIP. The report is of considerable interest in that it uses a metalanguage to define the actual language. In 1963, discussions started on a successor language, called ALGOL-X, by Working Group 2.1 of IFIP and the definition of this language, renamed ALGOL 68, was published as the "Report on the Algorithmic Language ALGOL 68". Although it bears considerable similarities to its predecessor, it is very much more powerful.

**ALGORITHM:** A formal description of the method of solving a specified problem. One method of doing this is by means of an algorithmic language, such as Algol.

**ALGORITHMIC:** Pertaining to the use of algorithms.

**ALLOCATE:** To assign system resources for the processing of a *job*.

**ALLOCATION:** The process of assigning system resources for the processing of a *job*.

**ALOHA:** An experimental packet-switched computer network at the University of Hawaii which uses satellite communication links in a broadcast mode. Much work has been done in this network to investigate optimal use of these links and these are described under *broadcast satellite techniques*.

**ALPHA:** Often used as an abbreviation for *alphabetic* (or sometimes, confusingly, for *alphanumeric*).

**ALPHABETIC:** An adjective describing characters in the set 'A' to 'Z' or 'a' to 'z'.

**ALPHAMERIC:** A synonym for *alphanumeric*.

**ALPHANUMERIC:** An adjective describing characters which are either numeric or alphabetic.

**ALTERNATE ROUTING:** A routing technique used in some computer networks when, in the event of failure of a primary route, an alternate route is provided.

**ALT-MODE:** A name sometimes given to the character (or key) known more often as *escape*.

**ALU:** An abbreviation for *arithmetic/logical unit*.

**AM:** An acronym for *amplitude modulation*.

**AMENDMENT FILE:** A file which contains the changes required to be made to a *master file*, performed in a batch environment. It consists of a set of *amendment records*.

**AMENDMENT RECORD:** One record which is a part of an *amendment file*, specifying the change(s) to be made to a record in the *master file*.

**AMENDMENT TAPE:** A tape (magnetic or paper) containing an *amendment file*.

**ANALOG(UE):** The representation of values by means of a physical variable, often a voltage level but could be, for example, a length (as in a slide rule). A number of early computers (and some current, special purpose, computers) are based on analog(ue) principles. One based on a combination of analog(ue) and digital principles is known as a "hybrid computer".

**ANALOG(UE) CHANNEL:** A transmission channel on which the data being transmitted is represented as an analog(ue) signal (for example, a telephone line).

**ANALOG(UE)/DIGITAL CONVERTER:** A device which converts between analog(ue) and digital signals.

**ANALOG(UE) NETWORK:** An electrical (electronic) circuit which is set up in order to solve a problem by analog(ue) methods.

**ANALYSER:** Something which performs analysis, for example, a syntax analyser (part of a compiler) which performs analysis of the *source code* according to pre-defined *syntax rules*.

**ANALYSIS:** The process of breaking down a problem into its constituent parts.

**ANALYST:** Usually used as an abbreviation for *systems analyst*.

**ANALYTICAL ENGINE:** A device invented in 1833 by Charles Babbage which is the forerunner of the modern computer.

**AND (1):** A Boolean operation which produces a value of TRUE only if both inputs are TRUE.

**AND (2):** A logical operation which gives the result 1 only if both operands are 1. It conforms to the following table:

| & | 0 | 1 |
|---|---|---|
| 0 | 0 | 0 |
| 1 | 0 | 1 |

**ANISOCHRONOUS TRANSMISSION:** Transmission of data where the transitions occur at irregular (unclocked) intervals.

**ANNOTATION:** Explanatory text added to a flowchart or program.

**ANSI:** The American National Standards Institute (formerly the American Standards Association). This is the USA member body of the International Standards Organisation.

**ANSWERBACK:** The response of a device (usually a terminal) to a specific enquiry (usually the WRU character) in order to verify the identity of the device.

**ANSWERBACK DRUM:** A component of a terminal (e.g. a Teletype) which automatically sends the terminal identification in response to an enquiry. Since this is a physical component, it provides some degree of security.

**ANTIOPE:** The French *videotex* system.

**APL:** An acronym for *A Programming Language*, a very high-level language developed by Iverson of IBM.

**APPLE:** A *home computer* made by Apple Computers Inc. A UK version is marketed as the ITT 2020.

**APPLICATION:** The problem for which computing is required.

**APPLICATION PROGRAMS:** Programs to solve problems. These should be contrasted with *systems programs* which are programs written to enable operation of computer systems.

**APSE:** An abbreviation for *Ada Programming Support Environment* which is, as the name implies, an environment in which programs written in the DoD language Ada are run.

**ARCHITECTURE:** The set of facilities and functional components visible to a programmer using the language of the machine and some of the principles used to realise this language.

**ARGUMENT:** Most commonly used to indicate values passed to a function or routine. For example, in the call:
$$y = \sin(x)$$
"x" is the argument of the function call.

**ARITHMETIC EXPRESSION:** An expression consisting of a number of values (or equivalent), joined by various *arithmetic operators*.

**ARITHMETIC/LOGICAL UNIT:** Part of a central processor unit which performs the arithmetic and logical operations on data. It is usually abbreviated to ALU.

**ARITHMETIC MEAN:** The result of adding together the items in a set of values and dividing by the number of items.

**ARITHMETIC OPERATION:** An operation on data using an *arithmetic operator*.

**ARITHMETIC OPERATOR:** One of the set of operators used to perform arithmetic operations, such as "+", "−", "*" and "/".

**ARITHMETIC SHIFT:** To shift the bits in a word, treating the value as a signed integer. A left shift of "n" places is equivalent to multiplication by $2^n$. Conversely, a right shift of "n" places is equivalent to division by $2^n$. It should be contrasted with other shifts such as a *logical shift* or a *circular shift*.

**ARITHMETIC STATEMENT:** A statement in a programming language to perform arithmetic operations.

**ARITHMETIC UNIT:** Part of the *central processor unit* which performs arithmetic functions. Usually this is combined with logical functions into the *ALU* (arithmetic and logical unit).

**ARPA:** The Advanced Research Projects Agency of the United States Department of Defense.

**ARPANET:** A packet-switched computer network, set up in 1969 by ARPA and now consisting of over 100 "Host" computers, mainly in the continental USA, with links to Hawaii, Norway and England.

Following the publication of a series of papers by Paul Baran of the Rand Corporation in 1964 and early experiments by Marrill and Roberts (1966) in the USA, ARPA decided to fund the setting up of a *packet-switched* network, connecting together various sites in the continental USA which were in receipt of ARPA grants. Various criteria were proposed for the network, such as that the end-to-end delay should be less than half a second, that there should be at least two physically separate paths between any two network nodes, that the communications cost should be less than 25% of the total network cost and that software costs should be minimised at each site. In early 1969, the contract for the network was awarded to a company in Cambridge, Massachusetts called Bolt, Beranek and Newman. The design of the network was that each computer to be connected ("Host") should be connected to a dedicated minicomputer which formed part of the communications sub-network. These node computers were called *IMPs* and were based on Honeywell-516 computers (later 316s). They were later superseded by *TIPs* — Terminal IMPs — which had facilities for terminal handling.

The first, four-node, experimental network was operational in early 1970 and expanded rapidly, including the provision of satellite links to Hawaii and London (1973). The network has provided a testbed for much research into computer networks and protocols but now is considered an operational (rather than research) network and is operated by the Defense Communications Agency (DCA).

Although ARPANET mainly provides a communications medium between various computers and terminals, there have been experiments in the concept of distributed operating systems, perhaps the best known of which is *RSEXEC*.

1. Baran, P. *et al.*, "On Distributed Communications", Rand Corporation, 1964.
2. Marill, T. and Roberts, L.G., "Toward a Co-operative Network of Time-shared Computers", *Proc.* AFIPS FJCC, **29**, 425–431, 1966.
3. Roberts, L.G. and Wessler, B.D., "Computer Network Development to Achieve Resource Sharing", *Proc.* AFIPS SJCC, **36**, 543–549, 1970.

**ARQ:** An abbreviation for "automatic request for repetition", an error detection and correction technique.

**ARRAY:** A linearly ordered set of data items, often used synonymously with "matrix".

**ARTIFICIAL INTELLIGENCE:** A branch of computer science concerned with the design of computer systems so that they have attributes associated with intelligence such as game playing.

**ASA:** An acronym for the *'American Standards Association'*, now known as ANSI.

**ASC:** A function provided in many implementations of BASIC which converts a character into its ASCII representation.

**ASCC:** An acronym for *Automatic Sequence Controlled Calculator*, an early computer (constructed around 1937 by Howard Aiken at Harvard University). It was also known as the "Mark I".

**ASCENDER:** The part of a character which projects above the body of the character.

**ASCII:** An acronym for *American Standard Code for Information Interchange* — a seven-bit plus parity character code established by the American Standards Institute (ANSI). A table of these codes is given in Appendix B.

**ASLIB:** An acronym for the *Association of Special Libraries and Information Bureaux.*

**ASR:** An acronym for *automatic send/receive*. A Teletype which has a keyboard/printer, together with a paper tape reader/punch which allows the automatic transmission of data.

**ASSASSIN:** An acronym for *A System for Storage and Subsequent Selection of Information.*

**ASSEMBLE:** To translate from a *source program* written in *assembly language* into *object code* by means of an *assembler*.

**ASSEMBLER:** The program which translates a *source program* written in *assembly language* into *object code*. Assemblers vary from extremely simple ones which perform little more than resolving label references and translating mnemonic operation codes, to extremely complex ones which allow *conditional assembly* and *macros*.

**ASSEMBLY:** The process of translating a *source program* written in *assembly language* into *object code* by means of an *assembler*.

**ASSEMBLY LANGUAGE:** A language which is usually the lowest level available on a computer and, in its simplest form, bears a one-to-one relationship to *machine code* but has additional facilities such as symbolic reference to *addresses* and *opcodes*. Very much more complex assemblers exist, including facilities for *conditional assembly* and *macros*. In recent years, the concept of *high-level assemblers* has appeared, designating languages which appear similar to conventional high-level languages but which translate directly into machine code, allowing the programmer to specify the actual code produced.

**ASSEMBLY LISTING:** The *listing* produced by an *assembler*, usually consisting of the input code, together with the *machine code* produced.

**ASSEMBLY PROGRAM:** A synonym for *assembler*.

**ASSIGN:** The operation of allocating part of a computer system to one user or dedicating it to a particular function.

**ASSOCIATIVE MEMORY:** Storage in which locations are accessed by means of their contents rather than an address.

**ASYNCHRONOUS DEVICE:** A device which operates asynchronously (e.g. a Teletype).

**ASYNCHRONOUS TRANSMISSION:** Transmission of data where time intervals between transmitted characters may be of unequal length. Transmission is controlled by start and stop bits framing each character. Also known as "start-stop" transmission.

**ATS:** An acronym for *Administrative Terminal System*.

**ATTACH:** To reserve a system resource for the sole usage of a process. Within the context of an operating system, the word is used to mean to create a sub-task and present it to the supervisor for execution.

**ATTENTION KEY:** A key on a terminal (particularly a Teletype) which draws attention to its being pressed by causing an interrupt. It is often used as a means of breaking into a program (especially one which is accidentally executing an *infinite loop*).

**ATTENUATE:** To reduce the strength of a signal.

**ATTENUATION:** The amount by which a signal strength is reduced over a transmission line, usually measured in *decibels*.

**ATTRIBUTE:** Some characteristic of an item, for example, a variable may have the attribute *integer*.

**AUDIO CASSETTE:** A ¼'' magnetic tape cassette used for recording audio signals (e.g. in a domestic hi-fi system). However, they are often used for storing digital data, particularly in microcomputer systems. In the latter case, the method of recording information known as the Kansas City interface has become a *de facto* standard.

**AUDIO FREQUENCY:** Frequencies which may be detected by the human ear (say, 20 Hz to 20 kHz).

**AUDIT:** To ascertain the validity of data in a system.

**AUDIT TRAIL:** A means of tracing the path of a transaction through a system from beginning to end.

**AUGEND:** One of the operations in an addition. The augend is added to the *addend* to produce the sum. In most computer systems, the addend remains unchanged throughout this operation, while the augend is replaced by the sum.

**AUTOCODE:** A name used for a group of languages which lie between assemblers and high-level languages. Such languages were popular in the early 1960s and two such were EXCHLF and Atlas Autocode. They frequently had very high-level facilities (such as string or matrix manipulation) while at the same time allowing access to machine facilities (for example, by allowing in-line assembly code).

**AUTODIALLER:** A synonym for *automatic call unit.*

**AUTODIN:** A US Department of Defense computer network with a major criterion being extremely high reliability and therefore about 95% of the total network cost is in the switching nodes.

**AUTOINCREMENT:** This word is used either as a verb to mean *to increment automatically* or as an adjective qualifying something which is capable of this function. Perhaps the most common usage is in the context of an *autoincrement register* (particularly on the PDP–11 series), a register which, after being accessed (usually as an index register), is automatically incremented by one thus allowing rapid access to sequential storage locations.

**AUTOMATIC CALL UNIT (ACU):** A device which may be attached to a computer enabling it to transmit data over the switched telephone network (PSTN). Also known as an *autodialler*. It is illegal to use in a number of countries.

**AVAILABILITY:** The period for which a system is usable, often expressed as a percentage of total time.

**AVL:** An abbreviation for *Adelson-Velskii and Landis*, two Russian mathematicians who, in 1962, proposed a new form of *balanced binary tree* which retains a good search tree while reducing the search and build time significantly (to the order of log(n) operations for searching or insertion).

**AZERTY:** A name for the layout of a keyboard, mainly used in European countries, derived from the letters on the top row (*cf.* QWERTY).

# B

**BABBAGE (1):** The inventor of the digital computer was Charles Babbage (1791–1871) who constructed the *difference engine* and the *analytical engine*.

**BABBAGE (2):** The block-structured, high-level assembler for the GEC 4000 series of mini-computers.

**BACK-ARROW:** A character often used to indicate that the previous character is to be deleted from the string or to be ignored.

**BACK-END STORAGE NETWORK:** A network (usually of very high bandwidth) connecting a number of computers to storage devices, often of very high capacity.

**BACKGROUND:** In broad terms, the process space of a computer, especially a time-sharing system, may be divided into two parts, the *foreground* and the *background*. The foreground consists of the high-priority processes whereas the background consists of lower priority processes, such as batch jobs and the device spoolers.

**BACKGROUND PROCESSING:** Processing of jobs in the *background* region.

**BACKGROUND PROGRAM:** A program which executes in the *background*.

**BACKING STORE:** Computer memory which is not *primary storage*. In general, it is storage which has larger capacity but slower access time than primary storage and usually refers to devices such as disks, drums or magnetic tape. The term is usually restricted to secondary storage and hence excludes paper tape, cards etc.

**BACKPLANE:** The part of a computer system into which the PCBs are plugged and which interconnects them. It usually implements some *bus* structure.

**BACKSPACE (1):** To move the printing head (on a hard-copy device) or cursor (on a VDU) back one character position, usually by the generation of a *backspace character* (in most cases, this is control-H).

**BACKSPACE (2):** To move backwards on a sequential storage medium, usually one unit (for example, on magnetic tape, one block).

**BACKSPACE CHARACTER:** The character which performs back-spacing. In the ASCII character set, it is control-H, binary 0001000.

**BACKUP (1):** To make a copy of data for security purposes. Also used as a noun to refer to that copy.

**BACKUP (2):** Sometimes used as a synonym for *backspace*, particularly in the case of magnetic tape.

**BACKWARD CHANNEL:** A *communications channel* operating in the opposite direction to that transmitting information and which is used for error and supervisory signals.

**BACKWARD READ:** A technique used in magnetic tape decks whereby data can be read when the tape is moving backwards.

**BADGE READER:** An input device used to read the data encoded on some form of badge.

**BAL:** An abbreviation for *Basic Assembler Language*, most commonly used to refer to a simple assembler (without macros or conditional assembly instructions) available on some IBM System/360s.

**BALANCED BINARY TREE:** A *binary tree* in which the number of nodes in the right and left subtrees of any node differ at most by one.

**BAND (1):** A set of tracks on some magnetic storage device.

**BAND (2):** A range of frequencies.

**BANDWIDTH:** The range of frequencies assigned to a channel. For example, speech usually requires a bandwidth of about 3 kHz, between 300 and 3400 Hz.

**BAR CODE:** A coding consisting of a sequence of thick and thin bars which can be read by a special device. In particular, this is used in shops and the *bar code scanner* can be connected to a terminal which can not only produce a bill but also update a database enabling goods to be ordered when they reach a certain critical level.

**BAR CODE SCANNER:** An input device used to read *bar codes*.

**BAR PRINTER:** An output device used for printing *bar codes*.

**BARREL PRINTER:** A printer in which the characters occur on the surface of a barrel which rotates. At any instant in time, all print positions have the same character on the barrel and those required are printed.

**BASE (1):** The value on which a number system is based. For example, decimal arithmetic uses a base of 10.

**BASE (2):** A number used in *floating point* representation of numbers.

**BASE (3):** A reference value.

**BASE ADDRESS:** An address used as a reference value, for example, in compilation, a value to be added to all relative addresses to produce absolute addresses.

**BASE-DISPLACEMENT (ADDRESSING):** A method of addressing in which the address is given in the form of a base address (often contained in a register) and a displacement from that base. This method has a number of advantages, including the fact that it is easily possible to write programs without knowing in advance where in memory they will be located. It is the principal method of addressing used in the IBM System/ 370 and, for example, the Assembler instruction:

L        1,X

might become, in machine code:

5810   D040

where "D" is the base register (13) and "040" is the (hexadecimal) displacement. The absolute address is calculated by taking the contents of the specified register and adding the displacement (and, in fact, masking to 24 bits).

**BASIC:** A high-level language developed by Kemeny and Kurtz at Dartmouth College, New Hampshire, USA in 1963, intended as a means to facilitate the use of a computer by non-computer science specialists, particularly engineers. The BASIC system consists of the language itself, an editor and a filing system, thus enabling the user to carry out all required operations within the BASIC system itself. The BASIC language is not block-structured but has many high-level features, for example, comprehensive string manipulation facilities. BASIC is the most common language available on microcomputers although the facilities available differ significantly from machine to machine. In many cases, the language is interpreted rather than compiled leading to an order of magnitude decrease in speed of execution. A standard for "Minimal BASIC" was published by ANSI Committee X3J2 in 1977 and is to be followed by other standards for versions of the language, such as a real-time BASIC.

　　1. Kemeny, J.G. and Kurtz, T.E., "BASIC Programming", John Wiley and Sons Ltd., 1968.

**BASIC ACCESS METHOD:** A method of accessing data held in a file with no I/O buffering. Each request for I/O actually produces such a request to the file.

**BASIC OPERATING SYSTEM:** A relatively simple operating system available on some small IBM System/360 machines.

**BASIS:** An acronym for *British Airways' Staff Information System*, a *videotex* system used for disseminating information by British Airways.

**BATCH:** A group of records processed as a single item (the word is also used as a verb with the corresponding meaning).

**BATCH PROCESSING:** In early computer systems, jobs needing a particular systems program (usually a compiler) were collected together into a batch and run. This is a particularly efficient way of running a computer system and has been used in modern systems (e.g. at the University of Waterloo) to give a "cafeteria service". More recently, the term *batch processing* has been used loosely to mean any non-interactive processing.

**BATCH TOTAL:** A check on the accuracy of operations on a batch of records by summing a set of values.

**BATS:** An acronym for *Basic Additional Teleprocessing Support*. A system available in the late 1960s to provide support for telecommunications processing on IBM System/360.

**BAUD:** A unit of signalling speed corresponding to one signal event per second. It is frequently used (incorrectly) as a synonym for *bits per second*. This is only true where each signal event represents one bit.

**BAUDOT CODE:** A five-bit code used in Telex communication.

**BCC:** An abbreviation for *block check character*.

**BCD:** An abbreviation for *binary coded decimal*.

**BCPL:** An abbreviation for *Basic CPL*, a systems implementation language developed in order to write a compiler for CPL. It was mainly developed by Martin Richards at MIT and Cambridge (UK) and is now available on a wide range of machines, particularly since it was designed to be easily portable.

**BCS:** An abbreviation for the *British Computer Society*.

**BDAM:** An abbreviation for *Basic Data Access Method*, a method of accessing data on IBM System/360 which provided no queuing facilities.

**BEARER CIRCUIT:** The high-bandwidth circuit used in communications into which many lower bandwidth circuits are multiplexed.

**BEBUGGING:** A technique for debugging programs whereby bugs are deliberately introduced into a program on the assumption that, while detecting these known bugs, other unknown bugs will also be found.

**BEL (1):** An abbreviation for *bell character*.

**BEL (2):** A measure of the strength of a signal, relative to a given reference level. More formally, it is the common logarithm (base 10) of the ratio of the signal to that of the reference level. In practice, the unit used is the *decibel*.

**BELL CHARACTER:** A control character (in ASCII, control-G, binary value 0000111) which gives an audible indication − genuinely a bell in some terminals such as the Teletype 33.

**BENCHMARK:** A means of assessing the power of a computer, usually by a suite of programs which can be run on a series of different machines.

**BENCHMARKING:** The technique of using *benchmarks* to evaluate performance of a computer system.

**BETA:** An acronym for *Business Equipment Trade Association*.

**BIAS:** A number added to the exponent of a floating-point number to modify the range of exponents which can be represented. See *excess-N* notation.

**BI-DIRECTIONAL PRINTING:** A method of printing used by some character printers with some intelligence. Lines are printed alternately left to right and right to left in order to obviate the delay in returning the print-head to the start of the line.

**BILLION:** Used in the USA to mean one thousand million ($10^9$). In Europe, it means a million million ($10^{12}$), the word "milliard" being used for the American billion.

**BIM:** An abbreviation for the *British Institute of Management*.

**BINAC:** An acronym for *Binary Automatic Computer*, built in the late 1940s by the Eckert-Mauchly Corporation.

**BINARY:** A means of representing integers in base 2 arithmetic. It is necessary to use two symbols, conventionally 0 and 1. Since most computer devices (e.g. core) are two-state devices, a binary representation of data is the most natural method available.

**BINARY ARITHMETIC:** Arithmetic operations in which the operands are represented in binary notation.

**BINARY CHOP:** A synonym for *binary search*.

**BINARY CODED DECIMAL:** A means of expressing decimal values whereby each digit occupies four bits (the combinations 1010 to 1111 being unused). This is a relatively inefficient method of representing numbers (for example, one byte can represent 0 to 255 if a binary representation is used, but only 0 to 99 in BCD). However, some computers have hardware which can operate directly on BCD integers.

**BINARY DIGIT:** One of the digits used in binary representation of numbers. Since the number of digits required in a number system with base "n" is "n", only two are required and these are conventionally 0 and 1. The phrase is usually abbreviated to *bit*.

**BINARY DUMP:** A copy of the contents of, for example, main memory or a disk file, without any interpretation of the contents. Strictly, it is such a copy in binary but, for convenience, it may be printed in hexadecimal or some related system. Its most common use is for debugging purposes but also is used for security backup when the result is not printed but is stored on a suitable device.

**BINARY NUMBER:** A number written using binary notation. For example, the number 123 decimal would be represented as 1111011 in binary.

**BINARY POINT:** The character (usually a full stop) used to separate the integral and fractional parts of a binary number. The equivalent (for a number represented in binary notation) of the decimal point.

**BINARY SEARCH:** A method of searching a sequence of items for a specified key. The sequence is collated in increasing order and the method consists of comparing the specified key with the value at the midpoint of the sequence. Depending whether the specified key is less than or greater than the value found, the process is repeated in the lower or upper half of the sequence until the key is found or shown not to be present. The number of comparisons required is of the order of the logarithm (to the base 2) of the number of entries in the table.

**BINARY SYNCHRONOUS COMMUNICATION (BSC):** This is a low-level communications protocol introduced by IBM in 1968. It is a half-duplex protocol allowing data transparency via the DLE mechanism.

**BINARY TREE:** A *tree* consisting of nodes which have, at most, two subtrees. More formally, a binary tree is a finite set of nodes which either is empty or consists of a root and two disjoint binary trees called the left and right subtrees of the root.

**BIPOLAR:** An adjective referring to a representation of two different states by means of alternate polarities.

**BIQUINARY:** A method of representing decimal numbers in two parts, the first representing 0 or 5, the second 0 to 4. This method is used on some versions of the *abacus*.

**BIQUINARY CODE:** A code representing digits by means of the *biquinary* method.

**BISAM:** An abbreviation for *basic indexed sequential access method*. An access method used on IBM machines.

**BISTABLE:** An element of a circuit which is capable of being in one of two stable conditions.

**BIT:** Abbreviation for *binary digit*. Smallest unit of information.

**BIT DENSITY:** The number of bits stored per unit of measurement (linear or area).

**BIT MAP:** A map where each item is represented by a single bit. For example, a file directory may contain a bit map, the presence of a 1 bit denoting that the block is being used, a 0 denoting that it is unused.

**BIT PARALLEL:** A method of data transmission where a number of bits are transmitted in parallel. Often, the number of bits transmitted in parallel is eight and the method is known as "bit parallel, byte serial".

**BIT PATTERN:** The pattern of bits in a string, often a computer word.

**BIT POSITION:** The location of a bit within a word. Usually this is done by reference to either the most significant or the least significant bit of the word, which is referred to as bit 0. Needless to say, these two totally opposite conventions lead to some confusion.

**BIT RATE:** The speed at which a device transmits data, measured in bits per second (see also *baud*).

**BIT SERIAL:** A method of data transmission whereby bits are transmitted in order, one bit at a time.

**BIT STREAM:** A sequence of bits being transmitted without regard to any meaning contained therein.

**BIT STRING:** A sequence of characters, each of which is "0" or "1".

**BIT STUFFING:** A method of *data transparency* used in protocols such as HDLC in which the sender of data inserts a "0" on detecting any sequence of five binary "1"s. Similarly, the receiver, on detecting a sequence of five "1"s examines the next bit and, if it is zero, removes it. In this manner, sequences of more than five ones can be used as special sequences and, in particular, the sequence "01111110" is used as a flag sequence to indicate the beginning and/or end of a *frame*.

**BLACK BOX:** Used to refer to one component of a system (hardware or software) whose functions are clearly defined but the internal workings are unknown.

**BLAISE:** An acronym for *British Library Automated Information Service*.

**BLANK (n):** A character representing a space. In ASCII, this is represented by the binary pattern 0100000.

**BLANK (adj):** A field containing no information and filled with a certain specified character — for example, a blank card is assumed to consist of space characters while blank paper tape consists of null characters.

**BLANK COMPRESSION:** A technique used (mainly in data transmission but also in data storage) whereby contiguous sequences of blanks (or, in fact, any character) are replaced by a marker together with a count of the number of occurrences of the character.

**BLISS:** An acronym for "Basic Language for Implementing Systems Software", *SILs* available on various DEC machines.

**BLISS-10:** A version of "BLISS" available on the DEC system-10.

**BLISS-11:** A version of "BLISS" available on PDP-11s.

**BLOCK:** A group of bits, transmitted as a unit over which an encoding procedure is applied for error control procedures. The above definition, which is strictly in the context of data communications, also applies in the more general context of data transmitted between main and secondary storage (and the storage of that data on the secondary storage device). The word is also used as a verb meaning to put data together into a block.

**BLOCK CHECK CHARACTER:** A check procedure (see *cyclic redundancy check*) used on a transmission block.

**BLOCK DIAGRAM:** A diagram representing the components of a computer system (hardware or software) at a fairly high-level giving little detail.

**BLOCK LENGTH:** The size of a block of data, measured in convenient units, usually bytes or words. Where the block comprises records, it usually contains an integral number of such records and the length is sometimes expressed as the number of records (see also *blocking factor*).

**BLOCK SIZE:** An alternative name for *block length*.

**BLOCK TRANSFER:** The transfer of data in blocks.

**BLOCKING:** The collection of records into blocks, usually for the purpose of transmitting to a peripheral device.

**BLOCKING FACTOR:** The number of records contained in a *block*.

**BNF:** An abbreviation for *Backus-Naur Form* (sometimes known as *Backus Normal Form*), a notation originally developed for the language Algol-60 in which it is possible to represent formally the syntax of a programming language. There are many extensions to BNF in common use.

**BOARD:** An abbreviation for *printed circuit board*.

**BOMP:** An acronym for *Bill of Material and Requirement Planning*.

**BOOLE:** The inventor (1815-1864) of *Boolean algebra*.

**BOOLEAN ALGEBRA:** An algebra for expressing logical relationships between truth values. It is named after George Boole, a nineteenth century mathematician.

**BOOLEAN LOGIC:** A synonym for *Boolean algebra*.

**BOOLEAN OPERATOR:** A logical operator for which the input(s) and the output may only be one of two states, usually represented by zero and one.

**BOOLEAN OPERATION:** One of the set of operations which can be performed in *Boolean algebra*, for example, *AND* and *inclusive-OR*.

**BOOTSTRAP:** Derived from the expression "to pull oneself up by one's own bootstraps", the word (which may be used as a noun, adjective or verb) indicates, in general, the use of a an extemely simple system to generate a more complex one and so forth. It is most commonly used in two contexts: one, the starting of a computer system and the other, generating compilers (see *half bootstrap* and *full bootstrap*). As an example of the meaning of the word, a computer system is "boot-strapped" in order to start it. This involves setting up a simple program (usually less than a dozen instructions) on the front panel of the computer by hand then instructing the processor to execute these. They will, in turn, execute a more complex program which itself will read in the entire system from backing storage and execute it. In most modern computers, the first step is now performed automatically when the computer is switched on or reset, the first bootstrap program being contained in a read-only memory.

**BOOTSTRAP MEMORY:** The ROM containing a bootstrap program.

**BORROW:** A negative carry. In subtraction, when it is not possible to perform the operation, one unit is "borrowed" from the next higher (more significant) character position.

**BOSS:** An acronym for *Burroughs Operational System Simulator*.

**BOUND:** Used in certain contexts to mean "limit", for example, when describing the limits of an array, these are often referred to as the "upper bound" and "lower bound".

**BPAM:** An abbreviation for *Basic Partitioned Access Method*, a data access method available on IBM System/360 computers.

**BPI:** An abbreviation for *bits per inch*, a measure of the bit density of a sequential storage medium, usually *magnetic tape*.

**BPO:** An abbreviation for *British Post Office*.

**BPS:** An abbreviation for *bits per second* (see *bit rate*).

**BRANCH:** A transfer of control within a program so that the next instruction to be executed is not that next in order. It is performed by means of a *branch instruction*.

**BRANCH INSTRUCTION:** An instruction within a program which causes a *branch* to be taken. See also *conditional branch* and *unconditional branch*.

**BREADBOARD:** A printed circuit board without any components.

**BREAK:** This term usually refers to a key on a terminal keyboard which has the effect of sending continuous binary zeros for a specified time and which is usually interpreted by the computer to which the terminal is connected as an interrupt.

**BREAKPOINT:** A point in a program (usually inserted by a debugging system) where control returns from the program to the debugging system or the user, enabling the current state of the program to be examined before proceeding.

**BROADBAND:** A band consisting of a wide range of frequencies.

**BROADCAST (vb):** To send the same message to a number of destinations.

**BROADCAST (adj):** Refers to an item which is broadcast.

**BROADCAST SATELLITE TECHNIQUES:** A method of data transmission which uses a satellite, usually geosynchronous. Data is transmitted to the satellite which then retransmits it, inevitably in a broadcast mode so that it may be received by all possible receivers. Various techniques have been evolved to maximise channel bandwidth. Many of these were first evolved in the ALOHA system of the University of Hawaii which was a packet radio system. Similar protocols are used in contention networks such as Xerox's ETHERNET.

1. Abramson, N., "Packet Switching with Satellites", *Proc.* AFIPS NCC, **42**, 695–702, 1973.
2. Binder, R. *et al.*, "ALOHA Packet Broadcasting – a Retrospect", *Proc.* AFIPS NCC, **44**, 203–215, 1975.
3. Metcalfe, R.M. and Boggs, D.R., "ETHERNET: Distributed Packet Switching for Local Computer Networks", Comm. ACM, **19**, 395–404, 1976.

**BS (1):** An abbreviation for *British Standard*.

**BS (2):** An abbreviation for *backspace*.

**BSAM:** An abbreviation for *Basic Sequential Access Method*, an access method available on IBM System/360 computers.

**BSC:** An abbreviation for *binary synchronous communications*.

**BSI:** An abbreviation for the *British Standards Institution*, the UK member body of ISO.

**BSN:** An abbreviation for *back-end storage network*.

**BT:** An abbreviation for *British Telecom*, the public corporation in UK formed to handle the telecommunication business of the British Post Office.

**BTAM:** An abbreviation for *Basic Telecommunications Access Method*, an access method available on IBM System/360 computers.

**BUCKET:** Used to describe an element of data storage which need not correspond to a physical unit.

**BUFFER:** A data area which is used to compensate for different characteristics of devices to provide increased efficiency. For example, data from a disk is read into a buffer in main memory which is then accessed by the program. This is necessary for two reasons; first, the data rate for reading from the disk is orders of magnitude slower than reading from memory and secondly, it is usually not possible to read single data items from the disk but only blocks.

**BUG:** An unexpected function of a program or hardware. A bug which is known but uncorrected is often known as a "feature".

**BULK STORAGE:** A secondary storage medium of large capacity, for example, a *terabit memory*.

**BURST:** To split continuous stationery into separate sheets.

**BURST MODE:** A method of transmitting data between a processor and a peripheral whereby a large amount of data (for example, a *block*) is transmitted as a single unit and hence cannot be interrupted.

**BURSTER:** A device for bursting stationery.

**BUS:** An electrical connection between the components of a computer system along which data is transmitted. Examples of buses are DEC's UNIBUS and Q-BUS and the *de facto* standard for microcomputers, the S-100 bus.

**BYTE:** A number of contiguous bits which are handled together. It is often best defined to be the number of bits required to hold one character. Frequently taken to mean eight bits (particularly on IBM machines); in data transmission, an eight-bit byte is usually known as an "octet".

**BYTE MULTIPLEXING:** A form of time division multiplexing in which bytes from the different channels occupy individual time slots.

**BYTE ORIENTED:** Describes some item which is addressed in terms of *bytes*. Two major uses of the term are in the context of *protocols* and *addressing*. In the former case, a byte-oriented protocol is one in which the transmitted data is assumed to consist of bytes. In the latter, it refers to a computer in which the unit of addressing is a byte.

# C

**C:** A high-level systems implementation language in which the majority of the Unix operating system is written.

   1. Ritchie, D.M. *et al.*, "The C Programming Language", Bell Syst. Tech. J., **57**(6), 1991–2019, 1978.

**CACHE MEMORY:** A very high-speed buffer memory into which instructions from main memory are buffered so that they may be executed at much higher rates than if executed directly from main memory.

**CAD:** An acronym for *computer aided design*.

**CADC:** An acronym for *Computer Aided Design Centre*, an installation located just outside Cambridge (UK) whose major function is CAD.

**CAFS:** An acronym for *content addressable file store*, an autonomous unit developed by ICL which can be attached to a mainframe computer as a peripheral, allowing very high searching rates of a database on primary and/or secondary keys.

   1. Maller, V.A.J., "The content addressable file store – CAFS", ICL Technical Journal, 265–279, Nov 1979.

**CAI:** An acronym for *computer aided (or assisted) instruction*.

**CAL:** An acronym for *computer aided learning*.

**CALCULATOR:** A device which performs, at the very least, ordinary arithmetic operations. Early calculators were mechanical but are now electronic. They vary in complexity from simple ones which perform the four arithmetic operations of add, subtract, multiply and divide up to complex ones which are programmable and hence are really computers. There is no clear dividing line between calculators and computers.

**CALL (1):** Within a program, the instruction which transfers control to a *closed subroutine*.

**CALL (2):** Used in data communications, the word is derived from the technology of telephone networks and refers to the interaction of two processes or devices over a communications network.

**CALLING SEQUENCE:** The sequence of machine instructions required to set up a call to a *closed subroutine*. In general, these will set up the parameters for the call and save the environment of the calling program.

**CAM:** An acronym for *computer aided manufacturing*.

**CAMAC:** An acronym for *Computer Automated Measurement and Control*, an instrumentation interface system for which standards have been proposed by the IEEE. There are currently four CAMAC standards, IEEE Std 583–1975 on "Modular Instrumentation and Digital Interface System", 595–1976 on "Serial Highway Interface System", 596–1976 on "Parallel Highway Interface System" and 683–1976 on "Block Transfer in CAMAC Systems".

**CAMBRIDGE RING:** A technology for distributed processing which uses a very-high bandwidth transmission facility with the topology of a ring. Devices are connected to the ring via an interface module and there is a master station controlling the ring. Data consisting of eight data bits and thirteen control bits is circulated around the ring and removed by the destination. The "Cambridge ring" technology (so named after the University of Cambridge where it was developed) is one of the technologies used in *local area networks* (see also *ETHERNET*).

**CAN:** An acronym for *cancel*, a control code whose value, in ASCII, is 0011000 (control-X).

**CAPACITY:** A measure of the amount of data which can be held on a storage device. Also used to mean the amount of processing which can be done by a computer or other device.

**CAPSTAN:** A part of a magnetic tape deck which actually drives the tape.

**CAPTAINS:** An acronym for *Character and Pattern Telephone Access Information System*. A Japanese videotex system.

**CAR:** An acronym for *channel address register*.

**CARD (1):** A form of tertiary storage consisting of a piece of thin cardboard with data stored by means of punched holes. The most common form has eighty columns, although some manufacturers (notably IBM) now use 96 column cards.

**CARD (2):** A form of secondary storage consisting of a magnetic card. This is used mainly on simple word processors or memory typewriters.

**CARD (3):** A part of a computer system, consisting of a printed circuit board, together with its associated components.

**CARD CODE:** The character code used when representing data on a punched card.

**CARD COLUMN:** A vertical section of a card which can be punched to represent a single character.

**CARD DECK:** A set of punched cards.

**CARD FEED:** The mechanism for transporting cards through a device for performing some function on those cards (e.g. a card reader). Also sometimes used to mean the compartment in which the cards are put prior to the appropriate function (see also *hopper*).

**CARD FIELD:** A sequence of contiguous columns on a card representing a single item of information.

**CARD IMAGE:** A set of contiguous locations in a computer's storage (primary or secondary) which contains an exact representation of the data on a punched card.

**CARD PUNCH:** A device for making holes in a punched card to represent data.

**CARD READER:** A device for reading the data from a punched card.

**CARD REPRODUCER:** A device for reproducing a sequence of punched cards.

**CARD ROW:** A horizontal section of a card.

**CARD STACKER:** A part of a card reader (or other device for punched cards) where the cards are put after having been read.

**CARD VERIFIER:** A device, similar to a card punch, which is used to verify that the data punched onto a deck of cards is correct. The cards are "repunched" by a second operator and, if the data typed the second time does not match the holes punched on any card, an error is signalled, enabling the card to be correctly punched.

**CARD VERIFYING:** The operation of checking the correctness of data on punched cards by means of a *card verifier*.

**CARD WRECK:** The result of a card jamming in a card reader or similar device.

**CARRIAGE:** The part of a printing device which holds and moves the paper.

**CARRIAGE CONTROL:** The means of controlling the movement of the *carriage* of a printing device. This is usually done by means of a single character (the *carriage control character*) sent to the device as the first character of each record. The following are the standard (ASCII) conventions:

| | |
|---|---|
| <space> | Single spacing |
| 0 | Double spacing |
| 1 | Jump to new page |
| + | Overprint |

**CARRIAGE CONTROL TAPE:** A continuous strip of tape (paper or plastic) which has holes punched in appropriate positions in order to control movement of the carriage on some printing devices.

**CARRIAGE RETURN:** The operation of moving the carriage back to the beginning of a line (or the actual character used to perform this function — in ASCII, it is 0001101, control-M). In many computer systems, the operation of the *carriage return key* transmits the carriage return character and the computer transmits the *line feed* character, thus generating a new line.

**CARRIAGE RETURN KEY:** The key on the keyboard of a terminal which transmits the *carriage return* character.

**CARRIER:** A (usually sine) wave which is modulated by a signal for transmission.

**CARRIER FREQUENCY:** The frequency of a carrier wave.

**CARRY:** A value to be added to a digit in an addition arising from the sum obtained by adding the digits in the next less significant position exceeding the number base. Also used as a verb in the same context.

**CASE STATEMENT:** A statement in a number of high-level languages (with varying syntax) which allows the operation of a multi-way switch, i.e. control is transferred to one of a set of statements depending on the value of some variable.

**CASSETTE:** Usually used in the context of a *tape cassette*, magnetic tape in a closed container which is used for audio recording but may also be used for recording data.

**CATALOG(UE):** A list of contents of some item, such as a library or a disk.

**CATALOGUED PROCEDURE:** A *library procedure* which is accessed by means of a catalogue. Usually refers to a set of job control language procedures.

**CATHODE RAY TUBE:** A vacuum tube (cf. a television tube) which exhibits data by means of an electron (cathode ray) beam striking the screen which is coated with a suitable phosphor material. In early computers, a cathode ray tube was sometimes used as a storage device. It is usually abbreviated as "CRT".

**CAW:** An acronym for *channel address word*.

**CBL:** An acronym for *computer-based learning*.

**CBX:** An acronym for *computer-controlled branch exchange*, a telephone exchange controlled by a computer (and thus offering various additional facilities to those available on an ordinary non-intelligent exchange).

**CCB:** An acronym for *channel control block*.

**CCD:** An acronym for *charge coupled device*, a technology for computer memories which are cheaper than semi-conductor memories but only offer serial access to data, the latency time being of the order of 100 microseconds.

**CCETT:** An acronym for *Centre Commun d'Études de Télévision et Télécommunications*, a French research establishment.

**CCITT:** An acronym for *Comité Consultatif Internationale de Télégraphique et Téléphonique.* An international standards committee.

**CCW:** An acronym for *channel command word.*

**CDC:** An acronym for *Control Data Corporation*, a large US manufacturer of computers, particularly large "number-crunchers" such as the CDC 6600 and, more recently, the Cyber 70 series and the CDC STAR.

**CE:** An acronym for *customer engineer.*

**CEEFAX:** The British Broadcasting Corporation's version of Teletext.

**CELL:** A word sometimes used to denote a storage location, i.e. a *word* or *byte.*

**CENTRAL PROCESSING UNIT:** The part of a computer system which performs the actual execution of instructions. Normally, it contains an *arithmetic/logical unit*, a number of *registers* and some dedicated memory.

**CENTRAL PROCESSOR:** A synonym for *central processing unit.*

**CENTRALISED PROCESSING:** The opposite of *distributed processing*, namely where all computation is performed at a central site. One major justification of centralised processing is *Grosch's Law.*

**CEPT:** An acronym for *Conférence Européenne des Administration des Postes et des Télécommunications.*

**CERN:** An acronym for *Centre Européenne pour la Recherche Nucléaire*, a research organisation, mainly concerned with nuclear physics, on the French-Swiss border. It has a large computer network.

**CHAD:** The pieces of paper or card which are removed from the medium when data is punched onto it.

**CHAIN:** A sequence of items, linked together into order. It is used, for example, in BASIC where it is a reserved word used to call one program segment from another.

**CHAIN FIELD:** A field attached to a data item which contains the address of the next data item in a *chain.*

**CHAIN PRINTER:** A printer where the characters are linked together into a chain which rotates at high speed and characters are printed when they are at the appropriate position in the line. The chains are often easily changeable, enabling different typestyles to be used.

**CHAINED LIST:** A sequence of items where each contains, in addition to its data, the address of the next item in sequence.

**CHAINED RECORD:** A *chained list* where each item is a *record*, usually stored on *backing storage*.

**CHAINING:** The technique of scanning through a sequence of chained items or linking items together into a chain.

**CHANGE FILE:** A synonym for *amendment file*.

**CHANNEL (1):** The part of a communication system connecting a message source to a message sink.

**CHANNEL (2):** A (semi-) autonomous part of a computer system (often a dedicated processor) which performs input-output functions.

**CHANNEL CAPACITY:** The amount of data which can be handled by a channel, usually measured in bits per second.

**CHANNEL CONTROL BLOCK:** A *control block* which controls the input or output of data via a channel.

**CHANNEL COMMAND WORD:** A word which is passed to a channel to indicate the functions which it should perform.

**CHANNEL STATUS TABLE:** A *table* which defines the status of the input-output channels of a computer.

**CHANNEL STATUS WORD:** A word which defines the status of a particular input-output channel. The *channel status table* consists of a number of "channel status words".

**CHARACTER:** One of the set of symbols which represent data within a computer system.

**CHARACTER CODE:** A method of representing characters by means of a unique value. The two most common character codes are ASCII and EBCDIC (see Appendices B and C).

**CHARACTER FILL:** To place a specified character into given locations — for example, to insert spaces after a text string to turn it into a *card image*.

**CHARACTER ORIENTED:** Usually applied to an addressing philosophy where the unit of addressing is one character (by definition, the same as *byte oriented*).

**CHARACTER PRINTER:** A printer which prints a single character at a time. This is a relatively slow method of printing (see, for example, *line printer*), but high quality print can be produced.

**CHARACTER READER:** A device which can read individual characters, for example, by means of *optical character recognition*.

**CHARACTER SET:** The set of characters available on a particular computer.

**CHARACTER STRING:** A sequence of characters, concatenated together.

**CHARACTER SUBSET:** A subset of a *character set*.

**CHARACTERISTIC:** A synonym for *exponent* when used in the context of a *floating point number*.

**CHARGE COUPLED DEVICE:** A technique developed recently for secondary storage.

**CHECK:** To validate the accuracy of any data, usually by means of a different method from that which was used to obtain the result.

**CHECK CHARACTER:** A character added to a string of characters in order to provide a check.

**CHECK DIGIT:** A digit added to a number in order to provide a check. There are many algorithms available to calculate a check digit, for example, adding together all the digits in the number, dividing by an integer and using the remainder as the check digit.

**CHECK OUT:** (Sometimes written as "checkout"). To perform checks on a system, usually the final checks before commissioning.

**CHECKPOINT (1):** An alternative name for a breakpoint.

**CHECKPOINT (2):** A point in a program to which it is possible to revert if necessary to restart the program.

**CHECKPOINT/RESTART:** Usually used in the context of "checkpoint/restart marker" meaning a marker placed at a *checkpoint* from which it is possible to restart.

**CHECKSUM:** A value, used for checking purposes, often calculated by adding together the values to be checked. More sophisticated methods are also used, for example, by performing a cumulative exclusive-or or, in order to perform a higher level of checking (i.e. to detect errors more accurately), a technique such as a *cyclic redundancy check*.

**CHILL:** An acronym for *CCITT High Level Language*, a high level language proposed by CCITT, particularly for real-time applications such as control of electronic exchanges.

**CHIP:** A small piece of pure silicon used as the substrate on which the appropriate circuits for a processor, memory etc. are etched.

**CICS:** An acronym for *Customer Information Control System*, a system available on various IBM computers.

**CIRCUIT(1):** A set of electrical/electronic components and their interconnections.

**CIRCUIT (2):** A communications link.

**CIRCUIT SWITCHING:** A method of communication in which there is an exclusive circuit set up between the two stations for the duration of the "call". Such a method is used, of course, in the ordinary (analogue) telephone network but is also used in a number of computer communication networks. In the telephone network, there are a number of problems, particularly the long call set-up and clear-down times; in a computer network, these delays are unacceptable and so techniques are used to minimise these delays ("rapid circuit-switching"). Some disadvantages still remain, such as the static allocation of the channel bandwidth, but these do not prevent computer networks being designed using circuit switching techniques, of which the best known are those of the Nordic countries.

1. "The Nordic Public Data Network", Tele, **1**, 1–28, 1976.

**CIRCULAR LIST:** A set of data items, linked together in a circular arrangement so that there is no first or last item. Such a list may be singly or doubly linked; in the case of the former, in order to find the predecessor of an item, it is necessary to search the entire list; in the latter, it is possible to search the list forwards or backwards.

**CIRCULAR SHIFT:** A method of shifting the bits in a location so that bits which are lost from one end reappear at the other. It is also known as "end around carry". For example, if a 16-bit word contains two characters and it is required to interchange them, a circular shift of eight (in either direction) is required. To give an example, consider a word containing the letters "AB" in ASCII. The following shows (in binary and hexadecimal), each step in performing a circular left shift of eight:

| | |
|---|---|
| 0100000101000010 | 4142 |
| 1000001010000100 | 8284 |
| 0000010100001001 | 0509 |
| 0000101000010010 | 0A12 |
| 0001010000100100 | 1424 |
| 0010100001001000 | 2848 |
| 0101000010010000 | 5090 |
| 1010000100100000 | A120 |
| 0100001001000001 | 4241 |

**CIU:** An acronym for *computer interface unit*.

**CLEAR:** To fill a specified set of locations with a given binary pattern, usually zeros in the case of locations which are to hold integers and space characters for strings.

**CLK:** An abbreviation for *clock*.

**CLOCK:** A device which generates signals at fixed intervals, usually to enable synchronisation of a system.

**CLOCK TRACK:** A track on a storage medium (e.g. *magnetic tape*) which contains synchronisation (clock) pulses in order to locate data accurately.

**CLOSE:** An operation which is performed on a file which is active. It "tidies up", performing such operations as writing out any buffered data and replacing a previous copy by the new version.

**CLOSED LOOP:** A sequence of instructions in a program from which there is no exit.

**CLOSED SUBROUTINE:** A sequence of instructions in a program which are self-contained and which are entered by a *call* and return control by a *return* instruction.

**CLOSED USER GROUP:** A set of users of a system who are able to treat the system as one dedicated to their particular purpose in that they have no access to facilities outside those available to the group, nor does a user who is not a member of the closed user group have access to any of its facilities.

**CMOS:** An acronym for *complementary metal oxide semiconductor*, a technology for fabricating semiconductor components. CMOS chips have the advantage of very low power consumption so are often used in such devices as electronic watches.

**COBOL:** An acronym for *Common Business Oriented Language* – a high level language designed for commercial applications, originally developed for the US Department of Defense. A very high proportion of all commercial programs are written in COBOL. It attempts to resemble English as closely as possible and is more verbose than many other languages.

**CODASYL:** An acronym for *Conference on Data Systems Languages*, a standards body concerned with database systems.

**CODE:** A term used in a wide variety of ways but most usually used to mean the instructions or statements of a program or the act of generating them.

**CODE GENERATOR:** That part of a compiler or translator which produces the *code* for the *object machine*.

**CODING SHEET:** A sheet of paper, ruled in a certain way (depending on the language being used) on which programs are written by hand in order for them to be transcribed into machine-readable form (usually by a "data preparation" group).

**COGO:** An acronym for *Co-ordinate Geometry Language*, a computer language used mainly by civil engineers.

**COHESION:** The least number of lines which must be removed from a network to fragment it into sub-networks (see *connectivity*).

**COLLATE:** To sort into a specified sequence.

**COLLATING SEQUENCE:** An ordering of a set of characters used to sort a set of items containing those characters. For example, the ASCII character set is often used as a collating sequence.

**COLLATOR:** A device used to *collate* sets of cards into a specified sequence.

**COLUMN:** A vertical sequence, usually used in the context of the punchings on a card or the elements of an *array*.

**COM:** An acronym for *computer output to microfilm* (or *microfiche* or *microforms*).

**COMMAND:** An instruction specifying an operation to be performed.

**COMMAND LANGUAGE:** A language designed to give commands to an operating system, usually when in an interactive mode (see *Job Control Language*).

**COMMAND PROCESSING:** The functions of analysing and executing *commands*.

**COMMENT:** A statement in a source program intended to explain the operation of the program but which does not become part of the *object program*.

**COMMERCIAL LANGUAGE:** A language designed for use in commercial applications, the best known of which is COBOL.

**COMMON:** An area of memory used for passing data between separate program segments, particularly in FORTRAN.

**COMMON CARRIER:** A company (public utility) which offers telecommunication facilities to the public, particularly in the USA (e.g. Western Union, Bell). The equivalent of the PTTs in Europe.

**COMMUNICATIONS SATELLITE:** A satellite, usually geosynchronous, which is used for communications purposes. The first commercial communications satellite was INTELSAT I, also known as "Early Bird". The name "Communications Satellite" is also the full name of a consortium, known as COMSAT which has been setup to implement this technology.

**COMMUNICATIONS CHANNEL:** See *channel*.

**COMPARE:** The operation of examining the relationship between two operands. The result is usually specified by a "condition code". The relationships usually considered are greater than, greater than or equal, equal, less than or equal, less than. The operations are usually applied to numeric values but can also be applied to strings of characters.

**COMPATIBLE:** Having the same functional characteristics. The term usually refers to computers which are able to run the same programs. See also *upwards compatible*.

**COMPATIBILITY:** The property of being compatible.

**COMPILE:** To translate from a *source code* program into *object code* by means of a *compiler*.

**COMPILE AND GO:** A technique for executing computer programs in which the program is compiled directly into memory and, immediately the compiler has completed its task, control is transferred to the program, thus obviating the use of *object modules* and a *link loader*.

**COMPILER:** A program which translates from a (usually high-level) language – the *source code* – into the *object code* of the *target machine* (or a related form such as relocatable code).

**COMPILER-COMPILER:** A program which, when supplied with a definition of a language in a suitable *metalanguage*, will generate a compiler for that language.

1. Brooker, R.A. *et al.*, "The Compiler Compiler", Ann. Rev. in Automatic Programming, **3**, 1963.

**COMPLEMENT:** A value obtained by subtracting one value from a second, the latter derived from the number base. In binary arithmetic, two such systems are used, *ones complement* and *twos complement*.

**COMPUTED GOTO:** A type of statement used in some high-level languages (e.g. FORTRAN) which is a "multi-way switch", i.e. has the function of transferring control to one of a number of statements depending on the value of the specified variable.

**COMPUTER:** A device, usually electronic, which operates on data (*input*) according to specified instructions (*program*), usually contained within the computer and producing results (*output*).

**COMPUTER AIDED DESIGN:** The process of design, using computers as aids. In particular, this is done interactively with the designer using a CRT and a *light-pen*.

**COMPUTER SYSTEM:** A computer with its associated equipment and programs.

**COMSAT:** An abbreviation for *Communications Satellite*, a consortium concerned with telecommunications via satellites.

**CONCATENATE:** To link together a number of items into a single sequence.

**CONCENTRATOR:** A device (either hard-wired or programmable) which interfaces between many low-speed (usually asynchronous) lines and a much smaller number of high-speed (usually synchronous) lines. Frequently, the low-speed lines may accommodate different speeds and character codes. The concentrator may also be able to handle such functions as polling.

**CONCURRENT:** Occurring at the same time.

**CONCURRENT PROGRAMMING:** A technique of programming whereby a number of programs are executing in a computer such that they are effectively running in parallel.

**CONDITIONAL ASSEMBLY:** Assembly of a program in which there are embedded directives which inform the assembler that parts of the program are or are not to be assembled according to specified conditions.

**CONDITIONAL BRANCH:** A *branch* which is executed if specified conditions are met.

**CONDITIONAL BREAKPOINT:** A *breakpoint* which is either ignored or taken, according to specified conditions.

**CONDITIONAL TRANSFER (OF CONTROL):** A synonym for *conditional branch*.

**CONDITIONING:** The upgrading of communication lines to certain specified standards.

**CONGESTION:** A condition on a communications line which occurs when the amount of traffic on the line is near the "capacity" of the line. In many computer networks (depending on the routeing algorithms used), it is possible to re-route data. Many schemes exist for minimising congestion.

**CONNECT TIME:** The (real) time in which the user of an interactive system is *logged-in* to the computer system.

**CONNECTIVE:** An operation (or, more formally, the symbol representing that operation) connecting two *operands*.

**CONNECTIVITY:** The least number of lines or nodes which must be removed from a network to fragment it into sub-networks (see *cohesion*).

**CONNECTOR:** A symbol (usually written as a single character within a small circle) which is put on two parts of a *flowchart* (usually because the two parts occur on different sheets of paper) to indicate that they are connected.

**CONSECUTIVE:** Occurring in sequence with no intervening operation.

**CONSOLE:** Usually the controlling terminal of a computer system (in large systems, often known as the operator's console). Sometimes used to mean the front panel of a computer.

**CONSOLE SWITCH:** A switch provided on the *console* of a computer. Such switches can be used to invoke various functions, such as *boot-strapping* the system, or their status can be read by program, enabling data to be communicated to the program.

**CONSOLIDATE:** Sometimes used to mean *link-edit*.

**CONSTANT:** A value which does not change. Usually used in the context of programming languages to indicate a value which is set at compilation time and not allowed to be altered during execution of the program. See also *literal*.

**CONTENT ADDRESSABLE FILE STORE:** See *CAFS*.

**CONTENT ADDRESSABLE MEMORY:** See *associative memory*.

**CONTENTION:** A state whereby a number of devices try to access the same resource simultaneously.

**CONTENTION NETWORK:** A computer communication network in which the communication medium is accessed on a contention basis. There are essentially three types of contention network, packet radio, satellite and some types of local area network. In all cases, the devices using the network contend for the transmission medium and various techniques are used to resolve clashes. These techniques differ for the various types of network, mainly due to the different delays experienced between a transmitter and receiver. Perhaps the best known example of a contention network is the *Ethernet* local area network, although the first such network was the ALOHA network.

1. Abramson, N. "The ALOHA System – Another Alternative for Computer Communication", *Proc.* AFIPS Annual Conference, **37**, 281–285, 1970.

2. Jacobs, I.M., Binder, R. and Hoversten, E.V., "General Purpose Packet Satellite Networks", *Proc.* IEEE, **66(11)**, 1448–1467, 1978.

3. Metcalfe, R.M. and Boggs, D.R., "ETHERNET: Distributed Packet Switching or Local Computer Networks", Comm. ACM, **19(7)**, 395–404, 1976.

**CONTIGUOUS:** Adjoining.

**CONTINUATION CARD:** Since punched cards have a restriction on the number of characters which can be punched on to them, it is sometimes necessary to continue a statement on a subsequent card which is known as a *continuation card*.

**CONTINUATION FRAME:** One page in a viewdata system may consist of a number of separate frames; these have the same page number and are distinguished by a (lower-case) letter suffix. Frames other than the first are known as continuation frames and can only be viewed in sequence although they can be accessed by editing software.

**CONTINUOUS STATIONERY:** Stationery (usually paper but also labels on backing sheets etc.) which forms one continuous piece, perforated at page intervals. It usually has sprocket holes punched along both edges and is fed by means of a *tractor feed* mechanism.

**CONTROL BITS:** Some bits which convey control information. Usually used in the context of transmission of messages when they are distinguished from "information bits". Sometimes known (in the latter context) as "supervisory bits".

**CONTROL BLOCK:** A set of (usually) contiguous locations in memory containing data which is accessed by various programs and provides control of the operation of the programs and may also contain status information about the programs. For example, a *data control block* may be used to control operation of a program which performs I/O to a file.

**CONTROL CARD:** A *card* (or *card-image*) which contains control information used in the operation of a *package* or a computer system (in which case, it is usually called *job control card*).

**CONTROL CHARACTER:** A character which performs a specific control function. In the ASCII character set, the name specifically refers to a character with a value less than 32 (for example, the ASCII synchronisation character SYN has a value 22).

**CONTROL CONSOLE:** In a system with multiple *consoles*, one is designated to be in control of the entire system, thus known as the "control console".

**CONTROL DATA:** Items of data which are used to control, for example, the execution of a *package*.

**CONTROL DATA CORPORATION:** See *CDC*.

**CONTROL LOOP:** A synonym for *carriage control tape*.

**CONTROL REGISTER:** A cpu register which holds the address of the next instruction to be executed. Also known as the *sequence control register* or the *program counter*.

**CONTROL SEQUENCE:** The order in which instructions in a program are executed.

**CONTROL STATEMENT:** A statement in a programming language which requests a certain action. Alternatively, a statement in *job control language*.

**CONTROL TAPE:** A synonym for *carriage control tape*.

**CONTROL WORD:** Used in the same context as *control block* when the block is a single word.

**CONVERGENCE:** This is a word recently coined to describe the merging of three different technologies, computers, communications and office automation.

**CONVERSATIONAL:** A synonym for *interactive*.

**CONVERSATIONAL MODE:** A mode of operation in which the user interacts with the computer system.

**CONVERSATIONAL REMOTE JOB ENTRY:** A (fairly efficient) method of running a computer whereby users can edit files interactively but jobs are submitted to the *background* and a user cannot interact with a running job.

**CONVERSION:** The translation of data in one format to another. Often used in the context of modifying programs from one computer to run on another computer.

**CONVERSION PROGRAM:** A program written to convert data from one format to another.

**COPY:** To reproduce source data in an identical form, although the medium on which it is stored may alter, for example, copying a paper tape onto a magnetic tape. The word "duplicate" is more commonly used when the output medium is the same as the input.

**CORAL 66:** A high-level real-time language developed by the Royal Radar Establishment at Malvern, Worcestershire, UK.

**CORE:** Often used as a synonym for *memory* but more correctly refers to a form of secondary storage consisting of ferrite cores on a wire matrix, the direction of magnetisation signifying zero or one. Core memory has the advantage of being non-volatile, although considerably more bulky than more modern developments such as bubble memories.

**CORE STORAGE:** Primary storage consisting of *core*.

**CORRECTIVE MAINTENANCE:** Maintenance of a computer system following discovery of a fault. It should be contrasted with *preventative maintenance*.

**COURSEWRITER:** A language used particularly in "computer aided instruction" systems.

**CPI:** An abbreviation for *characters per inch*.

**CPL:** An acronym for *Combined Programming Language*, a very high-level language developed in the early 1960s jointly by the University of Cambridge and the Institute of Computer Science, London.

**CP/M:** A fairly complex operating system (similar to that on the DECsystem-10) available on a wide range of microcomputers and now a *de facto* standard. "CP/M" is a trademark of Digital Research. It is an abbreviation for *Control Program for Microcomputers*. A multi-user system has been developed based on CP/M, known as MP/M.

**CPS (1):** An acronym for *characters per second*, a measure of transmission rate, usually between terminal devices and a computer. Because of the different number of bits required to represent a character, there is no simple correlation between bits per second and characters per second. For example, 10 characters per second is usually 110 bits per second, while 30 characters per second is 300 bits per second.

**CPS (2):** An acronym for *cycles per second*, i.e. Hertz.

**CPU:** An acronym for *central processing unit*.

**CR:** An acronym for *carriage return*.

**CRASH:** An unexpected failure of a computer system.

**CRC:** An abbreviation for *cyclic redundancy check*.

**CRITICAL PATH METHOD:** A method usually applied to project planning where a network of events and activities is drawn and the critical paths evaluated. Also see *PERT*.

**CRJE:** An acronym for *conversational remote job entry*.

**CRO:** An acronym for *cathode ray oscilloscope*.

**CROSS CHECK:** A method of validating the results of a calculation by repeating it using a different method.

**CROSS-COMPILER:** A *compiler* which generates code for a different *object machine* than that on which it is running.

**CROSS REFERENCE:** An index to, for example, a program which provides a list of all variables and labels, together with the lines on which they occur.

**CROSS-REFERENCED PAGE:** A videotex page which can be selected from a page which is not its parent.

**CROSS TALK:** Interference between one circuit and another nearby.

**CRT:** An acronym for *cathode ray tube*.

**CSECT:** An acronym for *control section*, used in some assemblers (particularly IBM System/360) to indicate a program segment.

**CSIRO:** An acronym for *Commonwealth Scientific and Industrial Research Organisation*, a research organisation in Australia.

**CSMA:** An acronym for *carrier-sense multiple access*, a protocol used in broadcast satellite networks.

**CSMA-CD:** An acronym for *carrier-sense multiple access − collision detection*, a protocol used in broadcast satellite networks.

**CSMP:** An acronym for *Continuous System Modelling Program*, a simulation system.

**CSW:** An acronym for *channel status word*.

**CTNE:** An acronym for *Compania Telefonica Nacional de España*, the Spanish PTT. The acronym is often used for the packet switching network of the PTT which was one of the earliest packet switching networks in Europe. The initial network was based on nodes in Madrid and Barcelona and its principal use was for the banking community.

**CTS:** An acronym for *clear-to-send*, a handshaking signal in a modem interface.

**CUG:** An acronym for *closed user group*.

**CURSOR:** A short line or character on a VDU indicating where the next character is to be typed.

**CURSOR CONTROL:** A facility in VDUs enabling the *cursor* to be moved around the screen. The control facilities usually implemented are move up, down, right, left and to the top left-hand corner of the screen (*cursor home*).

**CURSOR HOME:** The operation (or the control character causing the operation) of moving the *cursor* to the top left-hand corner of the screen.

**CUSTOMER ENGINEER:** The person employed by a computer manufacturer who is responsible for maintenance of the computer system (usually hardware and software) when installed in the customer's premises.

**CYCLE (1):** To repeat the same sequence of operations.

**CYCLE (2):** The basic time unit of a processor.

**CYCLE STEALING:** The means whereby a peripheral uses one or more processor cycles to access memory (when using *direct memory access*), locking out the processor from memory for that period.

**CYCLE TIME:** The time required for one *cycle*, usually between 300 nanoseconds and one microsecond.

**CYCLIC CODE:** A means of encoding integers in a binary notation whereby any two adjacent numbers differ by a single bit (e.g. *Gray code*).

**CYCLIC REDUNDANCY CHECK:** A method of detecting errors where the *checksum* is the remainder after dividing the bits in a block of data by a specified binary number. This number is the set of the coefficients of the "generating polynomial". For example, the CRC-16 generating polynomial is $X^{16} + X^{15} + X^2 + 1$ and hence the divisor is 11000000000000101.

**CYCLIC SHIFT:** A synonym for *circular shift*.

**CYLINDER:** A subdivision of the space on a disk, consisting of a number of *tracks*.

# D

**DAC:** An abbreviation for *digital to analog(ue) converter.*

**DAISY WHEEL:** A plastic or metal disk with characters embossed on the ends of the "petals".

**DAISY WHEEL PRINTER:** A printing device which prints by means of a hammer hitting the appropriate character of a *daisywheel* against a ribbon. Such devices usually print at 45 or 55 cps and achieve an extremely high quality, especially since they often allow facilities such as proportional spacing. For this reason, they are usually the printing device employed in *word processors.* The two best known manufacturers are *Diablo* and *Qume.*

**DAP:** An abbreviation for *Distributed Array Processor.*

**DASD:** An abbreviation for *direct access storage device.* See *direct access.*

**DATA:** Strictly a plural of the noun "datum" denoting an item of information. However, it is now common to use the plural word as if it were singular, to mean information.

**DATA ACQUISITON:** The obtaining of data but more often applied in the more restricted context of a peripheral device which performs input functions only from, for example, process control monitors. The word is also applied to an entire computer system consisting of a processor, together with peripheral devices as just described.

**DATA ADAPTOR:** A device for connecting one item of computer equipment to another and performing various functions such as changing voltage levels. Sometimes used to mean a *modem.*

**DATABASE:** A structured set of records (usually a large set) which can be accessed using various *keys.*

**DATABASE MANAGEMENT:** The techniques associated with the management of a *database.*

**DATA CAPTURE:** The act of obtaining data by means of peripheral devices (see *data acquisition*).

**DATA CELL:** A high-capacity storage device developed by IBM. The device (known as the 2321) is *random-access* and a typical storage capacity is 400 Mbytes, stored on magnetic strips. These strips are contained in a "subcell", ten strips to a subcell. Twenty subcells are housed in a "data cell" and ten data cells form a "data cell array". The access time is of the order of a few hundred milliseconds.

**DATA CIRCUIT-TERMINATING EQUIPMENT (DCE):** The equipment at the PTT end of a telephone circuit.

**DATA COLLECTION:** A synonym for *data capture*.

**DATA COMMUNICATION:** The transmission of data over *communication channels*, usually telephone lines.

**DATA CONTROL:** A department within a computer installation which is responsible for ensuring that programs (jobs) which are submitted are run and that any output is married up to the input before returning to the programmer.

**DATA CONTROL BLOCK:** A *control block* used to control input/output operations, usually associated with the filestore and consisting of, for example, the *record length*, *block size* and *file name*.

**DATA CONVERSION:** The copying of data from one medium (such as paper tape) to another (such as magnetic disk).

**DATA DESCRIPTION:** The section of a program which defines the data items to be used within that program, together with their *attributes*.

**DATA DIVISION:** Part of a COBOL program which contains the *data descriptions*.

**DATA ELEMENT:** One single item of data within a program, for example, an *integer* or *array*.

**DATA ENCRYPTION STANDARD:** This is a Federal Information Processing Standard (USA) used for encryption of non-classified data which has to be transmitted over communication links. It uses a 56-bit key with 8 additional parity bits and is based on a system developed by IBM. There are a number of variations on the standard which are intended to make the system more secure.

**DATA ENTRY:** The act of getting data into a computer system.

**DATA FLOW:** The path of data during its processing in a computer system.

**DATA FLOW MACHINE:** A computer architecture where processing is not controlled by a linear sequence of instructions (as in a *von Neumann machine*) but by the data itself.

**DATA FORMAT:** A description of the size of *data elements* and their respective positions in a more complex structure such as a *field*.

**DATAGRAM:** A packet of data which is sent through a network and comprises a complete message. It has no connection with preceding or subsequent packets and hence, if a number of datagrams are sent from a source to a destination, there is no requirement that they arrive in the order in which they were sent.

**DATA LEVEL:** The level of a *data element* when included in a hierarchical structure as in, for example, COBOL or PL/1.

**DATA LINK:** Usually used as a synonym for *communications channel* but often also refers to the operation of that channel including connection to and disconnection from the remote computer.

**DATA MANAGEMENT:** The functions of an *operating system* concerned with the handling of data within that system including, for example, input/output, file manipulation and maintenance.

**DATA MANIPULATION LANGUAGE:** A language especially designed for the manipulation of data within a database.

**DATA NAME:** Sometimes used to refer to the symbolic reference to a data item, consisting of a sequence of alphanumeric characters (occasionally including other characters such as *underline*).

**DATA PAD:** An input device to a computer. The term is used in many different contexts but refers, for example, to a simple input device consisting of numeric keys only. One particular application for a datapad is as an input device to a videotex terminal.

**DATAPHONE:** A trademark of AT&T in the USA referring to a modified telephone (including a modem) which allows data to be transmitted over the switched public network.

**DATAPLEX:** A service of British Telecom allowing multiplexing of data over high-bandwidth communication channels. FDM or TDM techniques are used depending on the specific service chosen. The Dataplex 1 service uses FDM and allows six or twelve terminal connections to be multiplexed together; Dataplex 2 uses TDM and allows a much larger number of channels (depending on bandwidth required, up to 1200 bps) to be multiplexed onto a bearer circuit of 2400 or 4800 bps.

**DATA PREPARATION:** The operation of transferring information in written form (usually on *coding sheets*) into a machine readable form, for example, punched cards or, more recently, disk (see *key-to-disk*). Also used to mean the department of a computer installation concerned with this operation. Often abbreviated to "dataprep".

**DATA PROCESSING:** A term used in a very wide context, often used to mean any operation of a computer (since it processes data) but used more specifically to refer to the commercial, rather than scientific, aspects. The term can also be applied to similar processing without the use of a computer but this usage is declining rapidly.

**DATA PROCESSING STANDARDS:** Standards applied to data processing (and all other aspects of computing). There are a number of committees of the British Standards Institution concerned with this and they were known as DPS/n where "n" was the committee number. These Committees have now been renamed OIS/n, standing for "Office Information Systems" and the numbers of the Committees have now been brought into line with the corresponding ISO Committee.

**DATA REDUCTION:** A pre-processing of (raw) data to transform it into a more compact representation for a particular program.

**DATA REPRESENTATION:** The methods by which data is represented, particularly the sequence of characters or the bit patterns used within a computer (i.e. the external or internal representations).

**DATA RETRIEVAL:** The extraction of data from a *database*, usually by means of *keys*.

**DATA SECURITY:** The techniques involved in preventing unauthorised access to data.

**DATA SET:** A synonym for a *modem*.

**DATASET:** A collection of data. A file.

**DATA SHEET:** A synonym for *coding sheet*.

**DATA SIGNALLING RATE:** The speed at which data is transmitted over a *communications channel*.

**DATA SINK:** One end of a *communications channel* which receives the data. The other is known as the *data source*. More specifically, it refers only to a *simplex* channel since, in a full-duplex channel, each end of the channel can be a source (for one half of the connection) and a sink (for the other).

**DATA SOURCE:** One end of a *communications channel* which transmits the data. The other is known as the *data sink*. More specifically, it refers only to a *simplex* channel since, in a full-duplex channel, each end of the channel can be a source (for one half of the connection) and a sink (for the other).

**DATA STATEMENT:** A *statement* in a source program which refers to the definition of a data item.

**DATA STORAGE:** Either used as a verb to mean the storage of data on an appropriate device or as a noun to mean the medium on which the data is stored.

**DATA SWITCHING EXCHANGE:** A part of a *packet switched* computer network which performs the switching and routing functions, corresponding to the *IMP* in the *ARPANET*. It usually consists of a mini- or micro-computer.

**DATA TERMINAL:** A device which can transmit and/or receive data from a computer. Although more often applied to a device such as a VDU or a Teletype (consisting of a keyboard together with a display device such as a screen or paper), the term can be used to refer to more complex devices such as another computer.

**DATA TERMINAL EQUIPMENT (DTE):** Equipment consisting of a *data source* and a *data sink*, e.g. a terminal or a computer. The user end of a telephone circuit.

**DATA TRANSMISSION:** The transfer of data between a *data source* and a *data sink*, usually over a communications channel.

**DATA TRANSPARENCY:** A technique whereby any pattern of bits, including those normally used for control may be sent in a block. In byte oriented protocols, two methods commonly used are a count field and *data link escape*. In the first method, any *control characters* within the specified length are treated as data. In the second, any control character is only treated as such if preceded by the control character DLE. This also applies to DLE itself and hence, to send this character, it must be sent twice. In bit-oriented protocols (e.g. HDLC), a technique of *bit-stuffing* is used. That is, after a sequence of five binary ones, the sender inserts a zero bit. The receiver removes any binary zero following a sequence of five ones.

**DATA VALIDATION:** The act of checking that data fits certain defined criteria.

**DATA VET:** Used to refer to a program which performs *data validation*. Occasionally used as a verb to mean the carrying out of the process of *data validation*.

**DATA WORD:** An item of data stored as a single word.

**DATEL:** A term, originally used by the British Post Office but now used in a similar context internationally, to refer to the various data transmission services offered by the PTT, varying from telex services to high-bandwidth computer-computer communication lines.

**DATUM:** A single item of information. The plural of "datum" is *data* which is itself more commonly used (incorrectly) as a singular noun.

**dB:** An abbreviation for *decibel*.

**DBMS:** An abbreviation for *Data Base Management System*.

**DC:** An abbreviation for *device control*. In particular, the acronym is used for the control characters which have the functions of device control. In the ASCII code, there are four such characters, known as DC1 to DC4 and having the bit patterns 0010001, 0010010, 0010011 and 0010100 respectively (control-Q to control-T). These characters are also known as "X-on", "Tape-on", "X-off" and "Tape-off". Often DC1 and DC3 are used to control output to a VDU screen to stop the output from the computer temporarily and to restart it.

**DCA:** An abbreviation for *Defense Communications Agency*, a part of the US Department of Defense which now runs *ARPANET*.

**DCB:** An abbreviation for *data control block*.

**DCE:** An abbreviation for *data-circuit terminating equipment*.

**DD:** An abbreviation for *data definition*. Its most common usage is in IBM's Job Control Language where it is used as a connective mapping between the internal name used in a program and an external I/O device.

**DD CARD:** A statement used in IBM's Job Control Language for data definition. An example of such a statement is:

    //MACROS        DD              DSN=SYS1.MACLIB,DISP=SHR

which states that the *library* known internally to the program as MACROS refers to the file SYS1.MACLIB and that it can be shared between multiple users.

**DDCMP:** An abbreviation for *Digital Data Communications Message Protocol*. A line level protocol of DEC forming the lowest level of DECNET. It is a *bit-oriented* protocol.

**DDD:** An abbreviation for *direct distance dialling*, the US equivalent of STD.

**DDL:** An abbreviation for *Data Definition Language*, a language used to define data structures within a database.

**DDNAME:** A contraction of *data definition name*.

**DDT:** A generic name for a debugging program – various acronyms have been invented to fit the initials. The facilities available vary significantly but usually include the creation and deletion of breakpoints, the ability to examine and change memory locations and registers, to single-step through programs etc.

**DEAD TIME:** The gap between the termination of one event and the commencement of another in order to ensure no overlap.

**DEB:** An abbreviation for a *data event block*, a *control block* used in asynchronous processing which is modified to signify the progress of the specified event.

**DEBLOCK:** To split a block of data into its constituent records, usually done on transferring data from a block-oriented storage device into main memory or onto a non-block oriented device.

**DEBUG:** The act of removing errors from a computer system. It is usually facilitated by various tools from a front panel on a computer to a highly sophisticated software package (e.g. DDT).

**DEC:** Digital Equipment Corporation, one of the largest manufacturers of computers, especially the PDP range.

**DECIBEL:** One tenth of a *bel*, a measure of signal strength relative to a given reference level. A decibel is ten times the common logarithm (base 10) of that ratio.

**DECIMAL NOTATION:** A means of representing numbers using a base of ten. The characters used are (in order) 0, 1, 2, 3, 4, 5, 6, 7, 8 and 9.

**DECISION BOX:** A symbol used in *flowcharts* to indicate a point where a decision is to be taken and, depending on the result, one path or another will be followed. The usual symbol used is a diamond shape.

**DECISION TABLE:** A table representing the relationship between various functions and the actions to be taken when those relationships are met. It is a way of solving problems (cf. *flowchart*) but can be automated to a considerable degree and programs can be driven by means of decision tables.

**DECK (1):** A pack of punched cards.

**DECK (2):** A synonym for a *tape drive*.

**DECLARATION:** A statement in a programming language which defines attributes of data used in the program.

**DECODE:** Besides the commonsense use of the word, it is more specifically used to mean the act of the processor splitting an instruction word into its component parts prior to executing the instruction.

**DECOLLATE:** To split multi-part stationery into its component sheets.

**DECOLLATOR:** A device to split multi-part stationery into its component sheets.

**DECREMENT:** To reduce the value of a variable. If no amount is specified, it is assumed that the variable is decremented by one.

**DECTAPE:** A magnetic tape used on many DEC computers. The tape is 1″ wide and occurs on small spools. Data is recorded to include a timing track and hence the tape is addressable, i.e. blocks of data may be read and written anywhere on the tape (see *magnetic tape*). Each tape holds about 700 blocks.

**DECUS:** An acronym for *Digital Equipment Corporation Users' Society*.

**DEDICATED:** Reserved for one particular function or assigned to one particular task. For example, a tape drive may be "dedicated" to a particular *job* in the computer system.

**DEFAULT:** A value assigned by the writer of a program to be used when the user of that program does not specify a value for the given variable.

**DEGRADATION:** A reduction in service of a computer system (or component) due to a partial failure. If occurring in a controlled fashion, it is known as "graceful degradation".

**DEGRADE:** To reduce the performance of a computer system.

**DEL:** An abbreviation for the *delete character*.

**DELAY DISTORTION:** Distortion of a signal due to differing speeds of transmission of the components of the signal (because of their differing frequencies) through the transmission medium.

**DELAY LINE:** A component of some early computer systems where transmission of a signal was delayed, usually to implement a form of storage. See *acoustic delay line*.

**DELAY LINE STORAGE:** A form of storage, now obsolete, using *delay lines*.

**DELAY TIME:** The time taken between the issuing of an instruction or command and its being acted upon.

**DELETE (1):** A synonym for *delete character*.

**DELETE (2):** To remove a specified set of data – a file from a filestore or a program from main memory, for example.

**DELETE CHARACTER:** A character used to indicate that the previous character is to be ignored. In the ASCII code, there is a specific "delete character" whose value is 1111111 and so, if overprinted on paper tape, will completely obliterate the character to be deleted. Many computer systems use characters other than *delete* to mean character deletion (a common one is *backspace*) and sometimes use *delete* for other purposes (e.g. delete a line).

**DELETION RECORD:** An *amendment record* which specifies that a record in the *master file* is to be removed.

**DELIMIT:** To specify the limits for some variable quantity, such as the extent of a field.

**DELIMITER:** A specified character (or bit pattern) used to denote the termination of a field.

**DEMAND:** A system whereby resources are allocated dynamically, as they are needed, and not on a fixed basis.

**DEMAND MULTIPLEXING:** A form of *Time Division Multiplexing* in which time slots are allocated according to demand, i.e. the volume of data to be transmitted by each sub-channel.

**DEMODULATE:** To take a composite signal, consisting of a *carrier wave* modulated by the required signal, and recover the original signal.

**DEMODULATOR:** A device which *demodulates* a composite signal. Usually found in conjunction with the device which performs modulation and the total device is known as a *modem*.

**DENOMINATOR:** A synonym for *divisor* in a *division* operation.

**DEPOSIT:** Usually used to mean *store* in the context "the value 10 was deposited in location **X**".

**DEQUE(UE):** A double-ended queue.

**DES:** An abbreviation for *Data Encryption Standard*.

**DESCENDENT PAGES:** A term used in a viewdata system to describe all pages below a specified page.

**DESCENDER:** The part of a printed character projecting below the body of the character (below the line). In many cheap matrix printers, descenders are omitted from characters as the matrix used is not large enough to permit this; the resultant output is not as clear as when descenders are printed.

**DESCRIPTOR:** A qualifier which serves to describe another item. For example, a data item may have an attached "descriptor" which defines its data type.

**DESTINATION:** The place to which something (usually data) is sent from the *source*.

**DESTINATION FILE:** A file to which data is sent, usually as the output of a program run.

**DESTRUCTIVE READ:** The operation of reading data from some storage device which results in the destruction of the data being read. In cases where this is not the required objective, the data is then immediately rewritten to the same location.

**DEUCE:** An acronym for *Digital Electronic Universal Calculating Engine*, an early computer built in the UK. Its predecessor was *ACE*.

**DEVELOPMENT SYSTEM:** A computer system consisting of various components such as central processor, memory, display screen etc. which can be used by a systems programmer with relative ease to develop computer systems. The term is most commonly used in the context of microprocessor systems and examples of such systems are "Intellec" and "Exorciser".

**DEVICE CODE:** A unique code (often eight-bit) which serves to identify an input/output device.

**DEVICE CONTROL:** The control of a peripheral device (for example, starting and stopping a tape reader) by means of special characters or interface signals.

**DEVICE CONTROL CHARACTER:** A character used to perform device control functions. In the ASCII character set, four such codes are defined, DC1 to DC4, and these are discussed in more detail under *DC*.

**DEVICE INDEPENDENCE:** Usually used to mean the technique of writing programs so that they perform input/output functions with no regard to the functional characteristics of the device actually used, thus allowing the device to be defined at a later stage.

**DIABLO:** A US manufacturer best known for its high-quality *daisy-wheel* printers.

**DIAGNOSE:** To determine the nature of a problem with a computer system by examining the effects of the problem. The term is more often used for hardware problems, while *debug* is more commonly used for software problems.

**DIAGNOSTIC CHECK:** The use of various tools, in particular, special purpose programs, in order to diagnose problems in a computer system.

**DIAGNOSTIC PROGRAM:** A special purpose program which can be run in order to determine problems occurring in a computer system.

**DIAGNOSTICS:** The results of a run on a *diagnostic program*.

**DIALOG:** A database enquiry system operated by Lockheed in the USA giving access to a number of databases.

**DIAL-UP:** Usually used as an adjective to describe a means of access to a remote computer system by use of the public switched telephone network.

**DIBIT:** A group of two bits, represented by a single signal (which thus requires four levels).

**DICHOTOMISING SEARCH:** A rarely used synonym for *binary search*.

**DICTIONARY:** Although sometimes used in the more general sense, the word is most often used to mean the list of names (rarely in alphabetical order) generated by a compiler in the process of compilation.

**DIFFERENCE ENGINE:** A precursor of the modern computer designed by Charles Babbage in 1822.

**DIGIT:** A character referring to a numeric value.

**DIGITAL (1):** Pertaining to the representation of values in a system by means of numeric values (cf. *analogue*).

**DIGITAL (2):** An abbreviation for *Digital Equipment Corporation*.

**DIGITAL COMPUTER:** A computer using digital principles to perform calculations. More specifically, all values in the computer are represented by discrete signals rather than by continuously variable values (*analogue*).

**DIGITAL DATA:** Data which is represented in discrete, two-state (usually) form as opposed to analogue data which is represented by continuously variable form.

**DIGITAL EQUIPMENT CORPORATION:** See *DEC*.

**DIGITAL NETWORK ARCHITECTURE:** An architecture for distributed computer systems, developed by DEC. The implementation of this architecture is known as DECNET.
> 1. Wecker, S., "DNA: The Digital Network Architecture", IEEE Transactions on Communications, COM-28(4), 510–526, 1980.

**DIGITISE:** To convert from an analogue signal into a sequence of digital values. This is usually done by sampling the analogue signal at fixed intervals (the sampling frequency) and converting the value so obtained into the nearest value on a quantised scale. This technique is used in data communications (*pulse code modulation*) and *facsimile transmission*.

**DIMENSION:** The number of elements in an array referenced by one subscript. Thus the array:

$$A[1:10,2:6,-1:1]$$

has three dimensions, 10, 5 and 3 respectively.

**DIODE:** An electronic component which has the feature that current may flow through it in only one direction.

**DIP:** An acronym for *dual-in-line package*, the package on which a *chip* in mounted.

**DIP HEADER:** A component which plugs into a printed circuit board which has a number of pins which may be interconnected by soldered wire connections.

**DIRECT ACCESS:** A descriptor applied to storage which indicates that the access time for any data stored on that medium is independent of its location. In general, primary memory is direct access, whereas disks are pseudo-direct access and tapes are not (they are sequential access).

**DIRECT ADDRESSING:** Synonymous with *absolute addressing*.

**DIRECT CODE:** A synonym for *absolute (machine) code*.

**DIRECT DISTANCE DIALLING:** See *DDD*.

**DIRECT MEMORY ACCESS (DMA):** A facility permitting input/output to and from computer memory without passing through the cpu. In order to do this, the peripheral locks out the processor from memory for the required time, known as *cycle stealing*.

**DIRECTIVE:** A statement within a program which instructs the compiler or assembler to take a specified action while it is compiling rather than generating code which is executed when the program is run. Examples of directives are "TITLE" which is often used to indicate a heading to be printed out as the first line of each page of listing and "END" which instructs the compiler to cease compilation.

**DIRECTORY:** A table giving some information about some data storage, sometimes in main memory but more often used for backing store. On a file-oriented device, the directory will give such information as the file-names, their addresses and sizes.

**DIRECTORY ROUTING:** A method of routing in a distributed computer network in which the preferred routes between nodes are predetermined according to the entries of a table (which may indicate second preferences to be used if the first preference is unavailable). It has the advantage of simplicity (and hence low overheads) but the disadvantage that a route may exist between two nodes but may not be accessible. This is the routing method used in the British Post Office's Experimental Packet Switched Service.

**DISABLE:** To prevent a function being recognised and/or acted upon. For example, to disable interrupts means that the processor will ignore any interrupts which occur and hence take no action. The opposite is *enable*.

**DISABLED:** The state of being unable to be recognised; for example, one might say "interrupts are disabled".

**DISK:** A secondary, pseudo-random access storage device which occurs in many forms. The two major divisions are between *hard* and *floppy* disks, the former being rigid using a metal or glass base, the latter being flexible and having a plastic base. The disk is covered by a magnetic material and the data is recorded on this material using read/write heads. The disk rotates at quite a high speed (for example, hard disks often rotate at 2400 rpm) and hence data can be accessed quite fast. In addition, the transfer rate is also high. The disk is logically split into *tracks* and each track is divided into a number of *sectors*.

**DISK OPERATING SYSTEM:** An *operating system* which is available on systems with a disk and relevant routines are loaded from disk as needed.

**DISK PACK:** A set of disks on a common spindle, handled as a single unit.

**DISKETTE:** A synonym for *floppy disk*.

**DISPATCHING PRIORITY:** A number assigned to processes within an operating system which decides their relative priorities in accessing the central processor.

**DISPLACEMENT:** The number of address locations between that specified and a reference location. It is usually used in the context of *base/displacement addressing*.

**DISPLAY CONSOLE:** An input/output device which usually consists of a screen and keyboard but often has additional features. It is most commonly used to examine (and perhaps modify) storage locations of a computer.

**DISTRIBUTED ARRAY PROCESSOR:** A device developed by ICL which consists of a matrix of a large number (of the order of 4096) of small processors enabling extensive calculations to be performed. It is attached as a peripheral to an ICL mainframe.

**DISTRIBUTED NETWORK:** A network topology in which all nodes are connected either directly or through intermediate nodes.

**DISTRIBUTED PROCESSING:** The processing of *jobs* at a number of geographically separated locations.

**DIVIDEND:** One of the operands in a division operation. It is divided by the *divisor* to yield a *quotient* and a *remainder*.

**DIVISION (1):** An arithmetic operation usually represented in high-level languages by the "/" operator. A *dividend* is divided by a *divisor* yielding a *quotient* and a *remainder*. For example, with a dividend of 11 and a divisor of 5, the quotient (result) is 2 and the remainder is 1.

**DIVISION (2):** A part of some entity, usually a program (for example, in COBOL, the program is divided into the *data division* etc.).

**DIVISOR:** One of the operands in a division operation. It is divided into the *dividend* to yield a *quotient* and a *remainder*.

**DLE:** An abbreviation for *data link escape*. A control character usually used to provide data transparency in that any control characters (e.g. STX, ETX and DLE itself) are only recognised as such if preceded by DLE.

**DMA:** An abbreviation for *direct memory access*.

**DNA:** An abbreviation for *Digital Network Architecture*.

**DOCUMENT (vb):** To write a description of the functions of a program.

**DOCUMENT (n):** Any written or printed information.

**DOCUMENTATION:** The set of descriptions of the functions of a program or set of programs.

**DOPE VECTOR:** A sequence of contiguous locations which are used to simplify access to a multi-dimensional array.

**DOPING:** The process of introducing impurities into the silicon substrate in order to construct semiconductor components.

**DOS:** An acronym for *disk operating system*.

**DOT PRINTER:** A printer which forms characters as a set of dots, usually by means of a matrix of needles (see *matrix printer*) but sometimes by a single needle or a line of needles which thus need to traverse the paper a number of times to form a single character.

**DOUBLE BUFFERING:** A technique of input/output buffering in which two buffers are used, one containing data which is being processed, the other containing data to be read to or written from the output device thus allowing these operations to be overlapped. After processing is finished on the buffers, their roles are exchanged.

**DOUBLE LENGTH:** The use of a storage location or register which is double the usual length, in order to perform *double precision arithmetic*.

**DOUBLE PRECISION:** The use of a *double-length* location in order to perform arithmetic with increased (not actually double) accuracy.

**DOUBLE PRECISION ARITHMETIC:** The use of *double precision* for arithmetic operations.

**DOUBLE PRECISION HARDWARE:** *Hardware* enabling *double precision arithmetic* to be performed.

**DOUBLEWORD:** A set of two contiguous locations in memory (*words* treated as a single entity for some purposes. For example, in the IBM System/360 and /370, a "doubleword" is 64 bits (eight bytes) long.

**DOWN-TIME:** The time for which a computer system is inoperative.

**DPM:** An abbreviation for *data processing manager*.

**DPMA:** An abbreviation for *Data Processing Management Association*. The UK DPMA has been merged into the *Institute of Data Processing Management*.

**DPS:** An abbreviation for *Data Processing Standards*.

**DRIVE:** The mechanical device which transports a recording medium e.g. tape or disk.

**DRIVER:** The routine(s) which perform low-level input/output functions for a particular I/O device.

**DROP-OUT:** A loss of signal, either in data communications or from a magnetic storage medium.

**DRUM:** A secondary storage medium which is in the shape of a drum with the recording surface on the outside. The drum rotates and the data is read by a number of heads parallel to the surface. A drum is a fairly fast device, particularly as there is no seek time, but is fairly expensive. To some extent, it has been superseded by fixed-head disks.

**DRUM PRINTER:** A *printer* which operates by means of a drum on which are embossed all the possible characters.

**DRY RUN:** A method of testing programs by attempting to simulate the flow of control in the computer by hand, off-line (that is, on a piece of paper rather than on the computer).

**DSE:** An abbreviation for *Data Switching Exchange*.

**DSECT:** An acronym for *dummy section*. In IBM Assembler (System/360 and System/370), a DSECT contains data declarations but does not actually reserve space for that data.

**DSN:** An abbreviation for DSNAME.

**DSNAME:** An acronym for *data set name*, the name given to a file in some system (particularly IBM).

**DTE:** An abbreviation for *data terminal equipment*.

**DTL:** An abbreviation for *diode-transistor logic*.

**DTSS:** An abbreviation for *Dartmouth Time Sharing System*. This is an interactive system developed by Dartmouth College, Hanover, New Hampshire, first operational in 1969. It was based on early interactive systems developed at Dartmouth since 1964 and ran on GE computers. These computers have been superseded by Honeywell 66 machines. The major feature of the system is that it provides a highly "user-friendly" system, enabling non-computer science specialists to use the system with little training. This is achieved, in part, by the integration of the monitor system, editors and language translators into one homogeneous package with a unified interface. This interface is commonly available on other computers for the BASIC language but, on DTSS, is available for the entire system.

  1. Kemeny, J.G. and Kurtz, T.E., "Dartmouth Time Sharing", *Science*, 223–228, Oct. 1968.

**DUMB TERMINAL:** A terminal which has no "intelligence" (cf. *intelligent terminal*).

**DUMMY INSTRUCTION:** An instruction which has no effect on the system and is often used when it is required to *pad* a program (for example, on CDC 6600 machines, due to the implementation of differing length instructions, it is sometimes required to put short dummy instructions to pad to a word boundary). Effectively the same as a *no-op instruction*.

**DUMP (n):** A bulk transfer of data from one medium to another, for example, the transfer of the contents of main memory to a line printer.

**DUMP (vb):** To perform a dump.

**DUMP/RESTART:** The technique of dumping of the variable part of a program to a storage device at frequent intervals so that, in the event of failure, the program may be restarted from the most recent dump.

**DUMP ROUTINE:** A routine which performs a *dump*.

**DUODECIMAL:** A number system using base 12.

**DUPLEX:** Loosely used as a synonym for *full-duplex*.

**DUPLEXING:** The duplication of resources, such as computers, usually for reasons of security.

**DUPLICATE:** Used either as a verb or a noun to mean an exact copy of an item (on the same medium) or the making of that copy.

**DVORAK:** A *keyboard* which is designed to be more efficient to use than a standard *qwerty* keyboard.

**DYADIC:** Used as an adjective to describe an item which pertains to two operands — for example, multiply is a dyadic operator.

**DYNAMIC:** Changing with time (cf. *static*).

**DYNAMIC MEMORY:** Computer memory which only retains its stored information for a short time and which hence has to be continually "refreshed". It is cheaper than "static" memory but less reliable and, with some processors, reduces processor throughput due to the need to refresh the memory.

**DYNAMIC MULTIPLEXING:** A synonym for *demand multiplexing*.

**DYNAMIC RELOCATION:** The moving of a program (or part of a program) within a computer's memory with all address references being modified as required so that execution can continue, effectively unaltered. In this way, the computer is able to use the memory more efficiently.

**DYNAMIC STORAGE ALLOCATION:** The allocation of storage on a dynamic basis, that is, storage is allocated and de-allocated as required thus providing a more efficient way of allocating memory which is a relatively rare resource but with the overheads of allocating and de-allocating the memory (see *garbage collection*).

# E

**EAM:** An abbreviation for *electronic accounting machine.*

**EAN:** An abbreviation for *European Article Number* – the computer coding (bar code) used for consumer products.

**EAROM:** An abbreviation for *Electrically Alterable Read Only Memory.* See *ROM.*

**EBCDIC:** An abbreviation for *Extended Binary Coded Decimal Interchange Code.* An eight-bit code used (mainly) on IBM equipment. An extended version of BCD.

**ECAP:** An acronym for *Electronic Circuit Analysis Program.*

**ECB:** An abbreviation for *event control block.*

**ECHO CHECK:** A means of checking transmitted data visually in which the data is transmitted back to the source so that it can be examined and compared with the original.

**ECHO SUPPRESSOR:** A device fitted to telephone lines (particularly long-distance ones) which suppresses echoing, especially needed in data transmission.

**ECHOPLEX:** A variation of *full-duplex* in which the characters typed are not printed directly but are echoed (from the remote end of the connection or some intermediate point) and then printed.

**ECKERT:** One of the designers of "ENIAC", one of the first electronic computers.

**ECL:** An abbreviation for *emitter coupled logic*, a technology for fabricating logic components. ECL components are faster than TTL ones.

**ECMA:** The European Computer Manufacturers' Association – a standards body.

**EDGE-PUNCHED CARD:** A card used for recording data by means of holes punched along one edge of the card.

**EDIT (vb):** To amend a file, using an *editor*.

**EDITOR:** A program to amend the text of a file. There are many variations of editors, ranging from that provided with BASIC systems, allowing whole lines to be inserted, deleted or replaced to highly sophisticated editors such as TECO which, for example, allows users to create macros and has a similar power to that of a programming language. In general, editors may be line (context) or character oriented. The usual facilities provided include (in either case) searching for a given string, replacing a string (either the first occurrence or globally), deletion, insertion and moving text within the file. The major function provided by *word processors* is editing.

**EDP:** An abbreviation for *Electronic Data Processing*. A term which refers to the processing of data by a computer system. The term is more common in the USA while in Europe, the term with the first word omitted is more often used.

**EDS:** An abbreviation for *exchangeable disk store*. A general term to cover disk storage (e.g. cartridges) which may be removed and replaced by another.

**EDSAC:** The Electronic Delay Storage Automatic Computer. This was one of the first electronic computers, developed in 1949 by the Mathematics Department at the University of Cambridge.

**EDVAC:** The Electronic Discrete Variable Automatic Computer, designed and built at the University of Pennsylvania in 1949.

**EFFECTIVE ADDRESS:** The actual address used when accessing memory, formed from the address given in the instruction, perhaps modified by index registers. For example, in the IBM System/370, an address may be given in terms of three components, a *base*, *displacement* and *index*. The effective address is formed by adding the contents of the base register, the contents of the index register and the displacement, then calculating the remainder, modulo 16 777 216.

**EFFECTIVE TIME:** The time during which a computer is performing actual work, excluding such items as diagnostic test runs.

**EFTS:** An abbreviation for *Electronic Funds Transfer System*, a generic name given to systems for performing various banking functions electronically and not requiring the transfer of large quantities of paper.

**EIGHTY-COLUMN CARD:** A punched card which has eighty columns. This is a *de facto* standard, although other cards (e.g. 96 columns) exist. As a result of this standard, files are often *card images* and consist of 80 character records.

**EIN:** An abbreviation for the *European Informatics Network*. This network was set up by the COST-11 agreement between a number of European countries and EURATOM as a research network based on five sites, London (National Physical Laboratory), Paris (IRIA), Zurich (ETH), Milan and ISPRA with a number of secondary sites. It is a heterogeneous, packet-switched network which uses the CII Mitra 15 as a node processor.

**ELAPSED TIME:** The time taken to perform a specified task, measured in real-time (i.e. clock time) as opposed to processor time.

**ELECTRIC PENCIL:** A proprietary word-processing package available on a number of microcomputers.

**ELECTRONIC MAIL:** A generic term referring to the distribution of mail by means of interconnected word processors or computers. In addition to virtually instantaneous transmission of the mail, together with confirmation of delivery, most electronic mail systems allow processing of received messages to enable them to be read selectively etc. There are a number of commercial products facilitating the sending and processing of electronic mail but its spread has been inhibited by its being illegal in various countries, including the UK (except under certain conditions). However, this is likely to change with the advent of computer networks.

**ELECTROSENSITIVE PRINTER:** A relatively cheap form of printer which prints by means of a print head moving across special paper and varying its potential.

**ELECTROSTATIC PRINTER:** A form of printer which is based on a similar principle to xerography. The appropriate characters are formed on the specially coated paper by an electrostatic charge which is then "fixed" by passing through a toner.

**EM:** An abbreviation for *end of medium*. An ASCII control character whose value is 0011001 (control-Y).

**EMULATE:** To perform the task of *emulation*.

**EMULATION:** The technique of making one computer behave as if it were another, usually achieved at the hardware level. It is common when a manufacturer produces a new range of computers which are not compatible with earlier models for the manufacturer to provide emulation of the earlier range on the new machines.

**EMULATOR:** Something which allows *emulation*, frequently a program in ROM.

**ENABLE (vb):** To permit a function to be recognised and/or acted upon. For example, to enable interrupts means that the processor will recognise interrupts and act on them. The opposite is *disable*.

**ENABLED:** An adjective describing the status of a device which is able to recognise and/or act upon a specified event or function.

**ENCODE:** To convert data in one form into another. The term is used in various contexts, for example, as a synonym for *encryption* or for translation from a computer language into *machine code*.

**ENCRYPT:** To perform the function of *encryption*.

**ENCRYPTION:** To transform data from *plaintext* into an encoded form in order to retain security of the data, particularly when sent over communication lines.

**END:** Often used as a reserved word in many computer languages to indicate the physical or logical termination of a program or program module.

**END AROUND CARRY:** A *carry* from the most significant position of a number to the least significant.

**END AROUND SHIFT:** A synonym for *circular shift*.

**END OF FILE MARKER:** A bit pattern used to indicate the logical termination of a file. Various such patterns are used, usually consisting of a single control character. The three most common are ctrl-A (binary 00000001), ctrl-D (binary 00000100) and ctrl-Z (binary 000011010). The last is used in the CP/M operating system.

**END OF FILE ROUTINE:** A software routine which assumes control when the end of a file is detected. Often such a routine is provided as part of the operating system but the user has the opportunity to substitute his own version.

**END OF TAPE MARKER:** In the context of magnetic tape, this term is used to refer to a physical marker such as a reflective strip which indicates the end of the area on which data may be recorded. In the case of a medium such as paper tape, this usually refers to a character (usually ctrl-D, the ETX character) which indicates the end of tape.

**END OF VOLUME:** A marker which indicates the end of a physical volume. Also used to refer to the software routine which takes control when that situation is detected.

**END MARK:** An indication that the end of a given item has been reached.

**END PAGE:** A term used in *videotex* to indicate a *page* which contains information and is not a *routing page*. Usually an end page will contain a very restricted set of routing choices.

**ENIAC:** The Electronic Numerical Integrator and Calculator, an early computer built at the University of Pennsylvania in 1946 by Mauchly and Eckert.

**ENQ:** An abbreviation for *enquiry*. A control character used particularly in line protocols (especially BSC) as part of the initialisation sequence. In ASCII, its value is binary 0000101 (control-E).

**ENTRY (1):** An item in a set of such items, e.g. a table.

**ENTRY (2):** A synonym for *entry point*.

**ENTRY CODE:** A set of instructions which are the first to be executed in a program module and which usually perform such functions as saving registers.

**ENTRY POINT:** The point (or points) in a program module which may be accessed externally and to which control may be passed.

**ENVIRONMENT DIVISION:** A part of a COBOL program which defines the computer system on which the program is to be executed.

**EOB:** An abbreviation for *end of block*.

**EOF:** An abbreviation for *end of file*.

**EOJ:** An abbreviation for *end of job*, usually referring to a specific delimiter which signifies the end of the set of data (including instructions and control statements) comprising a *job*.

**EOM:** An abbreviation for *end of message*, a control character used in data transmission indicating the termination of the data comprising the message. There is no specific code for this in ASCII but often it is equated with ETX.

**EOT:** An abbreviation for *end of transmission*. A control character often used in line protocols to signify the end of transmission. In ASCII, its value is binary 0000100 (control-D).

**EOV:** An abbreviation for *end of volume*.

**EPROM:** An acronym for *Erasable Programmable Read Only Memory*. ROM which can, however, be erased, usually by means of an ultra-violet lamp, and then rewritten.

**EPSS:** An abbreviation for *Experimental Packet Switched Service*, the British Post Office's experimental packet-switched computer network which went live in April 1977. The network consisted of three "packet-switching exchanges", in London, Manchester and Glasgow and allowed access by 166 terminals and 84 "Host" computers. The "packet switching units" in the PSEs were Ferranti Argus 700 computers. The network was designed prior to international agreement on protocols and hence the protocols implemented were non-standard.

**EQU:** A directive in a number of assemblers to indicate that one symbol is to be equivalenced to another.

**EQUALISATION:** The reduction of distortion on a communications line arising from attenuation and time delays which vary according to frequency.

**EQUIPMENT FAILURE:** Failure of a computer system due to hardware as opposed to software.

**EQUIVALENCE:** A logical operation which gives the result 1 if both operands are the same and 0 otherwise. It conforms to the following table:

| ≡ | 0 | 1 |
|---|---|---|
| 0 | 1 | 0 |
| 1 | 0 | 1 |

**ERASE:** To remove information on a storage medium, particularly magnetic tape.

**ERASE CHARACTER:** A character which indicates that some item is to be erased or deleted. Often the term is used as a synonym for *delete character*, particularly when the latter is *backspace*.

**ERASE HEAD:** A part of a magnetic tape drive which removes information from the tape prior to new information being written. It usually operates by means of a DC current or a high-frequency signal being superimposed on the tape.

**ERROR:** A discrepancy between an expected or theoretical value and that calculated. The word is also used as a synonym for *fault*.

**ERROR BURST:** A condition on a transmission line which gives rise to a large degree of noise resulting in errors in transmission.

**ERROR CHECKING CODE:** A code which checks data which has been transmitted and detects errors. One such example is a *cyclic redundancy check*.

**ERROR CODE:** A character or sequence of characters which define the type of an error which has occurred. For example, on IBM System/370, the error code 013 indicates an error while opening a file.

**ERROR CORRECTING CODE:** A code which is an *error checking code* but which is also able to correct any errors which are detected. This ability is restricted to a certain frequency of errors.

**ERROR DETECTING CODE:** A synonym for *error checking code*.

**ERROR DIAGNOSTIC:** A message printed indicating the cause of an error, usually produced by a systems program or by a language translator.

**ERROR MESSAGE:** The same as *error diagnostic.*

**ERROR RATE:** A measure of the number of bits transmitted over a communications line which are received incorrectly as a fraction of the total number of bits transmitted. Over ordinary telephone lines, the error rate is of the order of one part in 10 000 while in packet-switched networks, the undetected error rate is of the order of one part in $10^{10}$.

**ERROR RECOVERY:** The method of taking action following detection of an error which allows processing to continue as if the error had not occurred.

**ERROR REPORT:** A listing of the errors encountered during processing of a program.

**ERROR ROUTINE:** A sequence of instructions invoked upon detection of an error.

**ERROR TAPE:** A magnetic tape on which the *error report* is written for later analysis.

**ESC:** A control character whose value, in the ASCII code, is 0011011 (control-[). It is called "escape" or "alt-mode" and has a variety of uses in different systems. For example, it is often used in editors to denote the end of a block of text which is to be inserted into a file.

**ESCAPE CHARACTER:** See *ESC.*

**ETB:** An abbreviation for *end of transmission block.* A control character which, in ASCII, is binary 0010111 (control-W).

**ETHERNET:** A network technology devised by the Xerox Corporation at their Palo Alto Research Center in which a number of devices access the transmission medium (a co-axial cable) on a contention basis. Very high data rates (e.g. 10 Mbps) are possible and Ethernet is one technology for implementing *local area networks.* A draft standard was published in 1980 by a consortium of three manufacturers, Xerox, Intel and DEC for the 10 Mbps Ethernet and it is likely that this will form the basis of an international standard for this technology. A commercial version of Ethernet is marketed by Ungermann-Bass.

1. Metcalfe, R.M. and Boggs, D.R., "ETHERNET: Distributed Packet Switching for Local Computer Networks", Comm. ACM, **19**, 395–404, 1976.

2. "The Ethernet: A Local Area Network – Data Link Layer and
Physical Layer Specifications, Version 1.0", DEC/Intel/Xerox, Sep-
tember 1980.

**ETX:** An abbreviation for *end of text*. A control character to indicate the
end of a message. In ASCII, its value is binary 0000011 (control-C).

**EVEN PARITY:** A system of using *parity* to check for errors in which the
number of bits set, including the *parity bit* is even.

**EVENT:** An occurrence in a computer system such as the receipt of a
character from a terminal. The terminology is used in an asynchronous
computer system when the system "waits" for events to occur and takes
action when this happens.

**EVENT CONTROL BLOCK:** A *control block* which is used to indicate the
status of events which are expected to occur and to take appropriate
action in certain specified situations.

**EVENT DRIVEN:** Refers to a computer system which is asynchronous
and actions only take place when *events* are detected.

**EXCEPTION REPORTING:** The listing of deviations from expected
results.

**EXCESS-N NOTATION:** A method of representing integers in which the
number, represented in M bits, is stored as the sum of itself and $2^{m-1}$.
Thus, as used in the exponent of floating point numbers in IBM System/
370, seven bits are available and hence any number is stored as the sum
of itself and 64, the notation being called excess-64 notation. This
method is identical to 2s complement notation with the sign bit reversed.

**EXCHANGE BUFFERING:** A technique of buffering when the data
which has been read into a buffer, rather than being copied into another
buffer, is processed in the original buffer. In order to provide a free buffer
to continue reading, the processing program gives access to one of its
buffers in exchange for the system buffer which it is using.

**EXCHANGEABLE DISK STORE:** See *EDS*.

**EXCLUSIVE-OR:** A logical operation which gives a result 1 if both operands are different and 0 otherwise (it is also known as *non-equivalence* or
*addition without carry*). It conforms to the following table:

|   | 0 | 1 |
|---|---|---|
| 0 | 0 | 1 |
| 1 | 1 | 0 |

**EXECUTABLE:** A program statement which gives rise to machine code which is executed by the processor. It should be compared with *non-executable* statements, such as *directives*.

**EXECUTE:** To perform the functions specified by an *instruction*.

**EXECUTE CYCLE:** The part of a computer cycle in which the instruction is executed. This follows the *fetch* phase.

**EXECUTION:** The performance of the machine instructions comprising a program.

**EXECUTION TIME:** The time taken for a computer to carry out a sequence of instructions (for example, a program). It will usually differ from elapsed time.

**EXECUTIVE:** The software which controls a computer. The term is used in many different senses and is often used synonymously for *operating system* or *monitor*.

**EXIT (vb):** To cease execution of a program module and return control to the calling module.

**EXIT (n):** The point in a program module from which control is returned to the calling module.

**EXIT CODE:** The instructions which occur prior to the exit from a program module and which perform functions such as restoring registers to their values prior to entry to the module (cf. *entry code*).

**EXORCISER:** A development package for the Motorola M6800 microprocessor.

**EXPANDING OP-CODES:** In early computers, the operation to be performed by a machine instruction was specified by a fixed number of bits, usually at the beginning of the instruction. In some machines, this proved unsatisfactory (because the manufacturer wished to upgrade the machine and had provided insufficient bits in the op-code field for this or because bits in the instruction were wasted) and hence the technique of the "expanding op-code" was evolved, namely that a certain op-code, instead of relating to a single operation, referred instead to a whole family of operations, the specific operation being designated by additional bits.

**EXPANSION CARD:** A *card* which is added to a computer system to expand the facilities available, for example, to increase the memory capacity.

**EXPONENT:** The power to which a base is raised. See *floating point*.

**EXPRESSION:** A sequence of variables and/or constants, separated by operators, which can be evaluated to give a result.

**EXTENT:** A contiguous area on a secondary storage device comprising part of a file.

**EXTERNAL CLOCKING:** Transmission of data in which the rate of transmission is determined, not by the transmitter, but by some external agent, usually the *modem*.

**EXTERNAL DATA FILE:** A *file* containing data for use by a program, i.e. the required data is not contained within the program itself.

**EXTERNAL NAME:** A symbol within a program module which refers to (or may be referred to by) another module. When program modules are translated independently, all internal names are converted into addresses but external names are retained and are resolved only when the modules are *linked* together.

**EXTERNAL REFERENCE:** A reference to an *external name* in another module.

**EXTERNAL SORT:** A generic name for a set of sorting techniques in which the items to be sorted cannot be held at one time in the computer memory and therefore must reside on some form of backing storage.

**EXTERNAL SYMBOL:** A synonym for *external name*.

**EXTERNAL SYMBOL DICTIONARY:** A list of *external symbols*, together with any other pertinent information such as the modules with which they are associated.

**EXTRACT:** To remove a selected item (which may be, for example, a part of a computer word) from a set of such items.

# F

**FACE:** The printed side of a card or, by extension, a verb to mean sorting a *card deck* into order such that all printed sides are the same way round.

**FACSIMILE:** Used in the context of "facsimile transmission" to indicate the transmission of a copy of a document, usually to a remote location. This is (usually) achieved by scanning the input document at whatever resolution is required and transmitting the resultant output either as an analog(ue) or a digital signal. In the latter case, the analog(ue) signal is sampled at an appropriate rate (again depending on the resolution required) and the resultant sequence of values transmitted. Increases in speed of transmission can be achieved by such techniques as blank compression.
There is much standardisation work in this area and standards have already been agreed for some facsimile Groups. In particular, CCITT Group 1 (allowing an A4 page to be transmitted in 6 minutes) was agreed in 1967, Group 2 (3 mins) in 1977 and, in 1981, Group 3 using digital transmission and allowing an A4 page to be transmitted in under one minute (on wideband lines, in ten seconds).

**FAILSOFT:** A technique for ensuring that, in the event of a system failure, the minimal harm is done and it is possible to recover to a specified point with no loss of data integrity.

**FAIRCHILD:** The Fairchild Instrument Corporation, a large American manufacturer of computer hardware, possibly best known by its F8 microcomputer.

**FALLBACK:** Used as an adjective or a verb describing facilities (or their usage) which are available in the case of the primary facilities becoming unavailable.

**FAMOS:** An acronym for *floating gate avalanche injection MOS*, a technology for semiconductor components.

**FATHER FILE:** Refers to a system of file updating when the file to be updated is not destroyed and replaced by the new file but is retained as the "father file".

**FAULT:** An unforeseen error, the term usually referring to the occurrence of this in hardware (cf. *bug*) or in the design of software.

**FAX:** An abbreviation for *facsimile transmission*.

**FCC:** An abbreviation for *Federal Communications Commission*, a statutory body in the USA which regulates communications.

**FDM:** An abbreviation for *frequency division multiplexing*.

**FD(X):** An abbreviation for *full duplex*.

**FEASIBILITY STUDY:** An examination of a possible solution to a problem and the possibility of the problem being solved. It is usually the first step taken when considering the implementation of a computer-based system.

**FEED:** The mechanism for inputting tertiary storage media into a computer (e.g. card feed).

**FEEDBACK:** The operation (or the result of the operation) of obtaining output from one process and treating it as input to another (or itself).

**FEEDBACK LOOP:** A sequence of operations in which the output from one process is input to a previously occurring process in order to provide control of the entire system.

**FEED HOLES:** The small holes punched on a *paper tape*, roughly in the centre, which enable the tape to be driven through a reader (or, on non-mechanical readers, to define the position of the data holes).

**FEP:** An acronym for *front-end processor*.

**FERRANTI:** A British computer company based near Manchester. They were the major contractors for the British Post Office's Experimental Packet Switched Network (EPSS) using Argus mini-computers. They are also known for advanced machines in the late 1950s and early 1960s, particularly Atlas.

**FERRITE:** A magnetic material (an oxide of iron) which is used to make *ferrite cores*.

**FERRITE CORE:** A small toroid of "ferrite" used to construct early *core* *memory*. It has the considerable advantage of being *non-volatile* but is now being superseded (on price grounds) by semiconductor memories.

**FET:** An acronym for *field effect transistor*.

**FETCH:** To locate an item of data in storage and access it for processing.

**FETCH CYCLE:** The machine cycle in which data is "fetched" from memory into a cpu register prior to execution. For this reason, the combined cycle is known as the *fetch-execute cycle*.

**FETCH-EXECUTE CYCLE:** See *fetch cycle*.

**FF:** An abbreviation for *form feed*. A control character (in ASCII, it is 0001100 − control-L) which has varied effects depending on the output medium. For example, when sent to a line printer, it moves the paper onto the next sheet. On a VDU, the usual effect is similar, namely to clear the screen.

**FFT:** An abbreviation for *Fast Fourier Transform*.

**FIBRE OPTICS:** A means of transmitting data by means of modulating a coherent light source and transmitting it along a glass fibre cable. Very high bandwidths can be achieved in this manner, with the additional advantage that it is relatively immune from outside interference (and hence less susceptible to illegal interception).

**FIELD:** A group of contiguous locations (or columns on a card) which contain a single item or related group of items.

**FIFO:** An acronym for *first-in, first-out*. A queue is a FIFO list.

**FIGURE SHIFT:** A key on a keyboard (particularly a Telex) which changes the meaning of a set of keys to enable figures (and other characters not in the principal character set) to be generated. By extension, the phrase is also used to describe the control character which is transmitted to shift from one character set to another (more usually referred to as *shift-out*).

**FILE:** A collection of records which are logically related to each other and handled as one unit, for example, by giving them a single name.

**FILE CONVERSION:** The act of changing the format of one file into another.

**FILE GAP:** The area on a storage medium (particularly magnetic tape) between one file and the next.

**FILE IDENTIFIER:** The sequence of characters which serve to identify a file uniquely. The length of such an identifer is usually restricted to, say, eight characters and these characters usually follow the standard syntax for names (i.e. first character alphabetic, remainder alphanumeric). However, file stores are often hierarchical, in which case, the above discussion only applies within one level of the hierarchy and the full filename (i.e. defining its position within the hierarchy as well as giving its name within its own level) usually consists of the filename at each level of the hierarchy, separated by a single character (usually a "." or "/"). In IBM terminology, the full identifier is known as the *fully qualified name* and would have, for example, the following syntax:

USER.NOV.ASM

where the root of the tree is the "filename" (actually a directory) USER, the selector at the second level is NOV and the (simple) filename is ASM. This can be shown diagrammatically as:

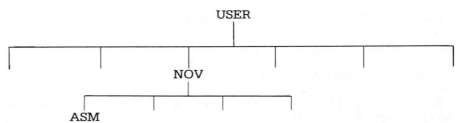

**FILE LABEL:** A record written at the beginning of the file giving information about that file, such as its name and length.

**FILE LAYOUT:** A specification of the internal arrangement of a *file*, usually forming part of a program which accesses the file.

**FILE MARK:** A special character (or sequence of characters) which are written to a tape to denote a special function, particularly the end of a file.

**FILE MAINTENANCE:** The updating of a *file*, together with other *housekeeping* tasks associated with this such as *garbage collection*.

**FILE NAME:** The sequence of characters which are uniquely assigned to a *file* and by which it may be referenced.

**FILE ORGANISATION:** A synonym for *file layout* but also used to mean a more general description of the layout, such as that the file organisation is *sequential* without any detail of the precise layout.

**FILE ORIENTED:** A generic term relating to a system where the data is handled in terms of files.

**FILE PROCESSING:** The set of operations which are performed on *files*.

**FILE PROTECTION:** The prevention of access to a file (particularly where that access would result in data within that file being modified or erased) usually carried out by software checks but also it is possible to provide file protection by hardware means, such as the *write protect ring* on a *magnetic tape*.

**FILE SEPARATOR:** A character (or sequence of characters) occurring between files denoting the logical end of one file and the start of the next.

**FILE STORAGE:** Usually used to refer to the device on which files are stored, such as a disk or a tape.

**FILING SYSTEM:** The set of (systems) programs which provide the facilities for accessing a *file oriented* set of data.

**FILL (vb):** To add specified characters to a set of characters to make the set a given length. Usually, the extra characters are added at the end in order to fill out to a known boundary and the fill character is often a space. In text processing, the extra spaces are added within a line of text in order to ensure a straight right-margin. In cases where the field to be filled is non-alphanumeric, the fill character is often binary zero (the null character) and the operation is known as "zero fill".

**FILL (n):** The character (or bit pattern) used to fill a field.

**FIRMWARE:** A word used to indicate something which is between software and hardware. It nearly always refers to programs which are held in ROM (read-only memory) and is becoming increasingly common, particularly in the field of microcomputers where it is not uncommon to find the operating system and/or various language compilers (e.g. BASIC or even Pascal) in *firmware*.

**FIRST GENERATION:** An adjective referring to the first set of electronic computers which were based on (a very large number of) thermionic valves. It is usually considered that the first generation of machines started with the Univac 1 in 1951.

**FIVE LEVEL CODE:** A means of coding information using five bits per character, used mainly on Telex machines (see *Baudot code*).

**FIX (vb):** To modify software or hardware, usually in a fairly minor way, in order to cure a fault or bug.

**FIX (n):** The set of instructions indicating how to "fix" a problem.

**FIXED AREA:** A permanently assigned area (usually of main memory but sometimes used for secondary storage) which is used to hold information which is frequently needed. In particular, when used to refer to main storage, the "fixed area" is used to describe the area of storage in which permanently resident parts of the operating system (sometimes referred to as the "nucleus") are kept. The remaining area reserved for the operating system and systems programs is sometimes known as the *transient area*.

**FIXED BLOCK LENGTH:** A system whereby each *block* has the same length.

**FIXED DISK:** A disk which is permanently fitted to the drive and not removeable. Often disk drives have one fixed and one removeable disk.

**FIXED FORMAT:** Used to refer to records in which the fields have pre-assigned positions. The most common usage of the term is in the case of card input in some languages (e.g. FORTRAN).

**FIXED-HEAD DISK:** A disk where the head doesn't move and therefore there is one head per track. In this manner, the seek time is eliminated but the cost of such a disk is considerably higher than non-fixed head disks. Except for the shape of the recording surface, a fixed-head disk is very similar to a drum.

**FIXED LENGTH:** Any item of data where its length is constant.

**FIXED LENGTH RECORD:** A record whose length is pre-assigned (often to be a *card image*).

**FIXED POINT:** A system whereby each number is represented by a sequence of digits with no explicit indication of the position of the radix point.

**FIXED POINT ARITHMETIC:** Arithmetic using *fixed point* numbers.

**FIXED POINT REPRESENTATION:** A representation of numbers where each is in *fixed point* format.

**FIXED ROUTING:** A technique of routing in a distributed computer network in which the routing is predetermined. See, for example, *directory routing*.

**FIXED STORAGE:** Storage which may not be altered (*read-only*).

**FIXED WORD LENGTH:** A computer system in which each word occupies a fixed number of bits.

**FJCC:** An abbreviation for *Fall Joint Computer Conference*, a series of conferences organised by AFIPS and now superseded by the "National Computer Conference".

**FLAG (1):** An indicator used to signify a particular condition or state. Often the state to be indicated is binary and hence the flag may be a single bit. Often instructions are provided in a computer's instruction set to allow testing of a single bit which facilitates their use as flags.

**FLAG (2):** A sequence of eight bits (01111110) used in HDLC to delimit *frames*.

**FLEXIBLE DISK:** A (rarely used) synonym for *floppy disk*.

**FLEXOWRITER:** An early form of I/O device which generated seven-hole paper tape (the machine was manufactured by Friden).

**FLIP-FLOP:** A device (or circuit) which is capable of being in one of two different states and which can be changed from one state to the other by an input signal.

**FLOAT:** To convert a *fixed point* number (or *integer*) into a *floating point* representation.

**FLOATING POINT:** A representation of a number in the general form:

$$(-1)^s \times m \times b^e$$

where "s" is the sign, "m" the mantissa, "b" the base and "e" the exponent. Most minicomputers or mainframes (but rarely microcomputers) have facilities for manipulating floating point numbers and converting them to and from fixed point. In general, the base is a power of two (often two itself) and is implicit. There are many ways of representing floating point numbers in a computer but the method used in IBM System/370 is fairly representative:

| s | e | m |
|---|---|---|

where the sign occupies one bit, the exponent seven bits (represented in *excess-64* notation) and the mantissa 24 bits. A *double-precision* representation is also allowed in which case the mantissa occupies 56 bits. The implicit base is sixteen. In most computers, it is necessary for the number to be *normalised*, that is, for the most significant bit of the mantissa to be 1. Floating point numbers are often represented by the "E" notation, whereby the mantissa and exponent are separated by the letter E where the base is implicit (and not necessarily the same as that used in the target machine, often it is 10). Thus 2.5E−1 is the same as a quarter.

**FLOATING POINT ROUTINE:** A set of instructions which are used to perform calculations on *floating point* numbers. In many machines, particularly smaller ones, no hardware is provided for floating point arithmetiç but software routines are provided instead.

**FLOODING:** A technique used in packet-switched networks whereby each node sends multiple copies of any received packets, one to each of its neighbours. Obviously this leads to very high network traffic and overheads in checking for and deleting duplicate received packets.

**FLOPPY DISK:** As the name implies, a disk which is flexible (hence, less commonly, known as *flexible disk*). Originally, such disks were 8″ in diameter but, more recently, *mini-floppies* have been used with a 5.25″ diameter. The disk is plastic, covered with the recording medium and enclosed within a protective envelope. There are three holes in this envelope, a circular one at the centre for the drive, a much smaller circular one near the centre for detection of the sector holes and an oval one for the read/write head. The capacity of a floppy disk varies significantly from about 70 Kbytes for a single-sided, single density mini-floppy up to over a Megabyte for a double-sided, double (or higher) density full-size floppy disk.

**FLOW:** A sequence of events, for example, the instructions executed within a computer.

**FLOWCHART:** A representation of a program (or, more generaliy, a solution to a problem) in a diagrammatic form, particularly indicating the flow of control.

**FLOWCHART SYMBOL:** A symbol used on a flowchart to indicate a particular operation. For example, a diamond shape is used to indicate a decision.

**FLOWCHART TEMPLATE:** A plastic rectangle in which holes are punched corresponding to the various *flowchart symbols* and which facilitates drawing of a *flowchart*.

**FLOW CONTROL:** Control of the flow of information, usually used in the context of data transmission networks to indicate the procedures used to ensure that data is transmitted only at a rate which can be processed by the receiver.

**FLOW DIAGRAM:** A synonym for *flowchart*.

**FLOWMATIC:** The first automatic programming language, developed for the UNIVAC computers.

**FLUB:** An acronym for *first language under bootstrap*, a simple language developed to facilitate the generation of compilers by means of boot-strapping techniques.

**FLYING SPOT SCANNER:** A device which is able to read by means of measuring the reflectance of a moving spot of light.

**FOLDING:** The technique of compacting a character set into a smaller one, usually in order to print it. For example, the full ASCII set can be folded into a 64 character set so that lower-case characters are transformed into their upper case equivalents.

**FONT:** A set of characters of the same size and typestyle. For example, the font in which this book is printed is Serifa.

**FORCE:** A synonym (now rarely used) for the logical operation *inclusive or*.

**FOREGROUND:** In general, a computer system may be divided into two parts, the *foreground* and the *background*. The foreground consists of the high-priority processes, particularly those concerned with interactive usage, whereas the background consists of lower priority processes, such as batch jobs and the device spoolers.

**FOREGROUND JOB:** A *job* which executes in the *foreground*.

**FORM FEED:** See *FF*.

**FORM FEED CHARACTER:** See *FF*.

**FORMAC:** An acronym for *Formula Manipulation Compiler*.

**FORMAT:** The layout of data. Also used as a verb to indicate the laying out of data in a specified manner.

**FORMAT EFFECTOR:** A control character which affects the format of printed data, as opposed to characters which are actually printed. Examples are *form-feed* and *horizontal tab*.

**FORMS TRACTOR:** A piece of equipment which is attached to a printer (e.g. a daisywheel printer) which allows continuous stationery to be used. It consists of various gears and two sets of *sprockets* which engage with the holes on the paper to ensure that it is fed correctly (the sprockets are driven by the platen).

**FORTH:** A high-level interactive multitask language developed in the late 1960s by Charles H. Moore. It is essentially a process control language and has a number of interesting features – in particular, the wide range of facilities from assembler to very high level. The Forth virtual machine is a stack machine with as much virtual memory as the machine allows, the programmer being relieved of the responsibility of transfer to and from backing storage (cf. the *one-level store* concept).

**FORTRAN:** An acronym for *Formula Translator*. Developed by IBM around 1957, there are many variations, the most common of which is FORTRAN IV which was standardised by the American Standards Association. A new standard, FORTRAN 77, is becoming more commonly available.

**FORWARD REFERENCE:** A reference in a programming language to an item which has not been defined previously, usually a label. This causes some problems in compilation since the address of the referenced item cannot be discovered until the item is defined and hence the compiler must make two passes over the source code or use a related method to resolve the references.

**FOUNT:** See *font*.

**FPLA:** An abbreviation for *field programmable logic array*, a programmable logic array which can be programmed by the user.

**FRAME:** A group of bits (cf. *block*). The word *frame* is preferred in the HDLC protocol. It is also employed in time division multiplexing to mean the set of bits consisting of the data in one time slot from each sub-channel, together with control information.

**FRAMING:** The enclosing of a block of data within *framing bits*.

**FRAMING BITS:** The bits (often eight) used to delimit a *frame*.

**FRED:** An acronym for *Frantically Rapid Electronic Device*, one of the earliest examples of a name chosen to fit an acronym.

**FREE FORMAT:** Layout of a set of characters where the actual positions do not matter (although there may be some restrictions regarding the separation of different items). Contrasted with *fixed format*.

**FREQUENCY:** The rate of change of a periodic variable, usually referring to a signal. It is usually measured in *Hertz*.

**FREQUENCY BAND:** A set of frequencies, for example, the frequency band of human voice is between 300 and 3400 Hz.

**FREQUENCY DIVISION MULTIPLEXING:** A form of analog(ue) multiplexing in which each sub-channel is modulated to alter its frequency. Since this gives rise to two signals for each sub-channel (one at higher frequency than the original signal, one lower), one is usually filtered out. The modulation frequencies are chosen to ensure that each sub-channel occupies a separate part of the frequency spectrum, separated by *guard bands*.

**FREQUENCY MODULATION:** A method of transmission whereby the frequency of the carrier wave is changed in response to changes in the signal.

**FREQUENCY SHIFT KEYING:** A method of signalling where one frequency is used for "0" and another for "1".

**FRICTION FEED:** One means of feeding paper through a printing device where the paper is retained in place by friction alone (as in a conventional typewriter). If more accurate registration is required, *pin feed* or *tractor feed* is used.

**FRONT-END:** Usually used as an abbreviation for *front-end processor* which is a computer interfacing between a mainframe and the outside world, usually with the purpose of removing some load from the mainframe. For example, a common use of a front-end processor (FEP), is in interactive systems where all terminals are connected to the FEP which is able to perform simple functions (such as character echoing, simple editing etc.) and multiplex the inputs for the mainframe.

**FRONT PANEL:** The set of lights and switches on the front of a computer which allow the operator (and engineer) to perform various functions, such as starting the machine and to perform some diagnostic procedures. The phrase is also used to indicate a software package which simulates the display just described.

**FS:** An abbreviation for *field separator*, a control character whose value in the ASCII code is 0011100.

**FSK:** An abbreviation for *frequency shift keying*.

**FTP:** An abbreviation for *file transfer protocol*, a protocol which allows files to be transferred between different computers.

**FULL ADDER:** See *adder*.

**FULL BOOTSTRAP:** A technique of *bootstrapping* whereby the bootstrap is performed on a single computer system and consists of starting with a minimal system then bootstrapping as many times as required until the appropriate result is obtained.

**FULL DUPLEX:** Simultaneous independent transmission in both directions of a connection.

**FULLWORD:** A variable which occupies a set of bits consisting of one whole word.

**FULLY CONNECTED NETWORK:** A computer network in which each computer is directly connected to every other computer in the network. Such a configuration is rarely used in practice due to the cost of the number of lines involved, although in certain applications, such as defence, these considerations may be outweighed by the greatly increased reliability.

**FULLY QUALIFIED NAME:** See *file identifier*.

**FUNCTION (1):** An operation to be performed by a computer, such as ADD.

**FUNCTION (2):** A mathematical description of the relationship between variables, e.g. the square function takes a variable and multiplies it by itself.

**FUNCTION (3):** A set of instructions in a computer program (cf. *routine*) which yield a result.

**FUNCTION KEY:** A key on a terminal which enables some function to be performed.

**FUSIBLE LINK:** A technology for generating *read-only memory* where metallic links are fused by a high current.

# G

**GAIN:** The ratio of an output signal to an input signal through an amplifier circuit. The opposite is *attenuation*.

**GAME THEORY:** A term coined by John van Neumann to describe the branch of mathematics concerned with probability and other aspects of games.

**GAP:** Used as an abbreviation for *inter-block gap*.

**GARBAGE:** Data which is incorrect in its context (for example, incorrect output data generated due to a hardware fault in the computer). See *GIGO*.

**GARBAGE COLLECTION:** In some circumstances, data items (particularly strings) which have been deleted are merely marked as having been so and left in memory. At some point, no new memory is available and it is necessary to actually delete all items which have been marked as deleted and to concatenate all contiguous areas of memory. This process is known as "garbage collection" and the same term is applied when the same process is used on disks and within files rather than in memory.

**GATE:** An electronic circuit which takes a number of inputs and produces the requisite output, depending on the function of the gate (for example, an *and gate*).

**GATEWAY:** An interface, usually a computer, between two computer networks which may have various functions such as access controls and protocol conversion.

**GE (1):** An abbreviation for *General Electric* (US).

**GE (2):** An abbreviation for *greater than or equal*, used as a reserved word in many computer languages.

**GEC:** An abbreviation for the *General Electric Company* (UK), best known for its range of minicomputers, the 4000 series (see *Babbage*).

**GECOS:** An acronym for *General Electric Comprehensive Operating System*, an early multi-processing operating system.

**GEIS:** An abbreviation for *General Electric Information Service*.

**GENERAL PURPOSE COMPUTER:** A computer which is designed to handle all applications, such as business and scientific, equally well rather than being specifically designed for one such function.

**GENERAL PURPOSE REGISTER:** A register which can be used for a multitude of purposes rather than being dedicated to a specific function such as an *index register*.

**GENERATE:** To produce some item. More specifically, the term is used in the context of generating a computer system from various given modules which are parameterised.

**GENERATION:** When a file is updated and the old file is not deleted but is retained, it becomes known as the *father* with the modified file becoming the *son*. This cycle is usually extended to three such levels, each known as a "generation", the earliest one being known as the *grandfather*.

**GENERATION NUMBER:** A number defining which *generation* a file belongs to. This information is usually kept in the *file label*.

**GENERATOR:** A program which creates further programs from standard, parameterised programs.

**GENESYS:** An acronym for *General Engineering System*.

**GEORGE:** An acronym for *General Organisational Environment*, a disk-based operating system produced by ICL for its 1900 series of computers.

**GET:** A word used in some systems to denote the action of obtaining a record from backing storage (for example, in IBM System/370, the macro for doing this is known as GET, the opposite being PUT).

**GIGA-:** A prefix denoting one thousand million ($10^9$).

**GIGO:** An acronym for *Garbage-in, garbage-out*. This, fairly descriptive, phrase indicates that, however good a system (usually a program) is, it cannot generate correct output from incorrect input.

**GLASS TTY:** A term used to apply to a VDU which has no facilities such as *cursor control* but is functionally equivalent to a *teletype* (although it may have some additional facilities such as higher speeds).

**GLITCH:** A transient condition affecting a computer system.

**GOLFBALL:** Specifically, the type element used in various typewriters from IBM and other manufacturers. It is a small sphere, about the size of a golfball, with the characters embossed on its surface. When typing, the golfball moves and strikes the paper. This leads to a fairly reliable system and, in addition, the golfball can be changed rapidly, leading to the ability to use multiple typefaces. The golfball typewriter was modified to be one of the first high quality I/O devices (e.g. the IBM 2741 terminal was based on the golfball). However, it operated at a speed of 14.7 characters per second (which is fairly slow) and was not highly reliable.

**GPSS:** An abbreviation for *General Purpose Systems Simulator*, a simulation *package*.

**GRACEFUL DEGRADATION:** The reduction in performance of a computer system (perhaps totally) in a controlled fashion, due to the failure of one component of that system.

**GRANDFATHER:** See *generation*.

**GRAPHIC:** An abbreviation for *graphic character* which relates to the set of characters which are neither control nor alphanumeric.

**GRAPHICS:** The part of computer science concerned with the representation of data in a pictorial form.

**GRAPH PLOTTER:** An output device which is able to draw graphs on paper by means of a moving pen.

**GRAY CODE:** A means of representing integers in a binary code in such a way that successive integers differ by only one digit (which is of help in analogue to digital conversion). In order to convert from binary to Gray code, start at the most significant end and copy the first digit. Then, if the binary digit changes, write a 1; if it does not, write a 0.

**GROSCH'S LAW:** A "law" suggested by Herb Grosch that the power of a computer increases as the square of its price and hence a powerful argument for centralised processing. In recent years, the law has become less valid due to the decreasing price of computer components.

**GROUP SWITCHING CENTRE:** Part of the UK's phone switching system at the level above local exchanges and below District Switching Centres.

**GS:** An abbreviation for *group separator*, a control character used to separate groups of data. In the ASCII code, its value is binary 0011101.

**GSC:** An abbreviation for *group switching centre*.

**GT:** An abbreviation for *greater than*, a reserved word in many computer languages for comparison operations.

**GUARD BANDS:** Frequency bands used in *frequency division multiplexing* to ensure that there is no overlap between the shifted sub-channel frequencies.

**GUTS:** An acronym for *Gothenburg University Terminal System*, an interactive system available on IBM machines, designed and implemented by the University of Gothenburg.

# H

**HALF-ADDER:** A hardware device in a computer which forms part of an *adder*. It takes the *augend* and *addend* and produces a *sum* and *carry*. It can use the carry in the place of the addend.

**HALF BOOTSTRAP:** A method of *bootstrapping* in which the bootstrap process takes place on another computer to the *target machine*. For example, in bootstrapping a compiler, one technique is to write a *code generator* for the target machine for a compiler on the *source machine*, then translate the compiler on the source machine via this modified compiler. This is a *half-bootstrap*.

**HALF-DUPLEX:** Transmission in both directions of a connection, but not at the same time.

**HALF-DUPLEX CHANNEL:** A *transmission channel* used in *half duplex* mode.

**HALFWORD:** A contiguous set of bits which can be addressed as a single unit and which form half of a *fullword*. For example, on IBM System/370, a *fullword* is 32 bits while a halfword is 16 bits. Halfwords are often useful for such items as loop counters etc. since they restrict the user somewhat in the range of integers which can be represented but, on the other hand, occupy significantly less space.

**HALT:** An instruction in a computer used to stop the processor which may be restarted (usually) by a switch on the console. In the case of a multi-programming system, the instruction is "privileged" and cannot be used by user programs.

**HALT INSTRUCTION:** See *halt*.

**HAMMING CODE:** An *error checking* code which detects errors and allows single-bit errors to be corrected. It operates by means of check bits which occupy positions in the word 1, 2, 4, 8 . . ..

**HANDKEYS:** A name sometimes used for the *console switches*. Also known as *sense switches*.

**HANDLER:** The routine which has responsibility for an input/output device.

**HAND PUNCH:** A mechanical device which enables a user to punch holes in cards manually. The term is occasionally used for a similar device for punching holes in paper tape, but this is more often known as a *unipunch*.

**HANDSHAKING:** A sequence of operations between two components (e.g. two processes communicating over a computer network) in which each takes turns in transmitting data.

**HANG-UP:** An unforseen situation where a program ceases to perform useful work, for example, by going into an *infinite loop*.

**HARD-COPY:** Output produced in a permanent form, usually by printing on paper.

**HARDCOPY LOG:** A *hardcopy* record of the operation of a computer system, usually printed at the *operator console*.

**HARD DISK:** A name for a conventional disk with the recording surfaces being on a rigid medium; the terminology is used particularly when it is required to contrast such a disk with a "floppy disk". For example, when referring to a disk on a large machine, it would be assumed automatically that it is a hard disk; when referring to a disk on a microcomputer, it would be assumed that it was a floppy disk, unless specified otherwise.

**HARD DISK ERROR:** An error occurring when reading data from a disk (whether a *hard disk* or a *floppy disk*) that recurs when re-trying the read operation a specified number of times (usually ten) and is therefore presumed to be irrecoverable.

**HARD-SECTORING:** A technique for determining the *sectors* on a *floppy disk* whereby small holes (*index holes*) are punched in the disk. Various formats for hard-sectoring are in common use – for example, mini-floppy disks use 10 or 16 sectors most commonly.

**HARDWARE:** The physical equipment comprising a computer system – the *mainframe*, *peripherals* etc. It should be contrasted with *software* and *firmware*.

**HARDWARE CHECK:** A check of the operation of a computer system, performed by "hardware". The term is also used to describe the condition which occurs when such a check detects an error, although this is more often known as a *machine check*.

**HARTLEY:** A logarithmic measure (to the base 10) of information content.

**HASH:** To calculate a *hash function*.

**HASH FUNCTION:** A function which operates on a sequence of characters to produce a result. There are two common ways in which this is used. The first is to provide a check that the data is correct. The second is to provide a method of distributing data in a *table*, for example, a *compiler's* dictionary. If data were stored in a dictionary according to, for example, alphabetic order, the distribution would be highly uneven. A well chosen hash function could be used to distribute the names evenly over a specified range. A simple-minded hash function to distribute names over the range 0 to 31 is to sum the ASCII characters of the name, then calculate the remainder modulo 32.

**HASH TOTAL:** A total used for the purposes of checking a set of values.

**HASP:** An acronym for *Houston Automatic Spooling Priority System*, a system which provides spooling and priority functions for IBM's Operating System. There are various modifications to the system such as HASP/RJE which permits the use of *remote job entry* terminals.

**HD(X):** An abbreviation for *half-duplex*.

**HDLC:** An acronym for *High-Level Data Link Control*. The line protocol which forms the basis of the X.25 standard. It is a bit-oriented protocol (that is, the data is not considered to be broken up into bytes but is treated purely as a stream of bits) allowing data transparency via *bit stuffing*.

**HEAD:** The part of a tape deck or disk drive which records and/or reads the data on the storage medium.

**HEAD CRASH:** The (usually catastrophic) failure of a disk drive (or drum) due to the *head* coming into contact with the recording surface, or with some obstruction such as dust on the surface.

**HEAD GAP:** The distance between a *head* on a tape deck or disk drive and the recording surface. This is usually extremely small and it has been said that it is equivalent to a 747 plane flying at an altitude of ten feet.

**HEADER (1):** The data placed at the beginning of a magnetic tape (or other sets of data) indicating the information contained on the tape.

**HEADER (2):** A sequence of bits at the start of a message containing various control information.

**HEADER LABEL:** See *header*.

**HEADER RECORD:** A record containing header information for subsequent records.

**HEADER TABLE:** A synonym for *header record*.

**HEAP:** A name given to a data area (usually used in execution of a high-level language, such as *Pascal*) in which there are no restrictions on access to the data. In such languages, there is often also a data area implemented as a "stack" in which access is restricted to the top.

**HEAPSORT:** A method of sorting in which the keys are arranged in a *heap* (in which case, the term implies a rather more structured heap than that used in compiler terminology) and then a selection procedure initiated. It is a fairly efficient method of sorting and has the interesting property that the time taken in the worst case is little different from the average case. For a large number (N) of items to be sorted, heapsort is of the order of $N \log N$.

**HEAT PRINTER:** A printer which uses a heated print element (usually a dot matrix) which is brought into contact with a heat-sensitive paper. Quite high speeds can be achieved but the special paper required is relatively expensive.

**HERTZ:** A unit of frequency equal to one cycle per second. Abbreviated to Hz.

**HETEROGENEOUS NETWORK:** A computer network in which the types of interconnected computers are different.

**HEURISTIC:** Strictly means an educational process whereby learning is through experience. This meaning has been modified in the context of computer programming to mean that the program is "self-learning" in that results from one run are retained and used to improve performance in a subsequent run. This is particularly useful in the field of artificial intelligence.

**HEURISTIC PROGRAM:** A program which has facilities for "self-learning".

**HEWLETT-PACKARD:** A (mainly mini-) computer manufacturer which is also particularly well known for programmable calculators.

**HEX(ADECIMAL):** A number system with a base of sixteen and thus requiring sixteen digits which are 0 to 9 and A to F. Since it requires four bits to represent a hex digit, hexadecimal notation is particularly useful as a compact method of representing eight-bit bytes which therefore require two hex digits.

**HIERARCHY:** A data structure where the data is ordered into ranks, each rank having a higher precedence than those below it.

**HIERARCHICAL NETWORK:** A computer topology in which computers are allocated to several levels, those at one level not being able to communicate directly with those on the same level but to one computer on a higher level and a (usually small) number at a lower level.

**HIGH LEVEL:** An adjectival phrase describing items which are far-removed from the computer hardware. See, for example, *high-level language*.

**HIGH-LEVEL ASSEMBLER:** A high-level language which nevertheless has the property that it translates directly into machine code (with no global optimisation) and hence can be used in exactly the same way as a conventional assembler while retaining the clarity of high-level language constructions. One example is GEC's Babbage.

**HIGH-LEVEL DATA LINK CONTROL:** See *HDLC*.

**HIGH-LEVEL LANGUAGE:** A language which is far-removed from the computer hardware and allows operations to be expressed in a relatively machine-independent manner, being far more dependent on the problem being solved. Such languages include Pascal, FORTRAN, COBOL and APL.

**HIGH ORDER:** The digits of a number which occupy the highest significant positions.

**HIGHWAY:** A synonym for *bus*.

**HIT:** A successful search for an item of data.

**HLL:** An abbreviation for *high-level language*.

**HMOS:** An abbreviation for *high-speed metal oxide semiconductor* memory.

**HOLLERITH:** Dr Herman Hollerith (1860–1929) who proposed the use of punched cards in order to complete the analysis of the US 1890 census. These cards are now in common use and the company he formed to exploit his invention became IBM. His card consists of eighty columns, each divided into twelve positions, designated X, Y and 0 to 9.

**HOLOGRAPHY:** A technique for recording images by means of transforming the waveforms, using a coherent light source (such as a laser) which has applications to data storage.

**HOME COMPUTER:** As the name implies, a small computer for use in the home, for example, for use in keeping accounts, playing games etc. In general, this is an eight-bit microcomputer with a moderate amount of memory (between 1K and 16K) with cassette tape as backing storage. The best known such machines are the Commodore PET and the Radio Shack (Tandy) TRS–80.

**HONEYWELL:** A well-known US computer manufacturer whose machines vary from the large Series 66 (used in the DTSS system) to the 16-bit 716, 516 and 316 machines (the last two being used as node processors for the *ARPANET*.)

**HOPPER:** A container used, for example, in card readers to hold the cards before being read and to retain them afterwards.

**HORIZONTAL TAB:** An abbreviation for *horizontal tabulation character*, a character which moves the print-head of a *hard-copy* device (or the "cursor" in the case of a VDU) horizontally to the right a specified number of spaces. In ASCII, it is a control character with a value binary 0001001 (control–I).

**HOST COMPUTER:** A computer, connected to a network node, which provides and/or uses network services.

**HOUSE-KEEPING:** A phrase used to mean the operations of a program (often an operating system) concerned with, for example, keeping track of memory used and optimising use of unused space. The term is also used in connection with the operation of a computer system, in which case it refers to those functions performed regularly (usually daily), such as backing-up disks.

**HPIB:** An abbreviation for *Hewlett-Packard Interface Bus*.

**HT:** See *horizontal tab*.

**HUB-POLLING:** A method of *polling* whereby devices are polled in turn.

**HUNTING GROUP:** A group of adjacent telephone numbers such that a user can dial any one of the group and will be routed to the next free number.

**HYBRID COMPUTER:** A computer which uses both digital and analogue processing, for example, in certain process control applications.

**HYPERCHANNEL:** A trade mark of Network Systems Corporation for a type of *local area network* technology which employs a contention scheme and operates at up to 50 Mbps.

**HYPERNET:** A generic term for a group of computers connected together into a network with data transmission rates in the megabaud range.

**Hz:** An abbreviation for *Hertz*.

# I

**IAn:** An abbreviation for *International Alphabet No. n* where the most common are IA2 which is a five-bit code mainly used in Telex systems and IA5 which is a seven bit code virtually identical to ASCII.

**IAL:** An abbreviation for *International Algebraic Language*.

**IBM:** An abbreviation for *International Business Machines Corporation*. Founded in 1911, IBM is the largest computer manufacturer in the world. Of its early machines, probably the 7090 and the 1400 are the best known, superseded by the System/360 in the early 1960s. This has been superseded by System/370 and more recent processors such as the 303x and 4331. It makes a wide range of machines but has only recently started to market microcomputers. IBM invented various languages, particularly FORTRAN and PL/1, and has also been very active in the field of communications with one of the first communications protocols, BSC (bi-sync). Within the last five years, it has offered a distributed processing concept, Systems Network Architecture (SNA).

**IC:** An acronym for *Integrated Circuit*.

**ICE:** An acronym for *In-Circuit Emulation (or Emulator)*.

**ICES:** An acronym for *Integrated Civil Engineering System*, a system for solving civil engineering problems.

**ICL:** An abbreviation for *International Computers Ltd*. A large British computer company formed during the lst 1960s. Perhaps best known for the System/4, the 1900 series and the 2900s.

**IDENTIFICATION:** A string of characters which uniquely define a data item.

**IDENTIFICATION DIVISION:** A part of the COBOL program which identifies various aspects of the program such as the author's name.

**IDENTIFIER:** See *identification*.

**IDLE:** Usually used as a verb to indicate the status of a computer when it is not undertaking useful work.

**IDLE TIME:** Time when a computer is not performing useful work. For example, in a communications environment, there may be idle time when data has been received and processed and the processor is waiting for more data. Often this idle time can be put to some useful purpose, such as performing internal checks (for example, one system which uses it to perform a CRC of programs in memory to ensure they have not been corrupted).

**IDP:** An abbreviation for *integrated data processing*.

**IDPM:** An abbreviation for the *Institute of Data Processing Management*, a UK professional body formed from the Data Processing Management Association and the Institute of Data Processing.

**IEE:** An acronym for the *Institution of Electrical Engineers*, a UK professional organisation.

**IEEE:** An abbreviation for the *Institute of Electronic and Electrical Engineers*, an American professional body. The IEEE is probably best known for its standardisation work (for example, the IEEE-488 standard which is often used for connection of peripheral equipment, particularly laboratory equipment, and which has been adopted by the *PET* personal computer). It also has a Computer Society which is very active.

**IF:** A reserved word in many computer languages signifying the start of a conditional statement. The most common use is of the form:

IF <condition> THEN <statement>

where the <statement> is executed if the condition is true. A derivation is:

IF <condition> THEN <statement-1> ELSE <statement-2>

where the first statement is executed if the condition is true and the second is executed if the condition is false. Because of possible ambiguities when parsing the two versions, some languages insist on the use of a terminator, often FI or ENDIF.

**IFIP:** An abbreviation for the *International Federation for Information Processing*. As the name suggests, an international federation of organisations concerned with information processing, one from each member country. It has a number of technical sub-committees.

**IIL:** An abbreviation for *Isoplanar (or Integrated) Injection Logic.*

**ILIFFE VECTOR:** A multi-dimensional array can be considered to be an array of arrays of lower dimensionality. An Iliffe vector is that (one-dimensional) array; in the case of a sparse array, the Iliffe vector may also contain descriptor information.

**ILLEGAL CHARACTER:** A character (or set of bits) which is not valid in a particular set of circumstances.

**ILLEGAL OPERATION:** An operation which is not valid in a particular set of circumstances, for example, as an *op-code* in an assembler program.

**ILLIAC:** An acronym for *Illinois Institute of Advanced Computation*, part of the University of Illinois, which has been concerned in the design and implementation of a number of "state-of-the-art" computers, the most recent being the ILLIAC IV (in which context, the abbreviation can also stand for "Illinois Automatic Computer"). This machine consists of 64 parallel processors and operates at about 200 million instructions per second.

**IMAGE:** An exact copy of some item. For example, a *card image* or a reproduction of some diagram via *facsimile*.

**IMMEDIATE:** Most often used in the context of operands in machine instructions. It refers to the operand being contained in the instruction (and thus is immediately available, not requiring a further access to memory). For example, the instruction:

$$3E41$$

on a Z–80 processor is a load immediate instruction which loads the eight bits (01000001 – hex '41') into register A.

**IMMEDIATE ACCESS:** A phrase which literally means storage with an access time of zero. In practice, no storage has this property and the phrase is used for storage with a very low access time.

**IMMEDIATE ADDRESS:** See *immediate*.

**IMIS:** An abbreviation for *Integrated Management Information System*.

**IMP:** Interface Message Processor, the node processor used in the *ARPANET*. Originally, a Honeywell-516 minicomputer but later replaced by the 316. More recently, the multi-processor Lockheed Sue has been used as an IMP.

1. Heart, F.E. *et al.*, "The Interface Message Processor for the ARPA Computer Network", *Proc.* AFIPS SJCC, **36**, 551–567, 1970.
2. Heart, F.E. *et al.*, "A New Minicomputer/Multiprocessor for the ARPA Network", *Proc.* AFIPS NCC, **40**, 529-537, 1973.

**IMPACT PRINTER:** A printer in which the output is produced by impact, such as occurs in a typewriter. Usually, the mechanism is similar to that of a typewriter whereby the metal type hits a ribbon and transfers the ink to the paper. Because of the mechanical nature of impact printers, they are restricted in speed, although *line printers* (which print a whole line at a time) often run at speeds in excess of a thousand lines a minute.

**IMPLEMENTATION:** The designing, testing and installing of a program or a system.

**IMS:** An abbreviation for *Information Management System*.

**INCLUSIVE OR:** A logical operation (also known as "force") which conforms to the following table:

| v | 0 | 1 |
|---|---|---|
| 0 | 0 | 1 |
| 1 | 1 | 1 |

**INCREMENT (vb):** Strictly, to increase, but often used more specifically to mean to increase the value of a variable by one.

**INCREMENTAL PLOTTER:** A *graph plotter* which is able to draw straight lines (and hence curves are drawn as a number of short straight lines).

**INDEX:** This word is often used in various contexts but the most common meaning is that used in everyday speech, namely a list, in a suitable order (usually alphabetical) of items.

**INDEXED ADDRESSING:** A mode of *addressing* in which the address is modified by an *index register*.

**INDEXED SEQUENTIAL:** A mode of file organisation on a *direct access* storage device in which a directory (index) is formed containing the address of each record and some means of identifying the record (a *key*). By using this directory, the relevant record can be accessed quickly.

**INDEX HOLE:** The small hole(s) near the centre of a floppy disk used by the hardware to detect the sectoring.

**INDEXING:** The accessing of data using an *index* or an *index register*.

**INDEX REGISTER:** A *register* used as a modifier during an address calculation. The contents of the index register are added to the address field to form the *effective address*. In some computers, the index register is automatically incremented after the data has been accessed.

**INDICATOR:** In the hardware sense, this word refers to some device which indicates the status of some aspect of the computer's operation. The term is also used to refer to software when it indicates a bit or sequence of bits which are also used to demonstrate the status of part of the computer system.

**INDIRECT:** An adjective which indicates that the specified data item does not contain the required data but contains a reference to the required data.

**INDIRECT ADDRESS:** An *address* which does not contain the required data but contains the address of the data. In fact, this process can be repeated an indefinite number of times so that the data is many levels indirect.

**INDIRECT ADDRESSING:** A technique of addressing in which the data is not referenced directly but instead the address of the data item is given.

**INFINITE LOOP:** A sequence of instructions in a computer which repeat indefinitely, usually due to a program error.

**INFIX NOTATION:** A means of representing operations in which the operator occurs between the operands, e.g. the expression A + B is written in infix notation.

**INFIXED OPERATOR:** The operator in an expression written using *infix notation*, e.g. in the expression A + B, the '+' sign is an infixed operator.

**INFORMATICS:** A word used, more or less synonymously, with *Information Technology*.

**INFORMATION:** The meaning attached to data.

**INFORMATION BITS:** The bits in a message which convey *information* rather than *control bits*.

**INFORMATION EXPLOSION:** A term used to describe the exponential growth of data and information.

**INFORMATION MANAGEMENT SYSTEM:** A system designed to handle all required operations on data, such as storing, retrieving and cataloguing. It is usually abbreviated as "IMS".

**INFORMATION PROCESSING:** The set of all operations on *information*, usually by means of a computer.

**INFORMATION PROVIDER:** A name given to those organisations who provide the information in the BT *Prestel* database.

**INFORMATION RETRIEVAL:** The aspects of computer systems involved with recovering specific information from stored data (e.g. a *database*).

**INFORMATION SCIENCE:** The study of all aspects of handling and processing information.

**INFORMATION SYSTEM:** A system involved with all aspects of handling information.

**INFORMATION TECHNOLOGY:** The technology associated with the handling of information. The UNESCO definition of this term is "the scientific, technological and engineering disciplines and the management techniques used in information handling and processing; their applications; computers and their interaction with men and machines; and associated social, economic and cultural matters". In the UK, 1982 was designated as Information Technology Year. In this context, the term is abbreviated to IT.

**INFORMATION THEORY:** The scientific discipline concerned with the transmission of information and the problems arising therefrom.

**INHIBIT:** To prevent from occurring.

**INITIAL PROGRAM LOAD:** The first operation(s) in the starting of a computer system (see *bootstrap*). Also used (particularly when abbreviated as "IPL") as a verb to indicate the starting of a computer system, usually after a *crash*.

**INITIALISE:** To set the value of a variable to a specified value at the start of program execution.

**INITIALISATION ROUTINE:** A sequence of instructions to "initialise" variables in a program.

**INITIATE:** To start some activity.

**IN-LINE:** *Instructions* or *statements* within the main sequence of a program.

**INLINE SUBROUTINE:** A sequence of *instructions* or *statements* which are contained within the main sequence of a program and therefore are repeated as often as required.

**INPUT:** The process of transferring data from some external medium into a computer. The opposite process is *output* and the two are sometimes referred to collectively as *transput*.

**INPUT AREA:** A region of storage which is reserved for data transferred from an external device.

**INPUT BUFFER:** A *buffer* used to transfer data from an external device (see *input area*).

**INPUT CHANNEL:** A *channel* which connects peripheral units to the central processor, through which data is transmitted.

**INPUT DATA:** Data which is to be processed and which is therefore transferred from an external device to the central processor.

**INPUT DEVICE:** Any *peripheral* which is used to transfer data from the outside world into a computer. Examples are *card reader*, *paper tape reader* and *OCR*.

**INPUT HOPPER:** A part of a *card reader* in which the cards are stored prior to being read.

**INPUT JOB STREAM:** The sequence of *jobs* prior to execution.

**INPUT-OUTPUT:** The means whereby a computer communicates with the outside world. The words (which, together, are sometimes called *transput*) are used as adjectives or verbs, either together or separately. Thus a Teletype is an "input-output device". To get data into a computer is known as "inputting" and conversely.

**INPUT QUEUE:** A synonym for *input job stream*.

**INPUT READER:** A part of an operating system which is concerned with obtaining data from an *input device* and stored in central memory.

**INPUT ROUTINE:** Sometimes used synonymously with *input reader* but, more often, used to mean a part of a user program which is concerned with reading *input data*.

**INPUT SECTION:** The part of a program which consists of all the *input routines*.

**INPUT STREAM:** A synonym for *input job stream*.

**INPUT WELL:** An area of main storage reserved for a set of *input buffers*. Usually this is used as an area for spooling data from input devices.

**INSTALLATION (1):** The totality of a computer system, the support equipment and the relevant staff.

**INSTALLATION (2):** The period during which a computer system is placed at a delivery site and commissioned.

**INSTRUCTION:** A sequence of bits (*word*) which, when interpreted by the *central processor*, are treated as an operation to be performed, together with the relevant operands. In practice, the term "instruction" is used also to mean the external representation of an instruction (for example, the sequence of characters used to represent an instruction in an assembly language program). In general, an instruction consists of an operation (code) together with zero or more operands.

**INSTRUCTION ADDRESS:** The *address* of the storage location which contains an *instruction*.

**INSTRUCTION COUNTER:** A counter (either a storage location or a register) which contains the *address* of the next *instruction* to be obeyed.

**INSTRUCTION FORMAT:** The number of bits allocated to each part of an *instruction*, together with their order. For example, one instruction format used on the CDC Cyber 70 computers is:

| Opcode | R1 | N |
|--------|-----|-----|

**INSTRUCTION MODIFICATION:** The altering of a part of an instruction so that it has a different effect when it is subsequently executed. Often the technique of address modification is used to access elements of an array in a computer which does not have an index register, in which case the address part of the instruction is incremented.

**INSTRUCTION REPERTOIRE:** A synonym for *instruction set*.

**INSTRUCTION SET:** The set of all *instructions* available on a particular computer.

**INSTRUCTION TIME:** The time it takes for an *instruction* to be executed, including fetching it from memory and decoding it.

**INSTRUCTION WORD:** A *word* which is occupied by an *instruction*.

**INTEGER:** A whole number, i.e. one without a fractional part. In most computers, integers (within certain specified ranges) can usually be represented accurately whereas *floating point* numbers cannot.

**INTEGRATED CIRCUIT:** An electronic circuit in which the various components (resistors, diodes, transistors etc.) are formed by depositing the required materials in the appropriate patterns (under the control of a *mask*) on a semiconductor substrate. The usual abbreviation is "IC" and a single IC can contain many thousand components (see *medium scale integration* and *large scale integration*). However, in general, the yield of such processes is very low but this is of little importance due to the extremely low cost of components made in this way.

**INTEL:** A large American company which is a major producer of microprocessors (its name derives from "Integrated Electronics"). Formed in 1969, it produced the first microprocessor, the four-bit 4004. This was superseded by eight-bit micros, the 8008, the 8080 and the 8080A. More recent micros include the 8085, 8048 and the sixteen-bit 8086.

**INTELLEC:** The registered name for the development systems developed by Intel.

**INTELLIGENCE:** A term applied to the ability of a device to perform certain functions. For example, a terminal is considered to have "intelligence" if it allows the user to edit data before sending it etc. This is achieved by means of enhancing the terminal with a processor and some memory.

**INTELLIGENT:** Pertaining to a device having some *intelligence*.

**INTELLIGENT TERMINAL:** A terminal which has been enhanced by the addition of a processor and some memory to give it *intelligence*.

**INTERACTION:** An exchange between two parties.

**INTERACTIVE:** An adjective applied to a computer system or a program which allows a user to communicate with a program in real-time, i.e. he receives "immediate" responses, rather than delayed ones.

**INTER-BLOCK GAP:** The distance between two *blocks* on a *magnetic tape* which facilitates reading the tape a block at a time. The gap is often 0.5'' or 0.75''. It is also known as an *inter-record gap*.

**INTERFACE:** A common boundary between two items, either hardware of software.

**INTERFERENCE:** The presence of spurious signals on a communication line which degrade service.

**INTERLEAVE:** To use the technique of *interleaving*.

**INTERLEAVING:** To overlap two (or more) functions. For example, memory can be arranged into a number of *stacks* and data accesses can be *interleaved* thus reducing the average time to access the data.

**INTERLOCK:** A device (usually a software flag) which prevents one device or process interfering with the operation of another. For example, when two processes wish to edit a file, an "interlock" is required to prevent this occurring.

**INTERMEDIATE RESULT:** The result of some operation which will be used as an operand for further operations.

**INTERMEDIATE STORAGE:** A synonym for *work area*.

**INTERNAL CLOCKING:** Transmission of data where the rate of transmission is controlled by timing pulses from the device performing the transmission.

**INTERNAL MEMORY:** The main memory of a computer.

**INTERNAL SORT:** A sorting technique when the data to be sorted can be contained in the computer main memory during the sort process.

**INTERNAL TIMER:** A part of the *central processor* which provides timing pulses to enable synchronisation of various parts of the system.

**INTERNATIONAL TELECOMMUNICATIONS UNION:** An international organisation founded in 1863 and now an agency of the United Nations. In 1925, it established CCIF (Comité Consultatif International des Communications Téléphonique à Grande Distance) and this merged with CCIT in 1956 to form CCITT.

**INTERPRET (1):** To print onto the top of a *punched card* the characters punched on that card.

**INTERPRET (2):** To implement the functions of an *interpreter*.

**INTERPRETER:** An interpreter is usually a program which directly executes statements in a high-level language (or, less frequently, a compacted version of the language). This method of execution is often used in microcomputers for some languages, notably BASIC, and has a number of advantages over compilation, particularly that program debugging and tracing can be facilitated. On the other hand, the speed of execution of an interpreted program is about one order of magnitude less than that of a compiler program.

**INTERPRETIVE:** A system whereby statements (or, often, commands) are *interpreted* rather than being *compiled* and acted upon immediately.

**INTER-RECORD GAP:** See *inter-block gap*.

**INTERROGATE:** To make an enquiry, for example, of a database system.

**INTERRUPT:** A priority signal generated in various ways, for example, by a *peripheral* completing a specified function, which is interpreted by the *central processor* in a special way, usually it suspends execution of the current program and transfers control to a specified location in memory (usually dependent on the type of interrupt) which then calls a routine to deal with the interrupt, then returns control to the interrupted program.

**INTERRUPT DRIVEN:** A system which transfers control from one process to another in response to *interrupts*, as opposed to *event driven*.

**INTERRUPT MASK:** A bit pattern which defines a set of *interrupts* which are to be ignored by the *central processor*.

**INTERRUPT TRAP:** The location (or sequence of locations, in which case it is more usually known as the *interrupt vector*) to which control is transferred in the event of an "interrupt" being detected.

**INTERRUPT VECTOR:** See *interrupt trap*.

**INTERRUPTABLE:** A process which is able to be interrupted or where *interrupts* are *enabled*.

**INTERVAL TIMER:** A device in the *central processor* enabling the interval between events to be measured under program control.

**INVENTORY CONTROL:** The control of stock levels, particularly by means of a computer system.

**INVERT:** To change some item to its opposite, particularly changing a bit value 0 to 1 and vice versa.

**INVERTED FILE:** A part of a database which indexes the database according to *secondary keys*. For example, in a book, the table of contents is the main means of access to the data and the index is the "inverted file".

**INVERTER:** A hardware device which takes a single binary input and produces the inverse as output (i.e. a zero input produces a one output and vice versa).

**INWG:** An acronym for the *International Network Working Group*. A Working Group of IFIP (WG 6.1) concerned with research on network protocols and interworking.

**I/O:** An abbreviation for *Input-Output*.

**I/O BOUND:** A term referring to a system (or a single program) in which the rate of operation is limited by the speed of input-output operations.

**I/O BUFFER:** See *input buffer*.

**I/O CHANNEL:** See *input channel*.

**I/O CONTROL SYSTEM:** A set of routines which are used to control the input and output of a computer system.

**IOCS:** An abbreviation for *Input-Output control system*.

**I/O INTERRUPT:** An *interrupt* generated by an input or output device.

**I/O LIBRARY:** A set of routines contained in a *library* which facilitate input and output operations and may be incorporated into user programs.

**IOR:** An acronym for *inclusive-or*.

**IP:** An abbreviation for *Information Provider*.

**IPL (1):** An abbreviation of *Initial Program Load*.

**IPL (2):** An abbreviation for *Information Processing Language*.

**IPS:** An abbreviation for *inches per second*. This measure is usually used for the speed of a magnetic tape.

**IPSS:** An abbreviation for *International Packet Switched Service*, a facility provided by British Telecom enabling users in the UK to access computers and networks abroad, initially in the USA but later extended to other countries (e.g. Spain).

**IR:** An abbreviation for *information retrieval*.

**IRIA:** An acronym for the *Institut de Recherche d'Informatique et d'Automatique*, a French research establishment which is one of the sites taking part in the EIN computer network.

**IRG:** An abbreviation for *inter-record gap*.

**IS:** An abbreviation for *Indexed Sequential*.

**ISAM:** An acronym for *indexed sequential access method*. A method of accessing data using *indexed sequential* techniques.

**ISARITHMIC CONTROL:** A technique of flow control used in packet-switched computer networks whereby an upper limit is set on the number of packets permitted to be in transit at any one time.

**ISO:** An acronym for the *International Standards Organisation* which, as the name implies, is an international standardisation body. Its member body in the UK is BSI and in the USA, ANSI.

**ISOCHRONOUS:** A synonym for *synchronous*.

**ISR:** An abbreviation for *information storage and retrieval*.

**IT:** An abbreviation for *Information Technology*, particularly when used in the context of Information Technology Year (1982).

**ITT:** An abbreviation for *International Telephone and Telegraphs*, a multi-national company concerned, *inter alia*, with telecommunications.

**ITERATE:** Literally, to repeat. It is quite often used to mean the process of performing the same set of instructions a number of times (i.e. a loop) but is also, more correctly, used to mean repeating a procedure with data derived from the last run of the procedure (i.e. using feedback) in order to obtain a more accurate value.

**ITERATIVE:** An adjective referring to a process which *iterates*.

**ITU:** An abbreviation for the *International Telecommunications Union*.

# J

**JCL:** An abbreviation for *job control language*.

**JDL:** An abbreviation for *job description language*.

**JFCB:** An abbreviation for *job file control block*, a *control block* which contains information about a particular job.

**JITTER:** An instability of short duration in a signal.

**JOB:** A number of tasks which constitute a single unit of work for a computer system. A "job" may, for example, consist of compiling a program, linking it with various library modules, loading it into memory and executing it. The flow of control during a job is regulated by control statements written in a *job control language*.

**JOB CLASS:** A subset of *jobs* which have similar characteristics (for example, they all require less than a certain specified *cpu* time) and which usually have a specific priority relative to other job classes.

**JOB CONTROL:** The function of controlling the execution of *jobs* within a computer system. This is usually carried out by a part of the operating system which is given relevant information from *jobs* by means of *job control statements*. The functions of this part of the operating system include allocation of storage and peripheral devices.

**JOB CONTROL CARD:** One card (or a *card image*) which contains information about *job control*.

**JOB CONTROL LANGUAGE:** A language which defines a *job* and the resources it requires from the computer system, including constraints on the job, such as time limits. The language is more often *interpreted* than *compiled*.

**JOB CONTROL STATEMENT:** One statement, written in *job control language*, which defines one aspect of a *job* and occupies one or more *job control cards*.

**JOB DEFINITION:** A set of *job control statements* which define a *job*.

**JOB DEFINITION LANGUAGE:** A rather more general term than *job control language* covering all aspects of defining a *job* to a computer system, whereas *job control language* often implies the specific language of various manufacturers, particularly IBM.

**JOB MANAGEMENT:** The functions of allocation resources to *jobs* and scheduling use of those resources, together with handling input-output requests.

**JOB NAME:** A sequence of characters which uniquely identify a *job* to an *operating system*.

**JOB QUEUE:** The set of all *jobs* currently in a computer system (or, more generally, the resources attached to the management of jobs, such as the space on disk reserved for them). In general, this is a *queue*, although the order of execution may be varied due to different priorities (or *job class*) or by resources not being currently available.

**JOB SCHEDULER:** The part of the *operating system* which manages the *job queue* and arranges the order of execution of the jobs.

**JOB STEP:** One part of a *job* which is self-contained, for example, the compilation step.

**JOHNNIAC:** An acronym for *John (von Neumann's) Integrator and Automatic Computer*.

**JOSS:** An acronym for *Johnniac Open-Shop System*.

**JOVIAL:** An acronym for *Jules' Own Version of IAL*, an algorithmic language developed by Systems Development Corporation which was used particularly in systems for the US Air Force.

**JUMP:** A transfer of control within a program so that the next instruction to be executed is not that next in order. It is more commonly known as *branch*.

**JUMP TABLE:** A *table* of addresses which define the destinations of a *jump* instructions depending on the value of a given variable, so that a multi-way branch may be executed. A more elegant way of achieving the same function is by means of a *CASE* statement.

**JUSTIFICATION:** The padding of a specified field in accordance with certain rules. For example, left justification of a binary pattern usually means to move the pattern so that the most significant digit appears in the leftmost character position. Similarly, to justify text means to pad each line with spaces so that the right margin appears straight.

**JUSTIFY:** To perform the process of justification.

# K

**K:** An abbreviation for *Kilo*, meaning one thousand as in 3 KHz being the same as 3000 Hz. Sometimes, the lower case "k" is used. However, in computer applications, K usually refers to $2^{10}$, i.e. 1024 and confusion sometimes arises, although the meaning is usually clear from context, e.g. 32 Kbytes means 32768 bytes and not 32000.

**KARNAUGH MAP:** A tabular method of representing logical relation-ships (i.e. a tabular *Venn diagram*).

**KB (1):** An abbreviation for *keyboard*.

**KB (2):** An abbreviation for *kilobit* or *kilobyte*. Although this seems likely to lead to confusion, the meaning is usually clear from the context.

**KEY (1):** A field (or set of fields) which may be used to identify a record in a *database*.

**KEY (2):** A sequence of characters (often a sequence of digits) which may be used to decode an *encrypted* message.

**KEY (3):** A button or lever on a machine, such as a Teletype, used to generate a signal on being depressed.

**KEYBOARD:** A group of *keys* arranged in a certain order (see, for example, *QWERTY*) which are used to generate a set of signals for input to a computer system.

**KEYBOARD SEND/RECEIVE:** A device (such as a Teletype) which has a *keyboard* and *printer* and hence is able to both send and receive data. It is abbreviated to KSR and should be contrasted with RO (receive only).

**KEYPAD:** A simplified *keyboard*, usually consisting of a small set of push-buttons (as on certain telephones or on the control unit of a *videotex* terminal).

**KEYPUNCH:** A device with a keyboard on which cards are punched with a particular pattern of holes to represent data.

**KEY-TO-DISK:** A means of inputting data directly from a machine similar to a *keypunch* directly onto magnetic disk rather than having to go via some tertiary medium such as printed cards.

**KEYWORD (1):** A single set of characters, used as a *key*.

**KEYWORD (2):** A *name* used to identify a parameter (see *keyword parameter*).

**KEYWORD IN CONTEXT:** An indexing method in which every significant word or phrase in a title (or even abstract or complete article) is used as a *key*. It is usually abbreviated KWIC.

**KEYWORD PARAMETER:** A parameter which is identified by means of a *keyword*. For example, in the following *job control statement*, the "datasetname" and "disposition" are both keyword parameters, the keywords being DSN and DISP respectively and their values being SYS1.MACLIB and SHR:

```
//MACROS        DD        DSN=SYS1.MACLIB,DISP=SHR
```

**KILO:** See *K*.

**KLUDGE:** A slang term used to denote a program or system put together in a haphazard fashion which works but is ill-designed and likely to contain many bugs.

**KSR:** An abbreviation for *keyboard send/receive*.

**KWIC:** An acronym for *keyword in context*.

**KWIC INDEX:** See *keyword in context*.

**KWOC:** An acronym for *keyword out of context*.

# L

**LABEL (1):** A sequence of characters, conforming to the rules for a *name* which are used to identify a particular instruction or statement in a program.

**LABEL (2):** Data placed at the beginning or end of a set of data (e.g. on a *magnetic tape*) indicating the information contained in that data.

**LAN:** An abbreviation for *Local Area Network*.

**LANGUAGE:** A means of conveying information. In the context of computers, there are *programming languages* and *natural languages*.

**LANGUAGE TRANSLATOR:** A means (e.g. a program) of translating from one language to another, for example, from a high-level language to assembler.

**LAP:** An acronym for *Link Access Protocol,* part of the CCITT X.25 recommendation.

**LATENCY:** This word is most often used in the context of disk operations where it describes the time taken for the disk to rotate to bring the appropriate sector under the read/write heads. The delay in accessing a disk also involves *seek time*.

**LAYOUT:** The specification of the ordering of data.

**LAYOUT CHARACTER:** A non-printing character which affects the *layout* of a printed page, for example, horizontal tabulation.

**LC:** An abbreviation for *lower case*, referring to characters within the range 1100001 to 1111010 inclusive in the ASCII character set.

**LCD:** An abbreviation of *liquid crystal display*, used in many calculators and watches. The display occurs fairly slowly and is not very bright (and hence often has to be illuminated externally). On the other hand, the power consumption is very low.

**LE:** An abbreviation for *less than or equal to*, used as a reserved word in many high-level languages.

**LEADER:** The blank section of tape (paper or magnetic) at the beginning of the recorded information, needed when threading the tape into a reading device.

**LEADING EDGE:** The edge of a *punched card* which is the first to be put into a *card reader*.

**LEADING ZERO:** A zero character which precedes the most significant digit in a number and which therefore itself has no significance, for example, the zeros in 000123.

**LEASED LINE:** A telephone line reserved for exclusive use which does not require exchange switching.

**LEAST SIGNIFICANT:** The character which occupies the rightmost position of a group of digits and which therefore has least weight. For example, in the number 123456, '6' is the least significant digit.

**LED:** An abbreviation for *light emitting diode*. A diode which glows with light (usually red or green) when supplied with the requisite voltage and thus often used in calculator and other displays. The resultant output is bright but consumes considerable power and is now being superseded in displays by LCDs.

**LEFT JUSTIFY:** To *justify* to a left-hand boundary.

**LEFT SHIFT:** To move the digits in a sequence (e.g. the bits in a word) to the left. There are various types of shift (e.g. *arithmetic, circular*) which have different effects.

**LEO:** An acronym for *Lyons' Electronic Office*, the first commercial computer.

**LETTER:** A character in the sets A . . . Z or a . . . z.

**LETTER SHIFT:** A key on a keyboard (particularly Telex) which changes the meaning of a set of keys to enable letters (and other characters in the principal character set) to be generated. By extension, the phrase is also used to describe the control character which is transmitted to shift from one character set back to the principal one (more usually referred to as "shift-in").

**LF:** An abbreviation for *line feed*, a control character which moves the paper (or equivalent) vertically upwards one line (without returning the carriage to the beginning of the line, known as *carriage return*). In ASCII, this has the value 0001010 (control-J).

**LIBRARY:** Besides the more obvious meaning of the word, it applies to a collection of programs (subroutines etc.) which are available in a relatively simple way to a programmer, allowing him to insert these standard programs into his own program. In addition to program libraries developed at each site, there are a number of libraries which are available over a wide range of machines, perhaps the best known of which is the NAG library.

**LIBRARY PROCEDURE:** A *procedure* contained within a *library*.

**LIBRARY PROGRAM:** A *program* contained within a *library*.

**LIBRARY SOFTWARE:** The set of all programs contained in a *library*.

**LIBRARY SUBROUTINE:** A *subroutine* contained within a *library*.

**LIBRARY TAPE:** A *magnetic tape* which contains a *program library*, especially used for the distribution of such libraries.

**LIFO:** An acronym for *last-in, first-out* a description of a certain type of list which is known as a *stack*.

**LIGHT-PEN:** An I/O device used with certain displays. It looks like a pen, connected to the device by means of a cable, and by using a photoelectric cell, can be used to indicate positions on the screen.

**LINE (1):** A sequence of characters terminated by *line feed*.

**LINE(2):** A colloquial term for a communications channel.

**LINE ADAPTOR:** A term used in the USA to mean a *modem*.

**LINE CONTROL:** The sequence of signals used to control a communications channel.

**LINE DELETE:** A control character used to signify that all characters typed on the current line are to be ignored. This character varies from system to system but is often "rub-out" or "control-U".

**LINE FEED:** The character (in ASCII, it is 0001010) which causes the output device to move vertically one line. Although used commonly in conjunction with the *carriage-return* character to perform a "new line" function, it is also often used on its own.

**LINE LEVEL (1):** The signal strength (usually measured in *decibels*) on a communications channel.

**LINE LEVEL (2):** An adjective used in the phrase "line level protocols" to denote *protocols* which are concerned with transmitting a transparent stream of bits along a communications channel.

**LINE NUMBER:** A sequence of digits assigned to a line within a program. In some languages (e.g. BASIC), they are mandatory and are equivalent to *labels*.

**LINE PRINTER:** An output device which has the property of printing one whole line of text at a time, often by means of a set of printwheels, one for each character position, which rotate to the required position, then print simultaneously. In this manner, quite high speeds (over a thousand lines a minute) can be achieved but line printers are not cheap. Although difficult to generalise, the maximum number of print positions is often 132.

**LINE SPEED:** This is strictly a misnomer which refers to the quantity of data which can be transmitted over a communications line. Correctly, it should be known as "line bandwidth". It is usually given in terms of "characters per second" or *baud* and, depending on the method of transmission, these may be synonymous.

**LINEAR PROGRAMMING:** A technique for determining the optimum values of functions subject to linear constraints.

**LINK (1):** Used as a noun, in the context of telecommunications, this refers to a communications channel.

**LINK (2):** Used as a noun in the context of programming, "link" refers to the location (or register) used to contain the return address from a subroutine.

**LINK (3):** See *link-edit*.

**LINKAGE:** A sequence of instructions that connects two separate program modules.

**LINK-EDIT:** To combine a number of independently compiled program modules (which are not fully compiled but retain information about external linkages) into a single module, resolving all inter-module linkages and performing other functions such as re-ordering the modules or globally changing names.

**LINK EDITOR:** A program which can *link-edit* program modules.

**LINKED LIST:** A list of items in which each item has appended to it the address of the next item. There are many varieties of linked lists, including "doubly linked lists" in which each item has a pointer both to its successor and predecessor and *circular lists*.

**LISP:** A list processing language (the name is an acronym for LISt Processing) where the data elements of the language are *atoms* or *lists*. The language is used particularly in the field of artificial intelligence.

**LIST (1):** A noun used to describe an ordered set of data.

**LIST (2):** A verb used to indicate the process of printing a complete set of data or the command in various languages (e.g. BASIC) to achieve this purpose. Also used as a noun to indicate the result of this process.

**LIST PROCESSING:** A technique of processing data which is repesented as *lists*. Many languages allow some list processing functions but some (e.g. *LISP*) are specifically designed to facilitate this.

**LISTING:** The output produced when doing a *list*.

**LITERAL:** A symbol in a programming language which is itself used as data rather than as a reference to data and hence, in many contexts, is identical to a constant. For example, a declaration could be:

abcd="ABCD"

where "abcd" is the name of the literal string "ABCD".

**LIVEWARE:** A rather unpleasant "pop" term used to mean the people associated with a computer establishment (cf. *hardware*, *software* and *firmware*).

**LOAD (1):** To enter data into storage locations in a computer.

**LOAD (2):** To prepare a peripheral device so that data can be accessed, for example, to put cards into a card reader.

**LOAD AND GO:** A technique of operating a computer whereby *compilers* do not produce *object code* but instead place their output directly into memory and, at the end of compilation, transfer control to that code so that it is immediately executed.

**LOADER:** A program (which is often considered part of the *operating system*) which takes a compiled (and *link-edited*) program and places it in memory prior to execution. In addition, it may perform such functions as *relocation*.

**LOAD MODULE:** The binary data (which may also include some linkage information) which is the output of a *link-editor* and which can be supplied as input to a *loader*.

**LOAD POINT (1):** The area on a magnetic tape to which it should be positioned when it is about to be read from (or written to). It is usually indicated by a metallic marker attached to the tape so that this positioning can be performed automatically by the *tape deck*.

**LOAD POINT (2):** The address in memory at which a program is loaded.

**LOAD SHARING:** A technique whereby the computers in a network share work to achieve a reasonably uniform distribution. The off-loading of jobs from a heavily loaded computer to one more lightly loaded.

**LOCAL AREA NETWORK:** As the name implies, a generic term applied to computer networks which operate over a small area (for example, one site of a company). In general, the data is transmitted at very high bandwidths (often megabits per second) and, although this technology is fairly recent, commercial versions are now becoming available. Two major technologies are used for such networks – the *Cambridge ring* developed at the University of Cambridge (UK) and *Ethernet* developed by the Xerox Corporation at their Palo Alto Research Center (Xerox PARC).

1. Cotton I.W. (ed), "Local Area Networking", Special Publication 500–31, National Bureau of Standards, Aug 1977.
2. Metcalfe, R.M. and Boggs, D.R., "ETHERNET: Distributed Packet Switching for Local Computer Networks", *Comm.* ACM., **19**, 395–404, 1976.
3. Wilkes, M.V., "Communication Using a Digital Ring", *Proc.* Pacific Area Computer Communications Network System Symposium, 47–56, Aug 1975.

**LOCATE MODE:** A mode of processing data (usually in input or output buffers) by providing the address of the data rather than moving it into the user's area (see also *move mode* and *exchange buffering*).

**LOCATION:** Often used as a synonym for *address*.

**LOCATION COUNTER:** Often used as a synonym for *sequence control register*.

**LOCKOUT:** To prevent access to a certain resource – for example, in a multi-processing system, it is necessary to prevent more than one program writing to the same data at the same time and hence one program "locks-out" the other(s). Similarly, the term is used to describe the inhibition of an interrupt.

**LOCK-UP:** A situation in which no further action may occur.

**LOG (1):** A record (usually in a *hard-copy* form) of a sequence of events, such as the jobs run through a computer system. The word is also used as a verb to mean the function of creating such a log.

**LOG (2):** An abbreviation for *logarithm*.

**LOGGER:** A device which creates a job, especially devices which perform this function automatically.

**LOGIC (1):** The scientific discipline concerned with reasoning and thought.

**LOGIC (2):** The use of truth tables to evaluate the solutions to problems.

**LOGIC (3):** An abbreviation for *logic circuits*, the set of electronic components which perform logical operations, on various inputs and which hence allow computations. By extension, the term "logic" is used to mean the electronic components of a computer system.

**LOGIC DESIGN:** The abstract design of a computer system in terms of symbolic logic rather than in terms of the hardware implementation.

**LOGIC DIAGRAM:** A representation of the *logic design* of the system.

**LOGIC ELEMENT:** A hardware component which performs a logic function (e.g. AND).

**LOGICAL COMPARISON:** A comparison of two data items, treating them merely as a sequence of bits, rather than taking those bits to be representing, for example, a signed integer.

**LOGICAL INSTRUCTION:** An instruction which executes a *logical operation*.

**LOGICAL OPERATION:** An operation which involves a *logical operator* such as *AND*.

**LOGICAL OPERATOR:** One of the set of functions which can be performed on logical variables such as *AND, OR, NOT*. The operands are considered as bit patterns and do not represent, for example, signed integers.

**LOGICAL RECORD:** A *record* which is defined in terms of its functions rather than the manner in which it is stored (*physical record*).

**LOGICAL SHIFT:** A *shift* which treats the operand as a bit pattern and not as a representation of some value, such as a signed integer. Thus, a left logical shift takes no account of the most significant bit being used as a sign bit, whereas an arithmetic shift would do so. Although the term "logical shift" usually refers to a shift wherein any bits shifted out of the word are lost and any required bits are assumed to be zero, the term can also be applied to shifts wherein bits lost at one end are fed back into the other end (a *circular shift*).

**LOGICAL SUM:** A synonym for *inclusive OR*.

**LOG-IN:** To connect to a computer system (usually a timesharing system, although the term is used in other contexts, for example, a remote job entry workstation *logging-in* to a mainframe). In this process of connection, the user supplies identification to the system, such as an identifier, account number and password.

**LOGO:** A high-level interactive programming language, developed at the Massachusetts Institute of Technology.

**LONGITUDINAL REDUNDANCY CHECK:** A form of error checking applied to a group of bits in which some function is applied to the relevant bits on generation and then checked on reading. The term is usually abbreviated as "LRC". A similar check is known as *vertical redundancy check*.

**LOOK-UP:** To search a set of values (usually a *table*) in order to find one which corresponds to the given input data.

**LOOK-UP TABLE:** A *table* which is used for the purpose of "looking-up" given data.

**LOOP:** A sequence of instructions which are executed more than once. Most, if not all, high level languages provide appropriate statements for loops. For example, in FORTRAN, a loop can be written:

$$DO \quad 10\ I = 1,\ 100$$
$$\ldots \text{(body of loop)} \ldots$$
$$10 \quad CONTINUE$$

**LOOP STOP:** An *infinite loop*, usually an instruction which jumps to itself, used to halt execution of a program (also known as a *soft halt*).

**LOOP TEST:** A test of communications hardware (especially *modems*) whereby the data, rather than being transmitted, is fed back into the receive side and thus checked without introducing the potential errors of transmission.

**LOW LEVEL:** A phrase used to mean near to the hardware level of a computer. Usually, this is used in the context of languages, when a "low level language" is one such as an *assembler* which is oriented towards the machine for which it was designed rather than the class of problems which it is meant to solve.

**LOW ORDER:** The digit(s) which have the least significance in a number.

**LOW ORDER POSITION:** The position in a number of the lowest order, i.e. the rightmost digit.

**LPM:** An abbreviation for *lines per minute*, a measure of the speed of printing of a *line printer*.

**LRC:** An abbreviation for *longitudinal redundancy check*.

**LSB:** An abbreviation for *least significant bit*.

**LSI:** An abbreviation for *Large Scale Integration*. A technology for constructing computer components in which a high packing density of logic elements is achieved on a single chip (of the order of 10,000 per square inch).

**LSI-4:** A computer manufactured by Computer Automation.

**LSI-11:** A 16-bit microprocessor manufactured by Digital Equipment Corporation, which has the same instruction set as the PDP-11 series and is used in the lower models of the range, such as the PDP-11/03. More recently, an LSI version of the PDP-11/34 has become available, known as the PDP-11/23.

**LT:** An abbreviation for *less than*, often used in high-level languages as a reserved word for the requisite comparison operation.

# M

**M:** An abbreviation for *mega*, a prefix indicating a million. As with "K", the term is used ambiguously to mean either a million or, more often, the nearest power of two to a million, namely $2^{20}$ which is 1 048 576. The meaning is usually clear from the context and so, for example, 16 Mbytes means 16 777 216 bytes.

**MAC (1):** An acronym for *machine aided cognition*, a large-scale project at the Massachusetts Institute of Technology.

**MAC (2):** An acronym for *multi-access computer*.

**MACHINE:** A term used as a synonym for *computer*.

**MACHINE ADDRESS:** A synonym for *absolute address*.

**MACHINE CHECK:** An *interrupt* caused by a malfunction of the *central processor* of a computer system.

**MACHINE CODE:** The sequence of binary patterns which are executed by the hardware of a computer. While most correctly represented in binary, it is more convenient to represent in more compact forms (either hexadecimal or octal, depending on the number of bits in the computer's word). However, once more sophisticated forms of representation are used (even to the extent of separating fields or using mnemonics), the representation should then be termed more correctly *assembly code*.

**MACHINE INDEPENDENT:** A term used to indicate that the item so specified (e.g. a program) is independent of any particular computer and hence will execute on any given computer. This implies that the program is written with regard to the problem which it is intended to solve, rather than the computer on which it will be run (see *high-level language* and *problem-oriented language*).

**MACHINE INSTRUCTION:** An *instruction* written in *machine-code*.

**MACHINE LANGUAGE:** The language consisting of the set of all *machine codes* for a particular computer.

**MACHINE READABLE:** Pertaining to any data which is in a form whereby it may be read directly by a computer, for example, data on a magnetic tape.

**MACHINE WORD:** One *word* on a particular computer.

**MACRO:** Usually used as an abbreviation for *macro-instruction*.

**MACRO-ASSEMBLER:** An *assembler* which allows the user to define and use *macro-instructions* and thereby give the appearance of an extended *instruction repertoire*.

**MACRO DEFINITION:** The statements which are used to define a *macro-instruction* to a *macro-assembler*. For example, in the assembly language for the IBM System/370, a macro-definition might be:

```
                  MACRO
     &NAME        STOP
       *
     &NAME        SVC             3
                  MEND
```

where the macro "STOP" will expand into the instruction "SVC 3" and, if a label qualifies the macro, it will also qualify the generated instruction.

**MACRO EXPANSION:** Either the act of expanding a *macro-instruction* into the basic assembler instructions or the instructions generated by such an expansion.

**MACRO-INSTRUCTION:** An instruction available when using a *macro-assembler* which is defined by the user (or by the system in a *macro library*) and which allows the user to specify the macro-instruction in the program. During the course of assembly, the macro is expanded into the relevant basic assembler instructions. There are many types of macro-instructions available but, in general, they share the fact of requiring to be defined (see *macro-definition*) before being used and allow the use of parameters when written in the program. Macros can be used to increase greatly the clarity of a program and serve to extend effectively the basic instruction set of a computer.

**MACRO LIBRARY:** A set of *macro-definitions* which are available to all users on a computer system. This is particularly helpful when it is necessary to refer to parts of the operating system. When the operating system changes, it is only required to change the relevant macros in the macro library and to re-assemble any affected programs.

**MACRO PROGRAMMING:** Programming in *assembly code* with *macro-instructions*.

**MACRO-10:** The (macro-)assembly language for the DECsystem-10 computers.

**MACRO-11:** The (macro-)assembly language for the PDP-11 range of computers.

**MAG TAPE:** An abbreviation for *magnetic tape*.

**MAGNETIC CARD:** A secondary storage device (often used in "intelligent" typewriters) consisting of a small card covered with a magnetic medium on which data can be recorded.

**MAGNETIC CORE:** A more accurate name for *core*.

**MAGNETIC DISK:** See *disk*.

**MAGNETIC DRUM:** See *drum*.

**MAGNETIC INK:** An ink which contains particles of a magnetic substance which can hence be detected by suitable sensors.

**MAGNETIC INK CHARACTER READER:** A reader which can detect characters which are printed in *magnetic ink*.

**MAGNETIC INK CHARACTER RECOGNITION:** A technique for input to a computer using characters printed in *magnetic ink* which can be read by a *magnetic ink character reader*. It is usually abbreviated as "MICR".

**MAGNETIC MEMORY:** A form of computer memory which relies on magnetic materials for recording data (see, for example, *core*).

**MAGNETIC STORAGE:** See *magnetic memory*.

**MAGNETIC TAPE:** A secondary storage medium which occurs in many forms. In general, it consists of a magnetic medium (usually an oxide, such as ferric oxide or chromium dioxide, but more recently, actual metal particles) on a plastic substrate. For some applications, the use of "cassette tape" is adequate (particularly with microcomputers, especially those for use in the home) but the most common type is reel-to-reel using tape of ½'' width, each reel holding 2400'. Some computers use wider tape, up to 1''. The major attribute of magnetic tape is that it is a sequential storage medium and hence large delays can be incurred in accessing data. In addition, most ½'' tapes are non-addressable. That is, a file cannot be read off the tape then written back with any guarantee of accuracy and hence data should only be written at the end of the data already written to the tape. However, some tape (e.g. DECtape) is addressable and the tape is divided into blocks which can be read/written.

Although methods of recording data on magnetic tapes vary, the following example (used by IBM) is typical. The tape is recorded in seven-track or nine-track format — that is, either seven or nine parallel tracks are recorded across the tape. One of the tracks is for a parity check, the remainder for data. In the case of nine-track tape, the mapping between computer memory and the tape is obvious, one byte having eight bits. With seven-track tape, two methods are used. The first is to record three bytes (3 × 8 bits) in four positions (4 × 6) on the tape. The second is to only record the lower six bits of each byte. Various recording densities are used, usually 200, 556 or 800 bpi for seven-track tapes, 800, 1600 or 6250 bpi for nine-track tapes. The abbreviation "bpi" stands for "bits per inch" but refers to the bits per inch PER TRACK and hence the actual data stored is greater by a factor of six or eight. In fact, for nine-track tape, the density equates to the total number of bytes per inch stored.

**MAGNITUDE:** The absolute value of a number, taking no account of its sign. One method of representing positive and negative numbers in a computer is *sign and magnitude*.

**MAINFRAME:** A name applied to any large computer (i.e. not a mini- or micro-computer).

**MAIN MEMORY:** The primary memory of a computer system. It usually has a fast access time (say, between 100 nanoseconds and 1 microsecond) and is random access. Due to the relatively high speed, it is relatively expensive and hence is restricted in size. In addition, its possible size may be restricted by the architecture of the computer (e.g. in IBM System/370, main memory is restricted to 16 Megabytes as the address field is 24 bits). Memory sizes vary from 1 Kbyte for a personal computer up to a number of Mbytes for a large mainframe.

**MAIN PROGRAM:** The controlling part of a program and that which is entered by the operating system when the program is executed.

**MAIN ROUTINE:** See *main program*.

**MAIN STORAGE:** See *main memory*.

**MALFUNCTION:** A failure in the operation of part of a computer system.

**MANAGEMENT INFORMATION SYSTEM:** A system (usually abbreviated MIS) which provides information as required and so facilitates management functions.

**MANIAC:** An acronym for *Mechanical and Numerical Integrator and Computer*, an early machine.

**MANTISSA:** See *floating-point*.

**MAP (1):** A representation of some item. For example, a memory map indicates the disposition of programs in memory (and, in some cases, the actual disposition of memory if it is not contiguous). Often a map merely shows if some item is present or absent, something which can be represented by a single bit and hence the use of *bit-maps*.

**MAP (2):** An abbreviation for *Microprocessor Awareness Project*. A project set up to increase awareness of microcomputers and their uses.

**MARC:** An acronym for *machine readable catalogue*.

**MARK (1):** Binary one condition on a telephone line.

**MARK (2):** A signal inserted into a stream of data to define a point which both source and sink may use for resynchronisation purposes, e.g. after an interrupt has been sent.

**MARK I:** An alternative name for *ASCC*, an early computer developed by Howard Aiken.

**MASK (1):** An alternative name for the logical operation *AND*.

**MASK (2):** Used in manufacturing ICs, the mask(s) define areas on the chip not to be etched.

**MASKED:** A synonym for *disabled*.

**MASKING:** The extraction of specified bits from a sequence of bits by means of a *mask*.

**MASS STORAGE:** Secondary or tertiary storage on a computer system. In the past, the term was used to indicate a large capacity backing store but, more recently, has been used to indicate extremely large storage (e.g. *terabit memory*).

**MASTER CLEAR:** A function provided on many computer systems, usually by means of a switch on the main console, which re-initialises the system and clears various registers and main storage.

**MASTER CONSOLE:** The *console* which has priority in a system with multiple consoles.

**MASTER FILE:** A *file* which acts as a source of information for some particular process and hence the information contained in it changes rarely.

**MASTER SCHEDULER:** The major *scheduler* in a computer system which may call processes which are themselves schedulers.

**MATCH:** To compare two items for identity. If they are found to be the same, this is a *hit*.

**MATHEMATICAL SUBROUTINE:** A subroutine which performs some mathematical function such as evaluating the sine of an angle.

**MATRIX:** A two-dimensional array (although the term *matrix* is often used to mean an array with two or more dimensions). In the case of two-dimensional arrays, each elements is identified by two values, designating the row and column respectively.

**MATRIX PRINTER:** A printer which, rather than pre-cast characters, uses a matrix of needles (frequently $9 \times 7$) from which all characters can be generated. The device may print by impact, heat or electrostatic techniques. If smaller matrices are used, the quality of the character is lower and, for example, may not permit lower case letters or, if permitted, they may not have descenders.

**MEDLARS:** A database available on the National Library of Medicine computers (and distributed by NLM to other centres) which has over two million citations to the medical literature.

**MEDLINE:** An abbreviation for *MEDLARS On-Line*, an interactive service (using the ELHILL program) to access the MEDLARS database which is available via the PSTN or various computer networks such as TELENET and TYMNET.

**MEGA-:** See *M*.

**MEMBER:** One file contained in a *library* or *partitioned data set*.

**MEMORY:** A word used to describe the storage capabilities of a computer system, in particular, the *main memory* of a system.

**MEMORY ADDRESS REGISTER:** An internal cpu register which contains the address of a data item (or instruction) to be accessed in the memory.

**MEMORY BUFFER:** A *buffer* which is contained in *main memory*.

**MEMORY CYCLE:** See *cycle*.

**MEMORY FILL:** A term used to denote the filling of a specified area of main memory with a given bit pattern, often binary zero.

**MEMORY MAP:** A *map* showing the allocation of programs to memory locations or, in some cases, a map showing where memory exists in the particular computer (for example, in some microcomputers, it is not uncommon for the memory supplied to occupy locations which are not contiguous).

**MEMORY MAPPING:** A technique whereby a peripheral is controlled by treating it as part of memory and addressing certain locations in memory causes it to perform various functions. For example, a "memory-mapped VDU" is one whereby writing to particular locations in main memory causes the data written to be output onto the screen and hence there is a mapping between the screen and memory.

**MEMORY PROTECT:** A facility whereby specified locations in main memory can be protected from reading and/or writing. In the event of attempted unauthorised access, an interrupt occurs or some similar action is taken.

**MERGE:** To combine two (or more) sets of data into a single set which has the same order as the input sets.

**MESSAGE:** An ordered set of characters which convey information.

**MESSAGE HEADER:** The first part of a *message* which contains information about the message, such as the source and destination.

**MESSAGE SWITCHING:** A technique whereby messages are sent into a network. The network stores the messages and then forwards them to the appropriate destination which is contained in a header block which precedes the data or message. Once the messages enter the network, the network itself takes responsibility for delivering them and the sending node need not retain a copy. However, the time for delivery may be long and hence message switching cannot be used in an interactive method of working. The SITA airlines network is perhaps one of the best known examples of a message switched network.

**METALANGUAGE:** An artificial language (e.g. *BNF*) used to define a language.

**METASYMBOL:** A symbol in a *metalanguage*.

**MFT:** An acronym for *Multiprogramming with a Fixed number of Tasks*, a multi-programming system available on IBM computers which divides memory up into a number of fixed partitions, in each of which one job is run at one time.

**MICR:** An abbreviation for *magnetic ink character recognition*, a means of input to a computer.

**MICRO (1):** A prefix, indicating one millionth.

**MICRO (2):** An abbreviation for *microcomputer* or *microprocessor*.

**MICROCODE:** The lowest level of a computer system above the hardware. It consists of instructions which perform such primitive functions as opening "gates" and hence a single *machine code* instruction is actually executed (if implemented in this manner) by means of a number of *micro-instructions*. Often the "micro-instructions" have long word lengths, the setting of each bit denoting an action to be taken ("horizontal microprogramming").

**MICROCOMPUTER:** A computer, based on a microprocessor, but including also memory and I/O facilities.

**MICROFICHE:** A sheet of photographic film about 6″ × 4″ on which a large number of printed pages are recorded in a reduced form (usually by a factor of 42 or 48). This is especially used for computer output.

**MICRO-INSTRUCTION:** One of the instructions in *microcode*.

**MICRO-MODELLER:** A financial modelling package available on a number of microcomputers.

**MICROPOLIS:** A manufacturer of computer peripherals, especially high-density, mini-floppy disk drives.

**MICROPROCESSOR:** A *central processing unit* implemented by means of a single (or occasionally more than one) chip using LSI or VLSI techniques. As the density of components increases, it is possible to include more functions on a microprocessor, for example, memory refresh. The term "microprocessor" should be distinguished from *microcomputer* which contains other components such as memory and I/O chips.

**MICROPROGRAMMING:** Programming, using *microcode*. Some computers allow the user some access to microcode and hence the basic instruction set of the computer can be changed.

**MICROSECOND:** One millionth of a second.

**MIDNIGHT LINE:** A facility which was made available for some time from the British Post Office whereby a user had use of a *leased line* during the night at a low cost.

**MILL:** A synonym for *central processor*, used in some computer systems, prticularly those from ICL.

**MILLI-:** A prefix indicating one thousandth part.

**MILLISECOND:** One thousandth of a second (i.e. one thousand microseconds).

**MIMD:** An acronym for *multiple instruction stream, multiple data stream*, a term applied to a number of computer architectures, of which perhaps multiprocessor systems are the most well known.

**MINICOMPUTER:** A word first used to distinguish smaller computers from *mainframes*. Although there is no agreed definition of a minicomputer, they are usually sixteen-bit machines with (at least the possibility of) a multi-user operating system, fairly sophisticated I/O and interrupt handling and costing from, say, £10,000 upwards. Perhaps one of the best known minicomputers is the DEC PDP-11.

**MINIMAL BASIC:** A standard for a minimal subset of the language *BASIC* defined by the ANSI Committee X3J2.

**MINUEND:** The number from which, during subtraction, a second number, known as the *subtrahend* is subtracted.

**MIPS:** An acronym for *million instructions per second*, a measure of the power of a computer system. Figures vary from about 1 mips for a moderately powerful minicomputer, to 20 mips for an IBM 360/195 to about 200 mips for an array processor such as ILLIAC IV.

**MIS:** An abbreviation for *management information system*.

**MISPUNCH:** The encoding of incorrect information onto a storage medium, usually a *punched card*, either due to the operator pressing the wrong key or the *card punch* having a fault which causes it to punch the wrong holes even though the correct key was pressed.

**MLC:** An abbreviation for *multi-line controller*, a piece of hardware which is added to an *ARPANET IMP* in order to give it facilities for handling up to 64 terminals at various baud rates (including automatic speed selection and character code recognition).

**MNEMONIC:** Something for aiding the memory but most commonly used in the context of "mnemonic instructions" where an assembler provides names for the machine operations.

**MODEM:** An abbreviation for *MOdulator-DEModulator*. A device used in data transmission for converting the computer or terminal digital signal into an analogue signal by modulation in order to transmit it via a telephone line.

**MODIFIER:** Some item (e.g. a *register*) which alters the value of another item (e.g. an *address*).

**MODIFY:** To alter some item, usually an *instruction* or *address* by means of a *modifier*.

**MODULAR:** Pertaining to a system which consists of a number of *modules*, i.e. separate units which have clearly defined functions and interfaces. This applies both to software and hardware.

**MODULAR PROGRAMMING:** A technique of programming whereby a program is broken down into a number of separate *modules*, each of which have clearly defined functions and interfaces and which can be programmed separately. In this manner, dependencies between modules should be significantly reduced and hence errors should be more localised.

**MODULATION:** A technique in data communications whereby, in order to transmit information, a *carrier frequency* is varied in accordance with the information signal.

**MODULATOR:** See *modem*.

**MODULE:** A separate unit (hardware or software) which has clearly defined functions and interfaces and hence can be implemented in isolation from the other components of the system.

**MODULO:** A mathematical function which yields the remainder when one operand is divided by another. Thus 79 modulo 11 is 2. Often it is required to find the modulus of a power of two and this can be done most easily by means of the logical *AND* operation due to the identity:

$$N \text{ MOD } 2^p = N \,\&\, (2^p - 1)$$

so, for example, 123456 MOD 32 is the same as 123456 & 31.

**MODULO N CHECK:** A means of checking data whereby an operand is divided by N and the remainder used as a check digit. Often N is taken to be 11.

**MOL:** An acronym for *machine oriented language*, a language which is oriented towards the computer on which it is to be run rather than towards the problem which it is intended to solve (see *problem oriented language*).

**MONADIC:** Pertaining to an operation which has a single operand. For example, in the expression $-3 \times 4$, the "$-$" is a monadic operator. It is also called a "unary operator".

**MONITOR:** An item which supervises the operation of a system. The term is usually applied to software, in which case, the "monitor" usually forms a part of the *operating system* (and often the two terms are used synonymously) but it can also be applied to hardware, particularly in the phrase "teleprocessing monitor".

**MONOSTABLE:** A device which has only one stable state (cf. *bistable*).

**MONTE CARLO METHOD:** A technique of numerical analysis whereby statistical sampling techniques are employed to obtain approximations to the correct solution, particularly in cases where the problem is not susceptible to purely analytical methods.

**MOP:** An acronym for *Multiple On-Line Programming*, an interactive operating system on ICL computers.

**MOS:** An acronym for *metal oxide semiconductor*.

**MOST SIGNIFICANT:** The character which occupies the leftmost position of a group of digits and which therefore has most weight. For example, in the number 123456, '1' is the most significant digit.

**MOTHERBOARD:** A part of a computer system into which the various PCBs are slotted and which may include such components as I/O interfaces, interrupt control and a real-time clock.

**MOUSE (AND KEYPAD):** An input device which is extremely simple to use and hence can be used by untrained operators. The mouse consists of a box, around the size of a human hand, which has a number (usually three) wheels; it is moved around a table by the operator's hand and the movement is detected by sensors attached to the wheels; this, in turn, is translated to a digital signal and used to move the cursor on the screen in a similar fashion to the movement of the mouse. The keypad is again an extremely simple device, usually consisting of about five levers which the user presses in combination, allowing access to a restricted character set.

**MOVE:** Transfer from one location to another.

**MP/M:** A multi-programming operating system (designed and sold by Digital Research) available on a range of microcomputers with a number of features such as output spooling and multi-tasking.

**MPX:** An abbreviation for *multiplex*.

**MSI:** An abbreviation for *medium scale integration*.

**MTBF:** An abbreviation for *mean time between failure*. A measure of the reliability of a (computer) system.

**MTS:** An acronym for *Michigan Terminal System*, an interactive system available on IBM System/360 and /370 computers, developed by the University of Michigan.

**MTTR:** An abbreviation of *mean time to repair*. A secondary measure of the reliability of a computer system (see MTBF).

**MULTI-ACCESS (SYSTEM):** A computer system which can serve multiple users, i.e. multiple users may access system resources.

**MULTICS:** An acronym for *Multiplexed Information and Computing Service*, a multi-user computer system developed by the Massachusetts Institute of Technology and now commercially available.

**MULTIDROP LINE:** A line connected to a number of devices (computers or terminals) each of which is polled in turn to determine whether it has any data to send.

**MULTIJOB:** An interactive operating system designed for some ICL computers.

**MULTI-PART:** An adjective describing stationery which has multiple sheets and hence multiple copies can be printed at once. Obviously this can only be used with "impact printers".

**MULTI-POINT:** A synonym for *multidrop*.

**MULTI-PUNCHING:** The technique of over-punching holes in a punched card so that, for example, lower-case letters may be represented.

**MULTI-REEL:** An adjective describing a file held on magnetic tape which, due to its size, spans more than one physical reel.

**MULTI-TASKING:** The execution of a number of *tasks* simultaneously. If a *task* is equivalent to a program, "multi-tasking" is synonymous with "multi-programming" but a task may often be a part of a program.

**MULTI-ADDRESS MESSAGE:** A *message* which is to be sent to more than one destination. If it is to be sent to all possible destinations, it is known as a "broadcast message".

**MULTIPLE-LENGTH ARITHMETIC:** In most computer systems, arithmetic is carried out in a single (or sometimes a double) word. In some applications, the restriction that this places on numbers is untenable and hence arithmetic is performed using multiple address locations giving greater precision or a wider range of numbers. This has to be performed, in nearly all cases, by software routines.

**MULTIPLE ON-LINE PROGRAMMING:** See *MOP*.

**MULTIPLE PUNCHING:** See *multi-punching*.

**MULTIPLEXING:** The division of a transmission medium into a number of channels. The two most common techniques are time division multiplexing and frequency division multiplexing.

**MULTIPLEXOR:** A device for performing *multiplexing*.

**MULTIPLICAND:** One of the two operands used in *multiplication*. It is multiplied by the *multiplier* to yield the product.

**MULTIPLICATION:** An arithmetic operation which takes two operands, the *multiplicand* and *multiplier* and yields their product.

**MULTIPLIER:** One of the operands in *multiplication*. Also used as the name for a hardware unit which performs multiplication.

**MULTIPROCESSING:** The technique of executing programs using multiple processors (see *multiprocessor*).

**MULTIPROCESSOR (SYSTEM):** A system which has a number of separate processors (*cpus*). These may be controlled in an integrated manner or may be autonomous to a large extent, perhaps sharing access to part of memory. In this way, a much higher throughput of instructions can be achieved.

**MULTIPROGRAMMING:** The technique of running multiple programs in a single computer (with a single processor) so that, while one program is awaiting some event (usually an I/O interrupt), another can be executing.

**MUX:** An abbreviation for *multiplex, multiplexor* or *multiplexing*, depending on context.

**MVT:** An acronym for *Multiprogramming with a Variable number of Tasks*, a multi-programming system available on IBM computers in which a variable number of *jobs* may be executing at one time, each occupying the space it requires (or, more accurately, the space it tells the operating system it requires) without any fixed partitions (see *MFT*).

**MYLAR:** A plastic which is often used as the base for magnetic tape or other storage forms (e.g. the Unicon laser memory).

# N

**NAG:** An acronym for *Numerical Algorithms Group*, a group who have produced a large set of library subroutines for various numerical functions which are available on a wide range of machines.

**NAK:** An acronym for *negative acknowledgement*. A control character usually used to indicate that an incorrect message has been received. In ASCII, its value is binary 0010101 (control-U).

**NAM:** An acronym for *Network Access Machine*, a general term applied to a computer (usually a minicomputer) which mediates between a user and a computer network in order to simplify access to that network. The term is derived from research at NBS, using a PDP-11 as the NAM.

1. Rosenthal, R.M., "Network Access Techniques – A Review", *Proc.* AFIPS NCC, **45**, 495–500, 1976.

**NAME:** A sequence of characters used to identify a data item. Although the syntax of names varies according to the programming language used, most languages insist that the first character of a name be alphabetic, the remainder being alphanumeric. Some languages also permit other *special characters* such as *underline*.

**NAND:** A logical operation which conforms to the following table:

|   | 0 | 1 |
|---|---|---|
| 0 | 1 | 1 |
| 1 | 1 | 0 |

**NAND GATE:** A logic element with two or more inputs whose output is 1 if any input signal is 0 and 0 if all inputs are 1.

**NANO-:** One thousand millionth part ($10^{-9}$).

**NANOSECOND:** One thousand millionth of a second, the same order of magnitude as current fast computer memories. To put it into perspective, it is approximately the length of time it takes light to travel one foot.

**NATIONAL COMPUTER CONFERENCE:** An annual conference in the USA organised by AFIPS and the successor to the Spring and Fall Joint Computer Conferences.

**NATIONAL SEMICONDUCTOR:** One of the largest US manufacturers of semiconductors who also make the SC/MP single board microcomputer.

**NATIONAL SOFTWARE WORKS:** A co-operative project between Massachusetts Computer Associates, Bolt Beranek and Newman and the Massachusetts Institute of Technology whose task is to design a distributed operating system for a heterogeneous computer network. It is, in some way, a successor to "RSEXEC".

1. Millstein, R.E., "The National Software Works: A Distributed Processing System", *Proc.* ACM Annual Conf., 53–58, 1977.

**NATURAL LANGUAGE:** A language such as English, French etc. which does not have the requirements of non-ambiguous, clearly defined syntax and semantics required (at present) by computer language processors. Some work has been done on the problem of allowing natural language input to a computer and perhaps thebest known example is the program ELIZA, implemented by the Stanford Artificial Intelligence Laboratory.

**NBS:** An acronym for the *USA National Bureau of Standards*, based at Gaithersburg, Maryland and Boulder, Colorado.

**NCC (1):** An acronym for *network control centre*.

**NCC (2):** An acronym for *National Computing Centre*.

**NCC (3):** An acronym for *National Computer Conference*.

**NCP:** An acronym for *network control program*, a program which permits process to process communication over a computer network.

**NCR:** An acronym for *National Cash Register Company*, a company which produces small to medium size computers.

**NE:** An abbreviation for *not equal to*, used as a reserved word in many languages.

**NEAT:** An acronym for *NCR Electronic Autocoding Technique*, a low-level language available on early NCR computers.

**NEEDLE:** The metal part used to generate the dot in a matrix printer (which is, rarely, known as a "needle printer" for this reason).

**NEGATE:** To perform the NOT operation, namely to invert the bit pattern. It is also used, more generally, to mean obtaining the negative of a specified number which is the same as the previous definition if the number is represented by, for example, ones complement.

**NEL:** An acronym for *National Engineering Laboratory*.

**NEST:** To embed routines, programs or groups of instructions within others to form a hierarchical structure. Often data within inner parts of such a nested structure are unavailable to outer levels.

**NESTED:** Pertaining to any suitably embedded data. See *nest*.

**NETWORK:** A number of computers, interconnected in some way.

**NETWORK ANALYSIS:** A method of determining critical paths in a project planning network. See *critical path method*. It is also used to mean the optimisation of the topology of a distributed computer network.

**NETWORK CONTROL CENTRE:** A site on a computer network which controls and, to some extent, monitors operation of the network.

1. McKenzie, A.A. *et al.*, "The Network Control Center for the ARPA Network", *Proc.* ICCC, 185–191, 1972.

**NETWORK CONTROL PROGRAM:** A program residing in each *Host* of a computer network enabling processes in the Host to communicate through the network.

**NETWORK MEASUREMENT CENTER:** A site on the *ARPANET* dedicated to measuring network performance, usually by means of relatively long-term experiments.

**NEWLINE:** A character in some character sets which combines the functions of *carriage return* and *line feed*, that is, to move the cursor or print head to the start of the next line.

**N-KEY ROLLOVER:** A feature of keyboards whereby input is buffered (to the extent of N key depressions) and hence the user cannot (if N is sufficiently large) type characters which are lost.

**NL:** An abbreviation of *newline*.

**NLM:** An abbreviation for the *National Library of Medicine* which, *inter alia*, provides access to a number of medical databases by means of interactive systems (e.g. TOXLINE, MEDLINE).

**NMC:** An abbreviation for *Network Measurement Centre*.

**NMM:** An abbreviation for *Network Measurement Machine*.

**NMOS:** An acronym for *N-channel Metal-Oxide Semiconductor*, a technology for making semiconductor components.

**NODE:** The intersection of edges in a network (a vertex). Often used to mean a small computer used for packet-switching functions in a computer network.

**NOISE:** Random signals on a transmission line.

**NON-DESTRUCTIVE READ:** A read operation which does not destroy the contents of the storage location from which the data is read. In cases where the read operation is destructive and it is required to retain the information, the data read is then immediately written back.

**NON-EQUIVALENCE:** A synonym for *exclusive-or*.

**NON-EXECUTABLE:** A statement within a program which is not executed, for example, a DATA statement in BASIC.

**NON-LINEAR PROGRAMMING:** A technique for determing the optimum values of functions subject to non-linear constraints.

**NON-NUMERIC:** Pertaining to any character which is not in the set 0 . . . 9 (i.e. *numeric*).

**NON-PRINTING CHARACTER:** A character which does not actually print but (usually) performs some control function (such as *device control*) or affects the layout (such as *backspace*).

**NON-VOLATILE:** used as an adjective to describe memory in which the data is not lost when power is turned off. It is most usually applied to primary memories and the most common non-volatile memory is core.

**NO-OP:** An abbreviation for *no-operation*, an instruction which has no action except to move to the next instruction. Such instructions are of use when it is required to "pad out" instructions to a specified boundary or, sometimes, in debugging.

**NOR:** A logical operation which gives the result 1 if and only if both operands are zero. It conforms to the following table:

|   | 0 | 1 |
|---|---|---|
| 0 | 1 | 0 |
| 1 | 0 | 0 |

**NOR GATE:** A logic element with two or more inputs whose output is 1 if all the input values are zero and 0 if any input is non-zero.

**NORMALISE:** Floating point numbers can be represented in a multitude of different ways but there are many reasons why a standard form should be used. The most common of these forms is known as normalised and is one where the mantissa of the floating point number has a non-zero most significant digit. This can always be achieved by shifting the mantissa to the left until the condition obtains and decreasing the exponent in accordance with the number of places shifted. In the case of some computers (notably the PDP-11), since the leftmost bit of the mantissa is known to be one (since floating point numbers are always stored normalised), it is not stored, thus allowing a small increase in precision.

**NORTH STAR:** A US manufacturer of microcomputers, notably the Horizon and the Advantage.

**NOS:** An acronym for *network operating system*, a general term used to describe a distributed operating system in a computer network.

1. Kimbleton, S.R. and Mandell, R.L., "A Perspective on Network Operating Systems", *Proc.* AFIPS NCC, **45**, 551–559, 1976.

**NOT:** A logical operator such that, if P is false, NOT P is true and vice versa.

**NOT GATE:** A logic element having a single input and a single output. The output is 1 if the input is 0 and vice versa.

**NOVA:** A minicomputer manufactured by Data General.

**NOVRAM:** An acronym for *non-volatile RAM*. Random access memory is a volatile medium (i.e. it loses its contents when power is turned off) and this is inconvenient in a number of circumstances. By a combination of ROM and RAM, it is possible (although expensive) to produce a component with the attributes of RAM but which is non-volatile.

**NPL:** Abbreviation for *National Physical Laboratory*, a UK Government funded establishment near Teddington, Middlesex which has been closely concerned with research into many aspects of computer science for many years.

**NRZ:** An abbreviation for *non-return to zero*, a technique for recording data on a magnetic medium.

**NRZ-C:** An abbreviation for *non-return to zero, change*, a technique for recording data on a magnetic medium.

**NRZI:** An abbreviation for *non-return to zero inverted*, a technique for recording data on a magnetic medium.

**NRZM:** An abbreviaion for *non-return to zero mark*, a technique for recording data on a magnetic medium.

**NSA:** An abbreviation for the (US) *National Security Agency*.

**NSW:** An abbreviation for *National Software Works*.

**NTU:** An abbreviation for *network terminating unit*.

**NUCLEUS:** A part of an *operating system* which is permanently resident in main memory.

**NUI:** An abbreviation for *network user identification*.

**NUL:** An abbreviation for *null*, especially in the context of the ASCII character consisting of seven binary zeros.

**NULL:** Used to mean "nothing", but dependent on the context. In particular, a character which, in ASCII, is seven binary zeros (0000000) and has the meaning of "do nothing". It can be generated on most keyboards by keying ctrl-@. When punched onto paper tape, it gives blank tape.

**NULL INSTRUCTION:** A synonym for *no-op*.

**NULL STATEMENT:** A statement which conveys no information and is usually used to terminate a group of statements.

**NULL STRING:** A string with no characters and a length of zero.

**NUMBER:** A set of *numeric* characters representing a value in a specified representation.

**NUMBER CRUNCHING:** A semi-slang phrase to indicate very fast computation on numeric quantities, for example, as used in much scientific computing. Many computers have been designed as "number crunchers", notably the CDC 6600, which are optimised for this type of work but are less efficient at the functions needed in business or systems applications such as string manipulation or decimal to binary conversions.

**NUMERAL:** A character or sequence of characters which represent a number.

**NUMERATOR:** A synonym for *dividend* in a division operation.

**NUMERIC:** Pertaining to a representation of a *number*.

**NUMERIC CHARACTER:** A synonym for *digit*.

**NUMERIC CODE:** A code which consists solely of *numeric characters*.

**NUMERICAL ANALYSIS:** A branch of mathematics concerned with the study and analysis of solving problems (whether or not analytical solutions exist) by means of numerical techniques. The term also includes the study of the errors and bounds of such solutions.

# O

**OBJECT CODE:** The output from a compiler which translates from *source code* to "object code". The object code may be pure machine code which may be loaded directly into memory or may be in various different forms, such as "relocatable binary" in which all addresses have not been resolved.

**OBJECT COMPUTER:** The computer on which a program is to be run, which may be distinct from that on which the program is compiled.

**OBJECT DECK:** A set of punched cards which contain the *object code* of a program.

**OBJECT LANGUAGE:** The language into which a program is translated. Usually this is *object code* but, in some circumstances, may be *assembler* or even a *high-level language*.

**OBJECT MACHINE:** A synonym for *object computer*.

**OBJECT MODULE:** A *module* of *object code*, usually produced as a file by a language translator and input to a *link-editor*.

**OBJECT PROGRAM:** The translated version of a program which is ready to run on a computer.

**OCR:** An acronym for *optical character recognition* or the machine which performs the recognition, an *optical character reader*.

**OCR WAND:** A hand-held *optical character reader*.

**OCTAL:** A number system using base 8 (in the words of Tom Lehrer, octal is the same as decimal if you're missing two fingers). It is perhaps slightly more comprehensible than hexadecimal but becoming less commonly used as computers are more often having a word length which is a multiple of four (the number of bits needed to represent a hex digit) rather than three (for octal). It is used, for example, on the DECsystem-10 (a 36-bit machine) but is also used on the PDP-11 series which are 16 bit machines.

**OCTET:** A term, usually used in data transmission, particularly in bit-oriented protocols, to mean a contiguous group of eight bits.

**ODD PARITY:** A system of using *parity* to check for errors in which the number of bits set, including the parity bit is odd.

**OEM:** An acronym for *Original Equipment Manufacturer*. A manufacturer who buys hardware which is incorporated into their own equipment.

**OFF-LINE:** Not connected to a computer or, more specifically, not under the control of the computer.

**OFF-LINE STORAGE:** Storage devices which are not under the control of a computer, such as a deck of punched cards which are not currently being read.

**OFF LOAD:** To transfer jobs from one computer to another which is more lightly loaded.

**OFFICE COMPUTER:** A term usually applied to a microcomputer-based system for use in an office environment. It is likely to be a similar machine to that used as a home computer but to have better storage facilities (for example, a hard disk rather than floppy disks or tape) and software developed for specific office functions.

**OFFSET:** The difference between two specified values, for example, the offset of the start of an array.

**OLRT:** An abbreviation for *On-Line Real Time*.

**OLTEP:** An acronym for *On-Line Test Executive Program*.

**OLTS:** An abbreviation for *On-Line Test System*.

**OMNIX:** A version of Unix, available on the Onyx range of microcomputers.

**OMR:** An abbreviation for *optical mark recognition* or *optical mark reader*.

**ON-LINE:** Directly connected to and under the control of a computer. The term is now more often used in the rather restricted sense of interactive systems.

**ON LINE STORAGE:** Storage which is under the direct control of a computer, such as a disk.

**ONE ADDRESS:** Pertaining to instructions in which a single address is specified. Since many operations require two operands, the second is implicit. For example, the "one address instruction".

ADD     X

means "add the contents of location X to the accumulator and retain the result in the accumulator".

**ONE ADDRESS INSTRUCTION:** See *one address*.

**ONE-LEVEL STORE:** The concept of arranging two levels of store (usually primary memory and backing − drum − storage) so that, from the programmer's point of view, it appears as a single level. This is achieved by *paging* or a related system. The "one-level store concept" was first introduced on the Ferranti Atlas computer.

**ONE PASS:** Pertaining to the operation of a language processor (*compiler*) which only reads the source text once.

**ONES COMPLEMENT:** A method of representing numbers in a computer (e.g. the Cyber 70 series) in which a negative number is formed by taking the absolute value of the number and inverting each bit. In this system, the range of positive and negative numbers represented is symmetrical but there are two representations of zero − all ones ("minus zero") or all zeros ("plus zero").

**O/P:** An abbreviation for *output*.

**OPCODE:** The part of a computer instruction which defines the operation to be performed.

**OPEN:** To prepare a file prior to reading from or writing to it. This usually involves ascertaining that the specified file exists and setting up the appropriate control blocks (including I/O buffers).

**OPEN SUBROUTINE:** A sequence of instructions which are inserted into a program each time they are needed. It should be contrasted with *closed subroutine*.

**OPERAND:** A data item which is operated on, usually in an instruction.

**OPERATING SYSTEM:** A set of software which controls the overall operation of a computer system, including such functions as accounting, data management, scheduling, storage management and I/O. Operating systems are generally complex, taking many hundreds or thousands of man-years to write.

**OPERATION:** An action which takes a number of *operands* and produces a result.

**OPERATION CODE:** See *opcode*.

**OPERATIONAL RESEARCH:** A branch of mathematics concerned with the allocation of resources to achieve optimum efficiency. Various techniques are employed in this, including *Monte Carlo* methods and *linear programming*. Usually abbreviated as *OR*.

**OPERATOR (1):** The description of the action to be performed on *operands*.

**OPERATOR (2):** The person who operates a computer system, including initiating various tasks and mounting tapes and disks.

**OPERATOR COMMAND:** A command, issued to a computer system by an *operator*, for example, to determine the status of storage devices.

**OPERATOR CONSOLE:** The *console* used by an *operator* to input *operator commands*.

**OPERATOR MESSAGE:** A message output on the *operator console* from a computer system indicating to an *operator* the status of (part of) the system or requesting him to take some action, such as mounting a tape.

**OPTICAL CHARACTER READER:** An input device which reads characters from a printed document (printed in special type founts, designated OCR-A and OCR-B).

**OPTICAL CHARACTER RECOGNITION:** The technique of recognising characters on a printed document.

**OPTICAL MARK READER:** An input device which recognises graphite marks (usually created by making the marks with a pencil) on a card.

**OPTICAL MARK RECOGNITION:** The technique of recognising graphite marks on an input document.

**OPTIMISE:** To write a program or design a system in such a way as to minimise or maximise the value of some parameter, especially cost, time or storage.

**OR (1):** A synonym for *inclusive-or.*

**OR (2):** An acronym for *operational research.*

**ORACLE:** An acronym for *Optional Reception of Announcements by Coded Line Electronics,* perhaps one of the most contrived acronyms. It is the IBA version of *Teletext.*

**ORDER:** To arrange a set of items in accordance with a given set of rules, for example, alphabetic order.

**ORIGIN:** The address (usually *absolute address*) of the lowest location of a program.

**OS:** An acronym for *operating system,* particularly that used by IBM on its System/360 and System/370 computers.

**OSCL:** An acronym for *operating system control language,* a general term for the language used for interaction with a computer system.

**OSI:** An abbreviation for *open system interconnection,* a general term used for the techniques for the connection of computer systems which may be different (i.e. heterogeneous). The International Standards Organisation (ISO) set up a sub-committee (TC97/SC16) in Sydney, Australia in 1977 to investigate this topic and it produced a draft proposal (DP 7498) defining the architecture for such interconnection. The architectural model consists of seven layers (and hence is often called the "seven-layer model") arranged in hierarchical manner. The lowest layer (Level 1) is the Physical Layer, Level 2 is the Data Link Layer, Level 3 is the Network Layer, Level 4 is the Transport Layer, Level 5 is the Session Layer, Level 6 is the Presentation Layer and the top level (7) is the Application Layer. A basic concept of the model is that one layer appears to communicate only with the corresponding layer in another computer, although the actual communication is through all lower layers on its own machine, through the communications link, then through the lower layers of the remote machine, up to the appropriate level. The lower layers of the model provide a "Transport Service" which ensures the reliable, error-free transmission of data through the communications service. The upper layers serve to provide the services necessary to communicate between applications processes.

In addition to the Draft Proposal, a number of protocols conforming to the model are expected to be standardised in the near future. The CCITT recommendations X.25 and X.75 conform to the lowest three layers of the OSI model.

**OUT OF LINE:** Pertaining to statements in a computer program which are not in the main line of the program, for example, *closed subroutines*.

**OUTPUT:** The process of transferring data from a computer system to some external medium or the product of this process. The opposite process is known as *input* and the two are sometimes referred to collectively as *transput*.

**OUTPUT AREA:** A region of storage which is reserved for data which is to be transmitted to an output device.

**OUTPUT BUFFER:** A *buffer* used to transfer data to an external device (see *output area*).

**OUTPUT CHANNEL:** A *channel* which connects peripheral units and the central processor, through which data may be transmitted for output.

**OUTPUT DATA:** Data which is the result of some computation on a computer and which is therefore transmitted from the central processor to an external device.

**OUTPUT DEVICE:** Any *peripheral* which is used to transfer data from a computer to the external world. Examples are *line printer* and *VDU*.

**OUTPUT HOPPER:** A part of a *card reader* in which cards are stored after being read.

**OUTPUT ROUTINE:** Sometimes used synonymously with *output writer* but, more often, used to mean a part of a user program which is concerned with sending data to an *output device*.

**OUTPUT STREAM:** The sequence of data to be transmitted to an *output device*.

**OUTPUT UNIT:** A synonym for *output device*.

**OUTPUT WELL:** An area of main storage reserved for a set of *output buffers*. Usually this is used as an area for spooling data destined for *output devices*.

**OUTPUT WRITER:** A part of an *operating system* which is concerned with taking data from central memory and transmitting it to an *output device*.

**OV:** An abbreviation for *overflow*.

**OVERFLOW:** The generation of a value (in an arithmetic operation) which is too large to be contained in the specified destination. Also used to denote that part of the result which cannot be contained.

**OVERFLOW RECORD:** A *record* which cannot be contained in the appropriate part of a database.

**OVERLAY:** To use the same area of main storage for different segments of a program, the segments being chosen so that they are not required to be active at the same time. In this manner, a large program can be contained in a much smaller amount of main storage, at the cost of the overheads associated with overlaying. The term "overlay" is also used to mean the segment which is overwriting the one currently in main storage.

**OVERLAY PROGRAM:** A program which is segmented so that segments may overlay one another (see *overlay*).

**OVERPUNCH:** To punch extra holes in a card column which is already punched, for example, to convert an upper-case character to a lower-case one.

**OVERWRITE:** As the word implies, to write data in the place of data which was previously there, often unintentionally.

**OWNER:** The entity which has control of a specified resource, for example, the owner of a file is usually the person who created it.

# P

**PABX:** An abbreviation for *private automatic branch exchange.*

**PACK (1):** To store data in a compact way, usually by removing redundancy. For example, it is possible to pack data by means of *blank compression.*

**PACK (2):** A set of punched cards.

**PACKAGE:** A program (or set of programs) which are designed to solve, in a general manner, a particular problem (or set of related problems) and which is available on a computer system in a *library.* The user need have no knowledge of the working of the package, merely the functions it performs and its interfaces.

**PACKET:** A group of bits transmitted as a single unit (cf. *block*) through a telecommunications network containing control information such as the destination address.

**PACKET INTERLEAVING:** A technique of multiplexing in a packet-switched environment whereby the packets from each sub-channel are multiplexed together. This technique is used in the X.25 standard.

**PACKET RADIO:** A system of packet-switching where communication takes place by means of radio transmission which therefore occurs in a broadcast mode.

**PACKET SWITCHING:** A technique whereby data is transmitted between computers on a network, the data being split into packets, each of which contains the destination address. The basic concepts of packet switching were proposed by Paul Baran in a series of papers for the Rand Corporation in 1964 describing a secure means of communication and, independently, by Donald Davies at the National Physical Laboratory in the UK. The first large scale application of packet-switching in a computer communication network was the US Department of Defense's *ARPANET* and, since then, many networks, particularly public networks, have been based on packet-switching principles (e.g. *PSS* in the UK).

1. Baran, P., "On Distributed Communications Networks", IEEE

Transactions on Communication Systems, **CS-12**, 1964.
2. Davies, D.W. *et al.*, "A Digital Communication Network for Computers Giving Rapid Response at Remote Terminals", *Proc.* ACM Symposium on Operating System Principles, Gatlinburg, 1-4 Oct 1967.
3. Roberts, L.G. and Wessler, B.D., "Computer Network Development to Achieve Resource Sharing", *Proc.* AFIPS SJCC, **36**, 543-549, 1970.

**PACKING DENSITY:** The amount of data stored on a recording medium expressed as a function of length or area. For example, the number of bits per inch on a magnetic tape or the number of electronic components on a *chip*.

**PAD (1):** To fill out a field to a given boundary or length (see *fill*).

**PAD (2):** An acronym for *Packet Assembly/Disassembly* facility. A component of a packet-switched network which accepts single characters from a terminal and assembles them into packets, together with the reverse function.

**PAD CHARACTER:** A character used when padding out a field to a specified boundary or length. See also *fill character*.

**PADDING:** The addition of *pad characters* to a field to extend it to a specified boundary or length.

**PAGE (1):** A single sheet of (non-continuous) stationery.

**PAGE (2):** An area of memory with a fixed size which is used for *paging*.

**PAGE PRINTER:** A printer which outputs a page at a time, usually by some optical or xerographic process.

**PAGING:** A technique whereby memory is divided into fixed-length areas (e.g. on the first commercial machine to implement this technique, the Atlas computer, the pages were 512 words each). Pages may occupy any locations in main memory (as designated by the operating system) or even on backing storage, without the user being aware of this *dynamic relocation*, since his programs are written in terms of *virtual addresses*. See also *one-level store*.

**PAM:** An acronym for *pulse amplitude modulation*, a means of reproducing an analogue signal by means of a sequence of pulses, the frequency of the pulses being at least double the bandwidth required, in order to achieve reasonable quality. PAM is the first step in the creation of a system to digitise analogue data and transmit it over, for example, telephone lines.

**PAPER ADVANCE:** The mechanism for moving paper on a printer or similar device. This is usually achieved by friction (*friction-feed*) or by means of sprockets engaging with holes in the recording medium, usually continuous stationery (*sprocket-feed*).

**PAPER LOW:** An indicator on a printer or similar device to show that the supply of paper has reached a specified critical level. The term is also used to mean the above condition.

**PAPER TAPE:** An early form of tertiary storage consisting of strips of paper, wound on a reel, which are punched according to certain conventions. This punching is performed either by a slow device such as the punch on a Teletype or a special high-speed punch. On a teleprinter, a five-hole code is used but, more commonly a seven-bit (e.g. on a Flexowriter) or an eight-bit (e.g. Teletype) code is used. These holes are in addition to the *sprocket holes* which define where the other holes are punched. Paper tape is relatively uncommon now, due to the reduction of price of secondary storage media but nevertheless still forms a useful input medium which can be prepared off-line.

**PAPER TAPE PUNCH:** An output device which punches holes in *paper tape*.

**PAPER TAPE READER:** An input device which reads holes punched in *paper tape*.

**PAPER THROW:** The movement of paper at a rapid speed through a printer, often applied specifically to the movement to the *top of form* (more strictly called *form feed*).

**PARALLEL:** Pertaining to the simultaneous occurrence of a number of events, for example, *parallel processing* or parallel transmission of data when a number of bits (usually a byte) are transmitted at the same time. The opposite is *serial*.

**PARALLEL COMPUTER:** A computer which has multiple processors (*cpus*) enabling it to perform processing in parallel.

**PARALLEL PROCESSING:** The technique of executing a number of processes in a computer in parallel. In this manner, the throughput of the computer can be increased but there are inevitable overheads to ensure that any sets of instructions which have to be executed serially (for example, because they depend on previous results) are not allowed to proceed in parallel.

**PARAMETER:** A variable which is assigned a value. For example, in the function call:

$$Y = SIN(X)$$

"X" is the parameter.

**PARITY:** A fairly simple form of error checking whereby a single bit is added to a stream of bits (usually a single word or byte) so that the total number of bits in the modified stream is odd (*odd parity*) or even (*even parity*).

**PARITY BIT:** The bit added for the purposes of *parity* checking.

**PARITY CHECK:** See *parity*.

**PARITY ERROR:** An error detected when a pattern of bits has the wrong *parity*.

**PARSE:** To analyse syntactically an input stream, according to the defined grammar.

**PARTITION:** A subdivision of some resource. In particular, the term is used to refer to areas of main memory in a multi-programming system and various *job classes* are run in each partition.

**PARTITIONED:** Divided into *partitions*.

**PARTITIONED DATA SET:** A file which is *partitioned* into subfiles which can hence be referred to as a single group or individually. In IBM System/370, a *partitioned data set* refers to a program library and, for example, the *partitioned data set* (abbreviated to *PDS*) SYS1.MACLIB consists of a number of macros as individual files, for example, OPEN which can hence be referred to as SYS1.MACLIB(OPEN).

**PASCAL (1):** A French mathematician (1623-1662) who designed and built an adding machine which operated with toothed gears using base 10 arithmetic.

**PASCAL (2):** A high-level, block-structured language, originally designed in 1968 and operational in 1970. It is related to Algol-60 and is available on a wide range of computers, including many microcomputers (the UCSD version of the language). A formal defintion of the language was published in 1973.

1. Wirth, N., "The Programming Language PASCAL", *Acta Informatica*, **1**, 35-63, 1971.
2. Jensen, K. and Wirth, N., "PASCAL User Manual and Report", Springer-Verlag, 1975.

**PASS:** One complete cycle, for example, in the compilation of a program, one pass refers to one complete reading of the source program.

**PASSWORD:** A set of characters which must be quoted before the user is given access to a specified resource, such as an interactive system or a file. Often passwords are encoded internally using a many-to-one mapping so that loss of the password may prevent access to the resource.

**PATCH:** Usually used to mean an *ad hoc* correction to a program to cure a *bug*.

**PATCHBOARD:** A board which allows the user to interconnect various components. It is most commonly used in two senses, first in interconnecting hardware components of a computer system for test purposes and second for interconnecting telephone lines.

**PATH:** A route between two points, usually used either in the context of a communications channel or a sequence of instructions in a program (as executed rather than as written).

**PATHNAME:** A more formal term for what is usually referred to as a *filename*, although *pathname* implies that the name indicates the *path* to the file. For example, the filename "SYS1.MACLIB" is really a pathname in that it denotes that the specified file is to be found in the first level directory SYS1.

**PATTERN RECOGNITION:** The recognition of shapes and other patterns by means of a computer. Used particularly in *artificial intelligence*.

**PATTERN SENSITIVE FAULT:** A *fault* (usually hardware) which only occurs when a certain pattern of bits is present and therefore often hard to detect since it appears to be an intermittent fault.

**PBX:** An abbreviation for *private branch exchange*, usually used synonymously with PABX.

**PC:** An abbreviation for *program counter*.

**PCB:** An abbreviation for *printed circuit board*.

**PCM (1):** An abbreviation for *pulse code modulation*.

**PCM (2):** An abbreviation for *plug-compatible manufacturer*.

**PDM:** An abbreviation for *pulse duration modulation*, a means of transmitting data.

**PDP:** An abbreviation for *Programmed Data Processor*, the name of a wide range of computer systems manufactured by Digital Equipment Corporation. These vary from the original PDP-1 to the large mainframe PDP-10 (more usually known as the DECsystem-10) and the well known range of minicomputers, the PDP-11s (although some of the PDP-11 range are now microcomputers – see *LSI-11*).

**PDS:** An abbreviation for *partitioned data set*.

**PE:** An abbreviation for *phase encoding*, a method of encoding data onto magnetic tape.

**PEEK:** An (non-standard) reserved word in many implementations of BASIC, particularly on microcomputers (and, more especially, on hobby or home computers) used to examine locations in memory. Sometimes, the word *peek* is used to mean the latter function without any implication of the method by which it is done or the language being used.

**PEPE:** An acronym for *Parallel Elements of Processing Ensemble*, a fairly early parallel processing system.

**PERIPHERAL:** An abbreviation for *peripheral device* (or *peripheral equipment*).

**PERIPHERAL BUFFER:** Either a *buffer* reserved in a computer's main storage for the sole use of a specified *peripheral device* or a buffer contained within the device itself, in both cases being used for input/output buffering.

**PERIPHERAL DEVICE:** The auxiliary equipment of a computer system, usually performing input/output functions, such as disk drives or paper tape readers. Peripheral devices usually work under the control of a central processor, although, in some systems, they work autonomously (see *peripheral processor*).

**PERIPHERAL PROCESSOR:** A processor, associated with one or more *peripheral devices*, enabling them to function (semi-) autonomously rather than under the control of the central processor. The term *peripheral processor* is especially used in the context of the CDC Cyber 70 and 6000 series machines, where they are abbreviated as *PP*.

**PERIPHERAL STORAGE:** A general term used to mean some form of *secondary storage*.

**PERMANENT ERROR:** An *error* which is reproducible and not transient. For example, in writing data to magnetic tape, if an error is detected, the operation is repeated a number of times (usually ten). If the error is found each time, it is known as a *permanent error*. More colloquially, the term "hard error" is used, especially in the context of disks (when the term used is *hard disk error* where the adjective qualifies "error" and not "disk").

**PERMANENT STORAGE:** Storage which is permanently associated with the central processor, i.e. primary storage.

**PERMANENT VIRTUAL CIRCUIT:** A *virtual circuit* leased from the PTT or other network owner between two users of a packet-switched network. The circuit is permanently available (for the period of the lease) and is directly analogous to a *leased line* in a circuit-switched network.

**PERSONAL COMPUTER:** A small computer available ready-built or in kit form. The best known personal computers are the Commodore PET, the Tandy TRS-80 and the Apple II. Such computers are based on microprocessors (usually the Z-80 or the 6502) and have relatively limited amounts of memory, although they can often be expanded and additional peripherals used.

**PERT:** An acronym for *Program Evaluation and Review Technique*, one technique for the control and management of projects. See *critical path method*.

**PET:** An acronym for *Personal Electronic Transactor*, one of the first *home computers*, manufactured by Commodore. It is based on the 6502 microprocessor and has many interesting features including a graphics capability. The early models had a touch-sensitive keyboard and a built-in cassette tape unit. In later models, this has been replaced by a standard keyboard and the cassette unit has been separated from the main body.

**PHASE MODULATION:** A means of transmitting information whereby the phase of a *carrier wave* is modulated in accordance with the information signal.

**PI:** An abbreviation for *program interrupt*, that is, an interrupt caused by a program (such as dividing by zero) rather than by some external event. The acronym is also used for "programmed interrupt", meaning an interrupt caused deliberately by a program, perhaps as a quick means of transferring control to an error routine.

**PICO-:** A prefix meaning one million millionth ($10^{-12}$).

**PICOSECOND:** A million millionth of a second.

**PILOT:** An interactive *computer aided instruction* programming language, developed by John Starkweather at the University of California in the late 1960s.

**PILOT RUN:** An initial execution of a program with a set of test data, in order to check the program's correctness.

**PINFEED:** A technique of feeding paper through a printing mechanism in which a set of pins exist at either end of the *platen* and engage with *sprocket holes* punched in the *continuous stationery*.

**PINS:** The connections between a *chip* and the PCB into which it is connected.

**PIO:** An abbreviation for *programmed input/output*.

**PIP:** An acronym for *Peripheral Interchange Program*, a name given to a series of programs available on DEC machines which transfer data from one device to another (e.g. copy files).

**PIPELINE:** Part of the *cpu* in some computers whose function is to speed up program execution by performing the various tasks required in instruction execution in parallel, for example, decoding the instruction and fetching the operands. The pipeline consists of extremely high-speed logic and is capable of holding a relatively restricted number of instructions (say 32). If one instruction performs an operation which affects instructions further along the pipeline (e.g. a transfer of control), it is necessary to "drain" the pipeline and refresh it with new instructions. If a loop within a program can be held entirely in the pipeline (known as "loop mode"), program execution is speeded up dramatically.

**PIPELINE DRAIN:** The action of clearing instructions from a *pipeline*. This is performed automatically in many circumstances but can be invoked by the programmer if required.

**PITCH:** A term used to describe the number of characters per inch in printing, usually ten or twelve.

**PL/1:** An abbreviation for *Programming Language 1*. A high-level, block structured language designed by IBM for both commercial and scientific applications but which is available on relatively few computers.

**PLA:** An acronym for *programmable logic array*, a network of logic components which can be programmed to perform required functions.

**PLAINTEXT:** Messages which have not been *encrypted*.

**PLANT:** To store a result at a specified location for later use, for example, in *self-modifying programs*.

**PLASMA DISPLAY:** A display relying on the discharge of high voltages through gas.

**PLATEN:** The cylindrical part of a printing mechanism around which the paper is rolled and which is hit by the print head to produce the characters.

**PLATO:** An acronym for *Programmed Logic for Automatic Teaching Operations*, a *computer-aided instruction* language and system.

**PL/M:** A high-level language developed by Intel for use on its microcomputer systems.

**PLOT:** To draw a diagram, using a *plotter*.

**PLOTTER:** An output device which can be connected to a computer to draw diagrams etc. There are various methods of achieving this, for example, by moving a pen across a moving sheet of paper.

**PLUG COMPATIBLE:** Most often used in the context of "plug compatible manufacturer" or "plug compatible peripherals", the former being makers of the latter. These are peripherals (including main memory) which, while not being manufactured by the computer manufacturer, are supposed to be fully compatible and hence merely plug in.

**PLUGBOARD:** See *patchboard*.

**PM:** An abbreviation for *prevent(at)ive maintenance, phase modulation* or *post mortem*, depending on context.

**PMOS:** An abbreviation for *p-channel MOS*, a technology for making semiconductor memories. The oldest form of MOS technology in which current flow is by means of positive charges which is slower than the more recent NMOS.

**POINTER:** A location (or *register*) which contains the *address* of the required item.

**POINT-TO-POINT:** A circuit which connects two devices together (cf. *multipoint*).

**POKE:** A (non-standard) reserved word in many implementations of BASIC, particularly on microcomputers (and, more especially, on hobby or home computers) used to store data in specified memory locations. Sometimes, the word *poke* is used to mean the latter function without any implication of the method by which it is done or the language being used.

**POLISH:** A notation for representing arithmetic operations designed by Jan Lukasiewicz, a Polish logician, in 1929 in which each operator precedes the operands on which it operates. It is also known as *prefix notation* but see also *reverse Polish*.

**POLL:** To perform the task of *polling*.

**POLLING:** To interrogate a number of devices (terminals or computers) to discover whether they have any data to send. There are many varieties of polling, such as "hub polling".

**POLLING CHARACTER:** The character (or set of characters) by which a central site interrogates the devices which it wishes to *poll*.

**POOL:** A set of resources, for example, a buffer pool which is space reserved for a number of buffers.

**POP:** To retrieve data from a stack (by definition, the top of the stack, since other locations are inaccessible) and to place it in the specified location or register, at the same time, decrementing the *stack pointer*. The opposite is *push*.

**PORT:** The socket on a computer to which I/O devices are connected and which is addressed by the central processor by a logical number.

**POS:** An abbreviation for *point-of-sale*, usually used in the context of I/O devices which are used in retail outlets.

**POSITIONAL PARAMETER:** A "parameter" whose significance or meaning is defined by the position it occupies.

**POST-MORTEM:** Usually used in the context of (or as an abbreviation for) a "post-mortem dump", a *dump* of storage locations and other pertinent data taken at the end of a computer run or, more often, after the occurrence of a fault. Abbreviated as *PM*.

**POWER:** The number of times a number is to be multiplied by itself, written as a superscript or, in most programming languages, as a number following two asterisks. For example, in the expression $10^6$, the power is 6 and the expression indicates that 10 is to be multiplied by itself 6 times, yielding one million.

**POWER FAIL:** The failure of the power supply to a computer system. This can be detected by suitable logic in the computer and an appropriate routine entered to save intermediate results.

**POWER SUPPLY:** Usually used to mean the set of circuits in a computer which are used to provide electricity at specified (usually regulated) voltages.

**PP:** An abbreviation for *peripheral processor*, the I/O processor used in various CDC machines (e.g. the CDC 6600).

**PPM:** An abbreviation for *pulse position modulation*.

**PRECEDENCE:** The order in which items have significance. For example, in an arithmetic expression, it is usual to evaluate it according to a fixed precedence amongst the operators, usually brackets, exponentiation, divide and multiply, addition and subtraction.

**PRECISION:** The degree of discrimination available in the specification of a value. Thus a number occupying eight bits can be precise to one part in 256. It should be contrasted with *accuracy*.

**PREFIX NOTATION:** See *Polish*.

**PRE-PRINTED:** Refers to stationery which is printed before being used in a computer printer, for example, pay-slips.

**PRESET:** To set up initially.

**PRESTEL:** The trade name for British Telecom's viewdata (videotex) service.

**PREVENT(AT)IVE MAINTENANCE:** Maintenance which is carried out at regular intervals in order (hopefully) to prevent faults occurring.

**PRIMARY CONTROL PROGRAM:** A simple form of operating system (particularly that available on early IBM System/360 computers) which does not allow *multi-programming*.

**PRIMARY GROUP:** A group of sub-channels multiplexed together.

**PRIMARY KEY:** A *key* used in information storage and retrieval on which the data is stored in order. Data may most easily be retrieved using the *primary key* but it may be required to access it using *secondary keys* and complex procedures have to be evolved to enable this to be done efficiently (for example, *inverted files*). For example, a list of people may be stored using their surnames as the *primary key*, but it may be necessary to retrieve them by their ages which is thus a *secondary key*.

**PRIMARY STATION:** A term particularly used in the X.25 standard (HDLC) denoting a controlling station (*master*) for one or more secondary stations (*slaves*).

**PRIMARY STORAGE:** See *main memory*.

**PRINT BARREL:** Part of a printer which has the characters engraved on a rotating barrel.

**PRINT CHAIN:** A chain used on a *chain printer*, on which the characters are engraved.

**PRINT FORMAT:** A specification of the way in which data is to be printed. This can be a written definition or by means of FORMAT statements in a program.

**PRINT POSITION:** The position along a line at which the specified character is printed.

**PRINTED CIRCUIT BOARD:** A board, usually plastic, on which is printed the requisite circuits (in some conducting medium, such as copper) and which has holes for the components to be soldered to the board. The components are located on the opposite side to the actual circuits. The board is often also printed with information about the components to be soldered into place. Abbreviated *PCB*.

**PRINTER:** An output device which transforms the signals from the computer into readable form. There are many varieties of printer, such as *chain printer* and *line printer*.

**PRINTOUT:** The output produced by a *printer*.

**PRINTWHEEL:** See *daisy wheel*.

**PRIORITY:** A value assigned to a task which defines the order in which that task, relative to others in the system, has access to system resources.

**PRIVATE WIRE:** A synonym for *leased line*.

**PRIVILEGED:** Pertaining to some resource or operation which can only be accessed or performed by specified tasks, often only the operating system.

**PRIVILEGED INSTRUCTION:** An instruction which can only be performed by the operating system, such as changing the limits of storage protection.

**PROBLEM ORIENTED LANGUAGE:** A language which is oriented towards the problem which is to be solved rather than the machine on which it is to be solved.

**PROBLEM PROGRAM:** A program which is not part of an operating system.

**PROBLEM STATE:** One of a number of states in which a *central processor* may be found, in which it is executing *problem programs*. It should be contrasted with *supervisor state*. The terminology is most commonly used in IBM System/370.

**PROCEDURE:** The sequence of steps used in solving a problem. See also *algorithm*.

**PROCEDURE DIVISION:** Part of *COBOL* program which contains the actual code.

**PROCESS (1):** To perform a set of operations on specified data.

**PROCESS (2):** A subtask of a system which performs specified operations to produce a required function.

**PROCESS CONTROL:** The use of a computer to control various (usually industrial) processes.

**PROCESSING:** The performance of a set of operations on specified data.

**PROCESSOR:** An abbreviation for *central processor*.

**PROCESSOR BOUND:** A state whereby the speed of execution of a specified program is limited by the speed of a central processor and it is not slowed down by the speed of a peripheral device. See also *I/O bound*.

**PROCESSOR TECHNOLOGY:** An early US microcomputer manufacturer, best known for the Sol computer.

**PRODUCT:** The result of multiplying two quantities (the *multiplicand* and the *multiplier*) together.

**PRODUCTION CONTROL:** The control of the production of items by means of a computer. This includes, for example, stock control, sales forecasting and invoicing.

**PRODUCTION RUN:** The routine execution of a program which is (hopefully) fully debugged. It should be contrasted with *pilot run*.

**PROGRAM:** A set of statements, including those for data definition and execution, which are executed by a computer (perhaps after some translation process) in order to solve a problem.

**PROGRAM CHECK:** An interrupt caused by a programming error, such as attempting to write to non-existent memory.

**PROGRAM CONTROL:** Pertaining to the control of some device by means of a program.

**PROGRAM COUNTER:** A register (or storage location) which contains the address of the next instruction to be executed. Also known as *sequence control register*.

**PROGRAM STACK:** A part of the main storage reserved for use by a program and treated as a *stack*.

**PROGRAM STATUS WORD:** A register (or number of registers or storage locations) used to define the current status of a program. It is abbreviated to *PSW*.

**PROGRAMMING LANGUAGE:** A language used for writing computer programs, such as BASIC or Algol. It should be contrasted with *natural language*.

**PROPRIETARY:** An adjective meaning held in private ownership but usually applied to software to indicate that it is the property of the author and may not be copied or re-sold.

**PROM:** An acronym for *programmable read-only memory*, ROM which can be erased (usually by ultra-violet light) and re-written.

**PROTECTED:** In the state of being unable to be overwritten, either in the context of main memory or backing storage. In the case of main memory, this is usually achieved by some form of *protection key*. In the case of backing storage, it is either by means of appropriate software or, more often, by some physical means, such as a *write ring*.

**PROTECTION KEY:** A value which is assigned to storage locations and, unless it matches the value for the program attempting to access these locations, the access is prohibited.

**PROTOCOL:** A formalisation of the methods used by which two parties communicate. A more formal definition was given by Roberts and Wessler in their early paper on the ARPANET (Roberts, L.G. and Wessler, B.D., "Computer Network Development to Achieve Resource Sharing", *Proc.* AFIPS SJCC, **36**, 543-549, 1970) as "the set of two processes' agreements on the format and relative timing of messages to be exchanged".

**PS:** An abbreviation for *picosecond*.

**PSE:** An abbreviation for *packet switching exchange*, used particularly in the context of the BPO's Experimental Packet Switched Service, referring to a group of network nodes ("packet switching units") at one location.

**PSEUDO-INSTRUCTION:** An instruction, used in a program (usually assembler), which does not correspond to a machine instruction but rather indicates that some action is to be taken (for example, "END" which indicates that assembly is to be terminated).

**PSEUDO-OPERATION:** An operation which appears to be available to the user but which is, in fact, not provided by the hardware and is simulated in some manner.

**PSEUDO-RANDOM NUMBER:** A number which is generated by a computer such that a set of numbers appear to be random but which are, in fact, deterministic and may be reproduced by re-running the program under the same conditions.

**PSN:** An abbreviation for *public switched network*, used synonymously with "PSTN".

**PSS:** An abbreviation for *Packet Switched Service*, the British Post Office's production packet-switched network which was operational in late 1980. It uses CCITT X.25 protocols and is based on the technology of TELENET, a US packet-switched network. The UK network contractors are Plessey. There are considerable expansion plans for the network and it is interconnected to IPSS and EURONET.

**PSTN:** An abbreviation for *public switched telephone network*.

**PSW:** An abbreviation for *program status word*.

**PT:** An abbreviation for *paper tape*.

**PTT:** An abbreviation for *Post, Telegraph and Telephone Administration*, a statutory body whose functions are to provide the specified facilities with (particularly in the UK) a monopoly of those facilities. There is no corresponding body in the USA, although the FCC regulates such matters.

**PUBLIC KEY CRYPTOGRAPHY:** A system of cryptography which requires two keys, one of which is public.

**PUBLIC SWITCHED TELEPHONE NETWORK:** The circuit-switched, analogue network used for voice communication by means of a telephone. It is usually abbreviated as *PSTN* (or, sometimes, as *PSN*).

**PUFFT:** An acronym for *Purdue University Fast FORTRAN*.

**PULSE CODE MODULATION:** A technique for representing an analogue signal by means of a sequence of digits. The signal is sampled at a regular rate and the resultant sample converted into a binary number which is then transmitted. In order to reconstitute the signal accurately, it is necessary to sample at twice the sending bandwidth and hence, for voice telephony, a sampling rate of 8 kHz is used.

**PUNCH:** Usually used as a verb meaning to make a hole in some medium such as paper tape or card in order to transmit information to a computer.

**PUNCH CARD:** A piece of thin cardboard which may be punched with holes in order to convey information to a computer. The most common such card has 80 columns, each of which has twelve positions and represents a single character.

**PUNCH POSITION:** One of the areas on a *punch card* where a hole may be punched.

**PUNCH TAPE:** Paper tape in which holes may be punched in order to transmit information to a computer. The most common paper tapes have five, seven or eight holes (plus a *sprocket hole*) for each character.

**PUNCH VERIFIER:** A machine which performs the functions of punching cards and verifying them.

**PUNCHED CARD:** A card (see *punch card*) which has had information punched onto it.

**PUNCHED TAPE:** A paper tape (see *punch tape*) which has been punched with holes to represent data.

**PUSHDOWN LIST:** An ordered set of data which has the feature that data being added to the list occupies the first position.

**PUSHDOWN STACK:** A synonym for a *stack*.

**PUT:** A word used in some computer systems to indicate the storage of a record in an output file.

**PWM:** An abbreviation for *pulse width modulation*.

# Q

**QBUS:** A *bus* used by *Digital Equipment Corporation*.

**QCB:** An abbreviation for *queue control block*.

**QED:** An abbreviation for *quick editor*, a simple, line-oriented editor.

**QISAM:** An abbreviation for *queued indexed sequential access method*.

**QSAM:** An acronym for *queued sequential access method*.

**QTAM:** An acronym for *queued telecommunications access method*.

**QUADRATIC PROGRAMMING:** A technique for determining the optimum values of functions which are subject to quadratic constraints.

**QUALIFIER:** A field (usually of one bit) which signifies the use to which another field is put. For example, in the HDLC protocol, a one-bit field is used to indicate whether the byte in which it occurs is data or control.

**QUERY:** To make a request for information, usually from an information retrieval database.

**QUEUE:** A linear list in which the first element to be entered is also the first to be removed (FIFO – *first in, first out*). This is used in computers in a multitude of ways; for example, the set of jobs awaiting processing by the cpu are formed into one (or more) queues (the *job queue*).

**QUEUE CONTROL BLOCK:** A *control block* which is used in processing the items in a *queue*. It is abbreviated as *QCB*.

**QUEUED ACCESS METHOD:** A means of access to data on secondary storage whereby I/O requests are "queued" and thus overlapped with processing, leading to a minimisation of delays due to I/O transfers.

**QUEUING THEORY:** A branch of mathematics concerned with the behaviour of items in queues, particularly used in *simulation*.

**QUICKTRAN:** A version of *FORTRAN*.

**QUME:** A US manufacturer of *daisy-wheel* printers.

**QUOTIENT:** The result of a *division* operation. When the *divisor* is divided by the *dividend*, it yields a *quotient* and a *remainder*. In integer arithmetic, the quotient is retained and the remainder discarded.

**QWERTY:** An adjective applied to the keyboard used in the UK and USA, so named because of the layout of the keys (the first row of alphabetic characters are QWERTYUIOP).

# R

**RADIX:** The value on which a number system is based; for example, the radix for decimal notation is ten.

**RAGGED RIGHT:** A description of the layout produced by text processors (or word processors) in which lines are not filled with spaces and hence the right-hand margin is not straight.

**RAM:** An acronym for *random access memory*.

**RANDOM ACCESS:** A description applied to a storage medium meaning that the access time for any data is independent of its location. Also known as *direct access*.

**RANDOM NUMBER:** A number selected entirely by chance and, when a set of such numbers is generated, the set satisfies various statistical criteria for randomness.

**RANDOM NUMBER GENERATOR:** A device or routine which generates *random numbers*. In practice, on most computer systems, the numbers generated are not random but are "pseudo-random". However, for example, the computer which generates prizes for Premium Bonds (ERNIE — Electronic Random Number Indicator Equipment) does use random numbers which are generated from the noise in electronic circuits.

**RANK:** To order a set of values according to relative importance. The term is also used to denote the position in such an ordered list.

**RASTER SCAN:** Pertaining to a means of generating output on a *VDU* in a manner similar to that used for a television picture, namely that the screen is scanned by a large number of horizontal lines.

**RBE:** An abbreviation for *remote batch entry*, referring to the ability to submit *batch* jobs via a *telecommunications* link.

**READ-ONLY:** Pertaining to a form of storage from which data may be read but not written. This may be a transient condition (for example, on a *magnetic tape* by removing the *write permit ring*) or permanent (for example, *ROM*).

**READ-ONLY MEMORY:** See *read-only*.

**READ-ONLY STORAGE:** See *read-only*.

**REAL TIME:** Pertaining to the use of clock time as a measure of time (rather than, for example, processor time). The term is used most often in the context of "real-time applications" which indicates applications where the calculations must be performed in real-time. Examples include process control and airline booking systems.

**REAL TIME CLOCK:** A device (often treated as a *peripheral*) which generates signals (usually *interrupts*) at fixed intervals and thus allow time intervals to be measured. If the time of day is made available to the system when it is initialised, the use of a *real-time clock* permits access to the current time of day.

**RECEIVE ONLY:** Pertaining to output devices which have no facilities for input as well. The most common example is a printer without a keyboard. It is usually abbreviated as *RO* and should be compared with *KSR* (*keyboard send/receive*).

**RECORD:** A number of related items of data which are considered as one entity.

**RECORD LAYOUT:** The manner in which data is placed within a *record*, including the length and position of each item. The term is also applied to the written description (particularly in a program) of such layout.

**RECORD LENGTH:** A measure of the size of a *record*, most often in terms of a unit related to the computer rather than the record (e.g. bytes).

**RECORD SEPARATOR:** See *RS*.

**RECORDING DENSITY:** A measure of the amount of information stored per unit length (or area) on a recording medium. The most common usage is in relation to magnetic tape when the density is specified in terms of "bits per inch" (which is, in fact, partially a misnomer since it refers to the bits per inch per track and, for example, on a nine-track magnetic tape with one bit for parity, the total density is eight times higher, i.e. bytes per inch). Common values for magnetic tape recording density are 200, 556, 800, 1600 and 6250 bpi.

**RECURSIVE:** See *recursive routine*. In more detail, the term refers to a process which calls itself (with some check for completion) and often uses the values obtained from a previous recursion. The most common example of recursion is the factorial function which may be defined as:

```
ROUTINE factorial (n)
     IF n=1 THEN 1
             ELSE n*factorial (n−1)
     END
```

**RECURSIVE ROUTINE:** A routine which allows recursion. Since the act of calling itself would overwrite the *return address*, it is necessary that action be taken to prevent this and the most common method of achieving this is to make use of a *stack* so that, for each call, the most recent return address (and any other status information) is pushed onto the stack and, on exit, the address on the top of the stack is popped off and used as the return address.

**REDUNDANCY:** The use of additional equipment or information to provide a means of checking or back-up. The term is most commonly used in data transmission where bits are added for error checking purposes (e.g. *parity*, *Hamming codes*) and these bits are *redundant* in the sense that they do not convey information.

**REEL:** The (usually plastic) spool on which magnetic tape is wound. The term is often used for the tape on a reel.

**RE-ENTRANT:** Pertaining to a section of code (e.g. a subroutine) which may be used concurrently by more than one other process.

**REFERENCE ADDRESS:** A synonym for *base address*.

**REFERENCE LEVEL:** A signal level used as a reference point for other signals on the same line.

**REFERENCE LISTING:** A synonym for *cross-reference listing*.

**REFRESH:** Used as a verb to indicate the process of re-transmitting information to some form of storage medium in which the recorded data decays. The two most common examples of the need for refreshing data are some forms of memory, particularly *dynamic RAM*, and certain VDU screens.

**REFRESHABLE (1):** Pertaining to a storage medium which is able to be (and needs to be) *refreshed*.

**REFRESHABLE (2):** A term sometimes used to pertain to a section of code (e.g. a subroutine) which can be replaced during execution and hence must not be able to be modified by itself or any other routine.

**REGISTER:** A high-speed storage location (usually forming part of the *cpu*) whose size is usually the same as the word-length of the given computer. Registers may be general purpose, in which case, they are usually used for the storage of intermediate results during processing, or they may have specific functions, such as an *index register*. Usually parts of an *instruction* specifically refer to registers but, in some machines, the registers are addressed as if they were main storage. Most computers have a relatively small number of registers, although some early machines (e.g. the *Atlas*) had well over a hundred.

**REGISTER ADDRESSING:** A method of *addressing* where the item addressed is a register (which often contains the address of a storage location).

**RELATIONAL EXPRESSION:** An expression which contains a *relational operator* (or more than one), the result of which is a Boolean value (i.e. TRUE or FALSE). An example of a *relational expression* is:

$$(A > B) \text{ OR } (A < C)$$

**RELATIONAL OPERATOR:** An *operator* which is used to compare two *operands*. These are, usually, greater than, greater than or equal, equal, not equal, less than or equal, less than.

**RELATIVE ADDRESSING:** A method of *addressing* where the location is specified in terms of a *base address* and a *displacement* (hence this method is also known as *base/displacement addressing*). However, the term is commonly used to mean *self-relative addressing* where the base is the address of the current instruction. If the base is specified in certain ways (e.g. a register or the current location), then the program may be *dynamically relocated*.

**RELATIVE ERROR:** The magnitude of an error, expressed in terms of the correct value.

**RELIABILITY:** A measure of the ability of a system (or part of a system) to operate without failure.

**RELOCATE:** To perform the process of *relocation*.

**RELOCATION:** The process of moving (part of) a program from one set of storage locations to another, adjusting any address references so that the program can continue to operate unchanged. This process is usually carried out to enable more efficient use to be made of main storage. In order for it to be able to be carried out, it is required that the program addresses be specified in certain ways (see, for example, *relative addressing*).

**REMAINDER:** In a division operation, the remainder is one of the two results and is equal to the difference between the dividend and the product of the quotient and divisor.

**REMOTE ACCESS:** The techniques involved in accessing a computer system from a device which is remote from it.

**REMOTE JOB ENTRY:** Submission of a batch *job* via a telecommunications link. Usually abbreviated as *RJE*.

**REMOTE STATION:** A device (or group of devices) which are remote from the computer system with which it communicates to perform processing. Often the term is applied to data collection devices which are connected via communications lines.

**REMOTE TERMINAL:** A *terminal* which is remote from the computer to which it is connected (via, for example, a telephone line requiring the use of *modems*).

**REPERTOIRE:** See *instruction repertoire*.

**REPORT:** A printed output which conveys information in an easily understood form.

**REPORT PROGRAM GENERATOR:** A special-purpose high-level programming language, enabling fairly naive users to generate reports and perform various other business functions relatively easily. It is usually abbreviated to *RPG*.

**REPRODUCE:** To make an exact copy of some item(s) on the same medium, for example, to copy a pack of cards for backup purposes.

**REPRODUCER:** A device which reproduces *punched cards* (also more commonly called a *card reproducer*).

**RERUN:** To repeat (part of) the execution of a computer program, usually because of some failure.

**RESERVED WORD:** A sequence of characters which have a particular significance in a language (usually a programming language) and which are hence unavailable to users of that language.

**RESET:** To restore some part of a computer system to its initial state. The term is also used for the more specific purpose of setting a bit (or contiguous sequence of bits, such as a word) to binary zero.

**RESIDENT:** Used as a synonym for *stored in (or on)*, for example, "the routine is resident on the systems disk". It is also used in the more restricted context of, for example, "memory resident" meaning that the specified item is permanently stored in memory (and hence easily accessible).

**RESOURCE:** Any facility of a computer system, hardware or software.

**RESOURCE MANAGER:** Software which is responsible for the allocation of *resources* within a computer system and which therefore forms part of the operating system.

**RESOURCE SHARING:** A term used mainly in the context of *distributed networks*, often to justify the building of such networks, denoting the ability of such a network to provide for the sharing of *resources* between a large number of installations and/or users. This is particularly important in the case of rare or unique resources, such as a large database or a *terabit memory*.

**RESPONSE:** The output from a computer as a result of some input.

**RESPONSE TIME:** The time between the initiation of a function and the start of the response to that function. The term is most usually used in interactive computer systems to mean the time between the depression of a key by the user and the first character of the response appearing at the terminal.

**RESTART:** To start execution of a group of instructions a second (or subsequent) time. This is used most often in the context of *checkpoint/ restart* where the system is *restarted* from a previously taken *checkpoint* following some failure in the system.

**RESTORE:** Often used as a synonym for *reset* but often used more restrictively to indicate the resetting of registers (and, perhaps, some storage locations) on exit from a subroutine to those values contained before execution of the subroutine.

**RETD:** An acronym for *Red Especial de Transmission de Datos*, the Spanish PTT *packet-switching* network, operational since 1971. The network now consists of six main centres connected via 9600 bps lines, to which are connected over 70 secondary centres, allowing access by up to ten thousand terminals. The main centres use Honeywell-716 computers. The major use of the network is for banking functions. It is expected that the network will be interconnected with other European networks in the early 1980s.

**RETRY:** To repeat an operation following detection of an error. The term is most commonly used in data transmission and in writing data to magnetic media.

**RETURN (1):** A synonym for *carriage return*.

**RETURN (2):** The instruction (or set of instructions) at the end of a *subroutine* which indicate that control is to be returned to the calling code. In many programming languages, *RETURN* is a *reserved word* for this particular function.

**RETURN ADDRESS:** The address to which control is to be returned after execution of a subroutine. It is also known as the *link*. There are many ways in which the *return address* is stored. The simplest one (implemented, for example, on the Digico M-16) is to store it *in-line* in the subroutine. A more elegant (safer) method is to store it in a particular register, either dedicated to that particular purpose or specified when calling the subroutine (as in, for example, the IBM System/370). However, both these methods prevent the subroutine being called recursively and, if this is required, it is necessary to use a mechanism such as a *stack*. Many computers (e.g. the DECsystem-10) allow the programmer to specify which of a number of alternative methods is preferred.

**RETURN CODE:** The sequence of instructions at the end of a *subroutine* which perform the necessary functions to return control to the calling program, *restoring* any values which are required. The opposite is *entry code*.

**RETURN INSTRUCTION:** The particular instruction which returns control from a *subroutine* to the calling routine. It usually performs an indirect jump via the *return address*.

**REVERSE CHANNEL:** In data transmission, a *channel* which operates in the opposite direction to that carrying data and which itself carries various control information and status reports. Often the *reverse channel* operates at lower bandwidth than the data channel.

**REVERSE POLISH:** Also known as *postfix notation*, this is a means of representing expressions in which the operations succeed the operands. Thus the expression:

$$(A+B) *C+D$$

would be represented, in *Reverse Polish*, as:

$$AB+C*D+$$

and this is a particularly convenient form for evaluating expressions, especially if a *stack* is available. See also *Polish*.

**REVERSE VIDEO:** A facility on many *VDU*s whereby the normal effect of light characters on a dark background can be reversed for emphasis.

**REWIND:** To return a *magnetic tape* to its *load point* or a *paper tape* to its beginning. By extension, the term is used to mean returning any item to its beginning and it is usual for the term to be used in the context of "rewinding a buffer", meaning resetting pointers to the beginning of the buffer.

**REWRITE:** To write data back to storage.

**RFC (1):** An abbreviation for *Request for Comments*, a series of informal working papers in the ARPANET community.

**RFC (2):** An abbreviation for *request for connection*, a term referring to two Host-Host protocol commands in ARPANET required to initiate a connection.

**RIGHT JUSTIFY:** To move data so that it occupies the right-hand locations of a specified field. In the context of *word processing* (or any other form of printing), the term means the moving of text and the requisite padding with spaces so that the right-hand margin is straight (text which is not *right justified* is said to have a *ragged right*).

**RIGHT SHIFT:** To move the digits in a sequence (e.g. the bits in a word) to the right. There are various types of shift (e.g. *arithmetic*, *circular*) which have different effects.

**RING NETWORK:** A network where the computers are connected in a ring structure. That is, each is connected to its two neighbours and to no other. There are now a number of network technologies which rely on the topology of the network being a ring, particularly the *Cambridge Ring*.

**RITA:** An acronym for *Rand Intelligent Terminal Agent*, a system for providing simple access to a computer network from a terminal, similar to the facilities provided by a *Network Access Machine*.

**RJE:** An abbreviation for *remote job entry*.

**RO:** An abbreviation for *receive-only*, a term applied to an output device which is able to receive data but unable to transmit.

**ROLLOUT/ROLLIN:** A technique for enabling high-priority processes to pre-empt lower priority processes currently executing whereby a lower priority process is suspended and copied out to backing store so that the higher priority process can then execute. After it has finished, the lower priority process is copied back and execution continues.

**ROM:** An abbreviation for *read-only memory*, that is, memory which may be read from but not written to, hence ensuring data or program integrity. Some varieties of ROM allow the user to re-program them, usually by erasing the information on them by means of an ultra-violet lamp, then rewriting by means of a high voltage. See *PROM* and *EPROM*.

**ROOT SEGMENT:** In a program which has been *segmented*, the *root segment* is the controlling one which therefore requires to be in main storage for the time the program is executing.

**ROUTINE:** A set of instructions which perform a clearly specified function and which are, to a large extent, self-contained. Routines (or *subroutines*, the terms are often used synonymously) may be *closed* or *open* (*out-of-line* or *in-line*).

**ROUTING CHOICE:** In *videotex* systems, a single digit which routes the user to a subsequent frame of information.

**ROUTING TABLE:** A table used by nodes in a distributed network to determine the routing of data. The table may be static (e.g. *directory routing*) or dynamic.

**ROW:** A set of data which occurs in a horizontal relationship, such as the holes on a *punched card* or the elements of an *array*.

**RPG:** An abbreviation for *Report Program Generator*.

**RRE:** An abbreviation for *Royal Radar Establishment*, perhaps best known for its work on the language *CORAL 66*.

**RS:** An abbreviation for *record separator*, a character used to delimit records. In the ASCII character set, it is binary 0011110.

**RSEXEC:** An experimental system developed on *ARPANET* whose purpose was to allow distributed processing over number of nodes on the network. It included facilities for creating global (network-wide) file directories, communicating with users on remote sites as if they were local and so on. The system ran mainly on PDP-10X computers, although implementations were carried out for Multics and the NASA-AMES 360/67. RSEXEC was superseded by a much more ambitious project, the "National Software Works", whose purpose was to permit distributed processing over a fully heterogeneous network.

1. Thomas, R.H., "A Resource Sharing Executive for the ARPANET", *Proc.* AFIPS NCC, **42**, 155-163, 1973.

2. Millstein, R.E., "The National Software Works: A Distributed Processing System", *Proc.* ACM Annual Conference, 53-58, 1977.

**RTOS:** An acronym for *Real-Time Operating System*, an operating system which has facilities for *real-time* operation.

**RTT:** An abbreviation for *Régie des Télégraphes et des Téléphones*, the Belgian PTT.

**RUBOUT:** A synonym for *delete character*.

**RUN:** Used either as a verb or as a noun to mean the execution of a computer program.

**RUN TIME:** Used either as a noun phrase to mean the time required for one *run* of a computer program or as an adjectival phrase to describe items required during the time a program is being executed.

**RUN TIME SYSTEM:** A set of systems routines supplied with various compilers to perform various functions which are required when programs written in the specified language are executed, such as I/O and fault trapping.

**R/W:** An abbreviation for *read/write*.

**RWM:** An abbreviation for *read-write memory*, a term rarely used to describe memory which can be read from or written to; the term most commonly applied to such memory is RAM (since it nearly always provides random access to data).

# S

**S-100 BUS:** A *bus*, originally designed for the Altair microcomputer which became a *de facto* standard for many microcomputer systems. In 1979, the IEEE published a formal standard for the bus.

**SAMPLING:** The technique of obtaining the value of some item at specified (usually regular) intervals.

**SAMPLING RATE:** The frequency at which *sampling* occurs. For example, in digitising speech, a sampling rate of 8 kHz is needed.

**SATELLITE (1):** A computer (usually small) which performs secondary functions for a main computer system. The term is used, for example, for a remote workstation.

**SATELLITE (2):** A synonym for *communications satellite*.

**SBS:** A abbreviation for *Satellite Business Systems*, a corporation formed by IBM and Aetna Life to use communications satellites for data transmission.

**SCALE FACTOR:** A value which is applied to a set of values so that they fall into a specified range.

**SCANNER:** A device which repeatedly examines certain items, such as communication channels.

**SCHEDULED MAINTENANCE:** Maintenance of a computer system at fixed intervals in order to increase its reliability.

**SCHEDULER:** A part of an operating system which is concerned with the order of execution of tasks within the computer, according to various criteria such as relative priorities.

**SCR:** An abbreviation of *sequence control register*.

**SCRATCH (vb):** To remove some data from storage.

**SCRATCH (adj.):** Pertaining to some item which is of transient use (for example, storage for intermediate results).

**SCRATCH FILE:** A file which is used for the storage of intermediate results and which is deleted after termination of the job.

**SCRATCH PAD:** An area of memory for intermediate results, especially used in the context of part of the cpu which thus enables instruction execution to be speeded up.

**SCREEN:** The front of a cathode ray tube on which output is displayed. Sometimes used as a synonym for *VDU*.

**SCROLLING:** Pertaining to the generation of output on a *screen* so that it moves upwards on the screen, appearing at the bottom and eventually disappearing off the top. It should be contrasted with page mode, whereby one screenful is written and then erased before more data can be written. VDUs which are *glass teletypes* implement scrolling.

**SDI:** An abbreviation for *selective dissemination of information*.

**SDLC:** An abbreviation for *synchronous data link control*, a line level, bit oriented protocol developed by IBM as its version of HDLC.

**SDM:** An abbreviation for *space division multiplexing*.

**SEAC:** An acronym for *Standards Eastern Automatic Computer*, an early computer.

**SEARCH:** To examine a set of items in order so that those which satisfy the specified criteria may be found.

**SEARCH KEY:** An item of data which is compared with each of a set of items in order to determine which contain the *key*.

**SEARCH TIME:** The time required to complete a *search* of a given set of items.

**SECOND GENERATION:** A term applied to computers (manufactured in the early 1960s) which consisted of solid-state discrete components (e.g. transistors).

**SECOND LEVEL ADDRESS:** Sometimes used as a synonym for *indirect address*.

**SECONDARY KEY:** A *key* which is not the same as that by which a set of items in a database are ordered (the *primary key*). For example, a set of personnel records might be ordered by surnames, their ages being a *secondary key*. In order to search a database on a secondary key, there are many techniques that can be used from sequential search to ones involving *inverted files*.

**SECONDARY CONSOLE:** In a system with multiple consoles, a *secondary console* is any one which is not the *master console*.

**SECONDARY STATION:** A term usually used in the HDLC protocol to indicate a station which receives commands from the *primary station* and acts upon them.

**SECONDARY STORAGE:** Used as a synonym for *backing storage*, referring to such items as *disks* and *tapes* which have slower access times than primary memory, but are considerably cheaper.

**SECTOR:** Part of a *track* on a *magnetic disk*. Each track is divided into a number of sectors (where the word is used in the conventional sense) and the sector boundaries may be defined by hardware (*hard sectoring*) or software (*soft sectoring*).

**SECURITY:** The prevention of unauthorised access to data.

**SEED:** A number used as a starting point for "pseudo-random number" generation.

**SEEK:** To move the read/write head of a *direct acess* storage device to the specified track (see also *latency*).

**SEEK TIME:** The time taken for the read/write heads on a disk to move to the selected track (hence the saying "on a clear disk, you can seek forever").

**SEGMENT (1):** A part of a program which is fairly self-contained but which has links to other program segments. It is necessary to code a program into segments in cases where the entire program will not fit into main memory and hence, when a segment has finished execution, it is overwritten by another segment from backing storage. One segment, the *root segment* is kept in primary memory all the time. The term is also used as a synonym for *page*, especially when the pages may be of variable sizes.

**SEGMENT (2):** A term used in data transmission (e.g. in *PSS*) to refer to a *packet* or part of a packet. In PSS, charging is by the segment.

**SEGMENTATION:** The process of splitting into *segments*.

**SELECTOR:** A device for initiating one of a number of possible alternative actions, depending on the data sent to it.

**SELECTOR CHANNEL:** An I/O channel which can transfer data to/from one peripheral at a time, as compared with a *multiplexor channel*.

**SELF-MODIFYING PROGRAM:** A program which, during the process of execution, modifies its own instructions. This technique is of some use on computers with a restricted set of features (such as the absence of an *index register*) in that it enables some operations to be carried out more efficiently. It is also used, for example, on IBM System/370 in order to move a variable length data item in memory. However, there are a number of disadvantages to the technique. The first is that code written in such a way cannot be *re-entrant*. Secondly, it leads to the possibility of over-writing code which is required to be unaltered (since it is not possible to protect code). Thirdly, in a *pipeline* machine, it is necessary to "drain" the pipeline, before executing the modified instruction, thereby decreasing efficiency.

**SELF-RELATIVE ADDRESS:** An "address" which is specified as a displacement from the current instruction. Code written using *self-relative addresses* can be easily *relocatable*. See also *relative address*.

**SEMANTICS:** The meaning attached to the code of a program, as opposed to its *syntax*.

**SEMICONDUCTOR:** A material whose resistance is between that of conductors (such as metals) and insulators (e.g. glass). Two well known semiconductor materials are silicon and germanium and these are used in the construction of computer components. The use of semiconductors may be divided into two: n-type and p-type. The former are semiconductors which have been doped with minute amounts of impurities which produce extra electrons (negatively charged, hence "n-type"); the latter are doped with impurities which produce "holes" (or acceptors which, being positive, give rise to the term "p-type"). Since these doping materials can be introduced in extremely small areas, it is possible to generate a very large number of computer components on a single chip of semiconductor material.

**SENSE:** To determine the state of some item, such as the presence or absence of holes in punched tape.

**SENSE SWITCH:** A switch on the *console* of a computer which may be set by an operator and interrogated by program. See also *handkeys*.

**SENTINEL:** A name sometimes given to a value outside the expected range of a parameter, used to indicate some exceptional condition. For example, if a program is to read a sequence of positive numbers, the number of which is unknown, a negative value may be used as a sentinel to indicate the end of the sequence.

**SEPARATOR:** A character which serves to separate two items. See also *delimiter*.

**SEQUENCE:** An ordering of a set of items, according to prescribed criteria (or the verb indicating to perform this ordering).

**SEQUENCE CONTROL REGISTER:** A synonym for *program counter*.

**SEQUENCE ERROR:** An error detected by an item not being in its correct place in a *sequence*.

**SEQUENTIAL:** Pertaining to the occurrence of a number of actions in time sequence with no overlap. The term should be compared with *concurrent* and *parallel*.

**SEQUENTIAL ACCESS:** Usually used to describe a storage device from which data can be read in the order in which it was stored, for example, *magnetic tape*.

**SEQUENTIAL COMPUTER:** A computer where instructions are executed one at a time (although there may be some overlap if *pipeline* techniques are used). Compare with *parallel processing*.

**SEQUENTIAL OPERATION:** The performing of functions in sequence.

**SEQUENTIAL PROCESSING:** The processing of data in a specified sequence.

**SERC:** An abbreviation for the *Science and Engineering Research Council*, a UK body (formerly the Science Research Council) which funds research into various aspects of science and engineering.

**SERIAL:** Pertaining to the *sequential* occurrence of a number of related activities.

**SERIAL ACCESS:** A synonym for *sequential access.*

**SERIAL COMPUTER:** A computer which processes bits within a word in sequence.

**SERIAL PROCESSING:** Pertaining to the processing of data in order, as opposed to *parallel processing.*

**SERIAL TRANSFER:** The transfer of data in which successive items are transmitted in sequence.

**SERIAL TRANSMISSION:** The transmission of data (usually over a tele-communications link) in which successive items are transmitted in sequence. For example, in data transmission, it is common for the sequence of characters to be transmitted one bit at a time (*bit-serial*) although they may be transmitted one character at a time ("bit-parallel, byte-serial").

**SERIALISE:** To change from a parallel data stream into a serial one.

**SERIALLY REUSABLE:** A phrase applied to routines which may be used serially, that is, after one process has called the routine and returned, another may do so. This implies that any required values in the routine are either initialised on entry or are passed as parameters.

**SERVICE ROUTINE:** A synonym for *utility routine.*

**SET (1):** To store a specified value in given locations. In the context of single bits, this term means to set them to binary one.

**SET (2):** Used in the mathematical sense of a collection of items, the term is a reserved word in some languages (e.g. *Pascal*).

**SHANNON:** A logarithmic (to the base 2) measure of information content.

**SHIFT:** To move the constituents of a data item (e.g. bits) to the left or right. There are many varieties of shift, such as *circular, arithmetic* and *logical.*

**SHIFT IN:** A control character used to change from a non-standard character set back into the base set. This was particularly necessary in early character codes which used a small number of bits (five or six) to represent data. In such cases, it was necessary to shift into another character set in order to represent, for example, lower case letters. It is usually abbreviated as "SI".

**SHIFT OUT:** A control character used to change from a standard character set into another. It is usually abbreviated as "SO". See *shift in*.

**SHIFT REGISTER:** A register which has the property of being able to shift data in it a given number of places.

**SHUGART:** An American manufacturer of disk drives.

**SI:** An abbreviation for *shift in*.

**SIDEBAND:** A frequency band generated by modulating a *carrier wave*. In fact, two *sidebands* are generated, the upper sideband having a frequency equal to the sum of the carrier frequency and the modulating frequency and the lower sideband equal to their difference.

**SIGN:** An indicator (or the symbol representing that indicator) used to define whether a value is positive or negative.

**SIGN AND MAGNITUDE:** A method of representing integers in a computer whereby the most significant bit is taken to specify the sign (0 if positive, 1 if negative) and the remaining bits are taken as the unsigned magnitude. Thus, in an eight-bit machine, using this notation, the value $+25$ would be represented as 000011001 while $-25$ would become 100011001.

**SIGN ON:** A synonym for *log-in*.

**SIGN POSITION:** The position which contains the sign of a number. In most binary representations, this is the most significant bit.

**SIGNAL:** An item which is transmitted in order to convey information.

**SIGNAL TO NOISE RATIO:** The ratio (usually measured in *decibels*) between the *signal* and *noise* on a communications link.

**SIGNALLING RATE:** The rate at which signals are transmitted over a communications link.

**SIL:** An abbreviation for *systems implementation language*.

**SILICON:** A *semiconductor* used in fabricating computer components.

**SILICONE:** A series of polymerised derivatives of silicon which are used, for example, as waterproof greases and which have no connection with computer components.

**SILICON VALLEY:** A term used to refer to an area south of San Francisco (near Sunnyvale) where many computer and semiconductor manufacturers are located.

**SIMPLEX:** Transmission in only one direction of a connection. The term is sometimes used (incorrectly) to mean *half-duplex*. It is equivalent to *channel*.

**SIMPLEX CHANNEL:** See *simplex*.

**SIMULATE:** To model the functioning of one system by another, for example, traffic flow can be simulated using a computer program.

**SIMULATION:** See *simulate*.

**SIMULTANEOUS:** Occurring at the same time.

**SINGLE ADDRESS:** Pertaining to a type of computer instructions which require a single address. See *one-address*.

**SINGLE SHOT:** A synonym for *single step*.

**SINGLE STEP:** Used as a description of one quantum of a computer program or, more commonly, as a verb to describe the process of executing a program one instruction at a time, usually by means of a switch on the front console of the computer, although (especially on microcomputers) sometimes under software control.

**SINK:** One end of a *channel* to which data is transmitted.

**SIR:** An acronym for *selective information retrieval*.

**SIMD:** An acronym for *single instruction stream, multiple data stream*, a term applied to a type of computer architecture, including vector machines, parallel processors with one control unit and many ALUs (e.g. ILLIAC IV) and some associative processors (e.g. STARAN).

**SISD:** An acronym for *single instruction stream, single data stream*, a term applied to conventional computer architectures.

**SITA:** The Société Internationale de Télécommunications Aéronautiques message-switched network.

**SJCC:** An abbreviation for the *Spring Joint Computer Conference*, a series of conferences held in the USA every spring which have now been superseded by the "National Computer Conference".

**SKIP:** To perform an unconditional transfer of control to the next instruction but one in sequence (or, more rarely, to transfer control to any subsequent instruction).

**SLANG:** An acronym for *systems language*, an early computer language.

**SLAVE:** Pertaining to some peripheral operating under the control of a *master*.

**SLOTTED ALOHA:** A technique used in contention networks (especially broadcast satellite networks such as ALOHA) in which the time domain is split into a number of time slots. In such a manner, quite a high channel utilisation can be achieved.

**SMF:** An acronym for *systems management facilities*, a set of utilities which are provided on a number of machines to facilitate management of the system, such as accounting routines.

**SNA:** An abbreviation for *Systems Network Architecture*.

**SNAPSHOT:** A dynamic dump of the contents of storage locations and registers being used during execution of a program. Also known as a "snapshot dump" and to be compared with a *postmortem*.

**SNOBOL:** A high-level language with extensive features for string manipulation.

**SO:** An abbreviation for *shift-out*.

**SOFTCARD:** A *card* which contains a Z-80 *cpu* and which may be plugged into an Apple microcomputer allowing it to run programs (particularly *CP/M*) which are only available for the Z-80.

**SOFT HALT:** An instruction which does not *halt* the central processor but has a very similar effect in that the processor cannot continue beyond the specified instruction unless an interrupt occurs. This is achieved by the instruction being an unconditional transfer of control to itself.

**SOFT SECTORING:** The marking of sectors on a (floppy) disk by means of software rather than by the presence of *index holes*.

**SOFTWARE:** Programs.

**SOH:** An abbreviation for *start of header*. A control character usually used to precede a block header. In ASCII, its value is binary 0000001 (control-A).

**SOL:** An early *home computer* made by Processor Technology.

**SOM:** An abbreviation for *start of message*. A control character used to indicate the start of a message.

**SORT:** To arrange a set of items into a fixed order given by specified criteria. There are many techniques for sorting, such as bubble sort, shell sort, tournament sort, heapsort and quicksort.

**SORT/MERGE:** To *merge* and *sort* a number of sets of data, or the program which carries out these functions.

**SOS (1):** An acronym for *Son of Stopgap*, a *line-oriented* editor available on many DEC machines.

**SOS (2):** An acronym for *silicon on sapphire*, a technology for fabricating semiconductor components.

**SOURCE:** The end of a *communications channel* from which data is sent. The other end is known as the *sink*.

**SOURCE CODE:** The input to a compiler (hence usually written in a high-level language, although the term is sometimes applied to assembly code) which is translated into *object code*.

**SOURCE COMPUTER:** The computer on which a *compiler* (or *assembler*) is run, as opposed to the computer for which it generates code (the *object computer*).

**SOURCE LANGUAGE:** The language in which a program is written (before it is translated into the *object language*).

**SOURCE MODULE:** A self-contained part of a program written in *source language*.

**SOURCE PROGRAM:** An entire program written in *source language*.

**SP:** An abbreviation for *space*.

**SPACE (1):** An area of memory consisting of blank characters.

**SPACE (2):** Used as a verb to mean the action of moving a printing device forward a number of print positions (cf. *horizontal tabulate*).

**SPACE (3):** In data communciations, binary zero condition on a line.

**SPACE CHARACTER:** A non-printing character used as a separator. It is usually abbreviated as "SP" and has the value 0100000 in ASCII (and hexadecimal '40' in EBCDIC).

**SPACE DIVISION MULTIPLEXING:** A means of multiplexing whereby individual circuits occupy physically separate paths.

**SPC:** An abbreviation for *stored program control (or computer)*.

**SPEC:** An abbreviation for *specification*.

**SPECIAL CHARACTER:** A somewhat loosely defined term but most generally it means any printing character which is neither *alphabetic* or *numeric*. Thus *special characters* include "£", "%" and "&".

**SPECIFICATION:** A formal, detailed definition of a set of requirements.

**SPOOL (n):** A synonym for *reel*.

**SPOOL (vb):** To read data from (and write it to) peripheral devices in parallel with normal job processing via a faster medium. For example, card input may be spooled via a disk (i.e. cards are read, not directly into memory, but are copied first onto a disk whence they can be read much faster).

**SPROCKET:** Part of a device which consists of a number of metal pins around the circumference of a wheel which engage with holes in the appropriate medium (e.g. *continuous stationery* or *paper tape*).

**SPROCKET FEED:** A means of feeding an I/O medium (e.g. *continuous stationery* or *paper tape*) by means of *sprocket holes* which engage with a *sprocket*.

**SPROCKET HOLES:** The small holes punched near the centre of paper tape to engage with a *sprocket* on the reader (if mechanical) to define the position of the data. The holes are also used by non-mechanical readers to define the position of the data holes.

**SRC:** An abbreviation for the *Science Research Council* which funds research in the UK into, *inter alia*, computer science. It has been renamed the *Science and Engineering Research Council*.

**STACK:** A *LIFO* list, that is a *list* where the last item added is the first to be retrieved. In the general sense, there is no need for the elements of the list to be contiguous and a stack may be implemented, for example, as a *linked list*. However, in most applications, the stack occupies contiguous storage locations. The act of adding an item to the stack is usually known as *pushing* and retrieving an item from the stack is *popping*. In some computers, a stack is implemented in hardware.

**STACKER:** An abbreviation for *card stacker*.

**STACK ADDRESSING:** A mode of addressing whereby the *stack* is implicitly addressed (and thus this is a *zero address* instruction). If, for example, the specified instruction were "ADD", two data items would be "popped off" the stack, added together and the result "pushed onto" the stack.

**STANDARD INTERFACE:** Usually used in the context of hardware to mean an interface which conforms to a formal standard (e.g. the CCITT V.24 or EIA RS232C standards).

**STANDARD SUBROUTINE:** A *subroutine* which is of general use and which forms part of a *subroutine library*.

**STANDARDS:** A formal set of rules which enable uniform practices to be implemented at different sites. There are a number of standards bodies, particularly ISO which has member bodies in many countries. In addition, there are bodies such as CCITT which do not promulgate standards but merely recommendations which neverthless have the force of standards (e.g. the V.24 recommendation).

**STANDARDISATION (1):** The process of formalising standards.

**STANDARDISATION (2):** A synonym for *normalise*.

**STANDBY:** Used a an adjective pertaining to equipment which is ready to take over in the event of a failure of the primary equipment, or as a noun applied to such equipment.

**STAR NETWORK:** A network where a central computer is connected to each peripheral computer, each of which is not connected to any other. Frequently used where the central computer is fairly large and the peripheral computers perform some local processing and job entry to the mainframe.

**START ELEMENT:** The one bit used in *asynchronous* data transmission to denote the start of a character.

**START/STOP TRANSMISSION:** A synonym for *asynchronous transmission*.

**STATE VECTOR:** A set of parameters which serve to define unambiguously the state of a program at any point in its execution. Such parameters would include the *program counter* or *program status word*. The process of execution or interpretation can be considered as the ordered set of changes to the state vector.

**STATEMENT:** A sequence of symbols in a programming (or related) language which form a meaningful, self-contained expression or instruction (or a set of such).

**STATEMENT NUMBER:** A sequence number allocated to some (or all) *statements* within a *source program*. In some languages (e.g. BASIC), the *statement number* corresponds to a *label*.

**STATIC:** Pertaining to any item which does not alter with the passage of time.

**STATIC STORAGE:** Storage whose contents do not decay with time and hence do not need to be *refreshed*.

**STATUS WORD:** See *program status word*.

**STD:** An acronym for *Subscriber Trunk Dialling*, a system available from telephones in the UK enabling the user to dial long-distance numbers directly. The US equivalent is *DDD*.

**STEP:** One single operation.

**STEP COUNTER:** A variable which is used to count the number of times an operation (e.g. the execution of a *loop*) is executed.

**STEPPING MOTOR:** A motor used, for example, in disk drives or character printers.

**STOP:** To cease, often used in the context of execution of a program. In early computers, it meant to halt the cpu but, in multi-programming systems, this would not be very helpful to other users and it is interpreted as a special exit to the *supervisor*. See also *halt*.

**STOP BIT:** A bit used to define the end of a character in *asynchronous transmission*.

**STOP ELEMENT:** A synonym for *stop bit*.

**STORAGE:** Any device into which data can be written then retrieved (read) at a later stage.

**STORAGE ALLOCATION:** The function of assigning areas of storage to particular programs.

**STORAGE BLOCK:** A contiguous area of storage. Often storage is divided up into blocks to simplify the problems of *storage allocation*.

**STORAGE CAPACITY:** The number of data items which can be stored on a given storage device, usually measured in terms of the addressing unit of the computer to which it is attached (e.g. bytes).

**STORAGE DENSITY:** The *packing density* of a storage medium.

**STORAGE DEVICE:** A device which can be used for storing data within a computer system, for example, a *magnetic tape* or *floppy disk*.

**STORAGE KEY:** A means of protecting data such that a value is associated with each block of storage and only programs whose key matches that value are allowed to access that storage.

**STORAGE PROTECT:** The means of protecting *storage* against unauthorised access.

**STORE (1):** A synonym for *storage*, particularly *primary storage*.

**STORE (2):** To enter data into a storage device (and, in many *assemblers*, used as the operation for moving data from *registers* into *main memory*).

**STORE AND FORWARD:** A technique used in data transmission (e.g. *message switched networks*) in which data is stored in an intermediate node for later onward transmission. An early form of *store and forward* was *torn tape networks*.

**STORED PROGRAM COMPUTER:** A computer in which the instructions controlling the computer are stored internally in exactly the same way as data, rather than being on some external medium. The concept of the *stored program computer* (usually abbreviated *SPC*) is usually attributed to John von Neumann.

**STORED PROGRAM CONTORL:** Pertaining to the control of a computer by means of an internally stored program.

**STRING:** A contiguous sequence of characters, treated as a whole (and sometimes with additional information such as the number of characters).

**STRING FUNCTION:** A function which may be applied to a string, for example, extracting part of the string.

**STRING MANIPULATION:** The techniques and operations using strings, such as concatenation.

**STRINGY FLOPPY:** A continuous loop tape cartridge system which provides access speed and cost somewhere between a cassette tape and a floppy disk.

**STRUCTURE:** The inter-relationships between various data items.

**STX:** An abbreviation for *start of text*. A control character usually used to precede the text of a message. In ASCII, its value is binary 0000010 (control-B).

**SUB:** An abbreviation for *substitute character*.

**SUBPROGRAM:** A part of a program. The term is not clearly defined but most often taken to be synonymous with *subroutine*.

**SUBROUTINE:** A sequence of instructions which are self-contained (but may be *open* or *closed*). Control is never passed directly from the *supervisor* to a subroutine.

**SUBROUTINE CALL:** The instruction (or set of instructions) which pass control to a *subroutine*.

**SUBROUTINE LIBRARY:** A set of *subroutines* which are of general application and are stored in a *program library* so that they are accessible to a wide range of programs. See, for example, *NAG*.

**SUBSCRIPT:** Strictly, an item which is written below other characters but which is most commonly used to mean a value which identifies one member of an *array* and which is written in parentheses. Thus, if there is an array X, the tenth member is repesented as X(10) with the "10" being the "subscript".

**SUBSET:** A part of a set.

**SUBSTITUTE CHARACTER:** A control character which is used to replace any incorrect character. In the ASCII character code, it is represented as the bit pattern 0011010 (control-Z) and is used in some systems (e.g. CP/M) to denote the end of file.

**SUBTASK:** A *task* spawned by a higher-priority task and which can proceed in parallel with its controlling task.

**SUBTRACT:** To carry out the process of *subtraction*.

**SUBTRACTION:** The arithmetic operation which evaluates the difference between two values, the *minuend* and *subtrahend*.

**SUBTRAHEND:** One of the two operands in *subtraction* which is subtracted from the *minuend* to yield the result.

**SUITE:** A set of programs which are closely related.

**SUM:** The result of performing the *addition* operation on an *addend* and an *augend*.

**SUPERSCRIPT:** Some item which is written above the line, for example, to represent a power. As it is not usually possible to reproduce this in computer input, other means have to be used and, for example, powers are often represented following two asterisks or an *up-arrow*.

**SUPERSET:** A *set* which consists of another set with additions. For example, many computer installations implemented versions of FORTRAN IV but included some additional facilities, thus the language implemented was described as a "superset" of FORTRAN IV.

**SUPERVISOR:** A program (usually used in the context of a multi-programming environment) which controls the operation of the computer. It is sometimes used synonymously with *operating system* and/or *monitor* or can be used to mean the permanently resident part of the operating system, although this is more often called the *nucleus*.

**SUPERVISOR CALL:** An instruction which can be issued by a user program to request the *supervisor* to perform some function which the user program is not allowed to perform for itself (for example, input/output). There are various synonyms for a supervisor call (abbreviated *SVC* in some systems, e.g. IBM System/370), such as *UUO*.

**SUPERVISOR PROGRAM:** A synonym for *supervisor*.

**SUPERVISOR STATE:** A state of the central processor in which it is allowed to perform certain *privileged operations*.

**SUPERVISORY BITS:** In data transmission, a number of bits which convey control information. See *control bits*.

**SUPERVISORY SEQUENCE:** In data transmission, a series of characters (or bits) which serve to control the transmission of the data.

**SVC:** An abbreviation for *supervisor call*.

**SWAP:** To interchange two items but used more often to mean *swap-in* or *swap-out*. It is sometimes used to mean the interchanging of two variables in storage and this can be achieved without using intermediate storage by the use of three "exclusive-or" instructions:

```
I    : =  I    XOR   J
J    : =  J    XOR   I
I    : =  I    XOR   J
```

**SWAP IN:** To copy from backing storage into main storage a section of a program. See *swapping*.

**SWAP OUT:** To copy from main storage to backing storage a section of a program. See *swapping*.

**SWAPPING:** The technique of copying programs (or parts of programs) from main memory to backing storage to enable more efficient use to be made of the relatively limited amount of main storage available. See also *virtual memory*, *one-level store* and *segmentation*.

**SWIFT:** An acronym for *Society for Worldwide Interbank Financial Telecommunication*, a banking network which transfers financial information between the participating countries. The network is based on two nodes (Burroughs 4800 computers) in Brussels and Amsterdam.

**SWITCH (1):** A device which connects or disconnects an electrical circuit.

**SWITCH (2):** To invert a bit.

**SWITCH (3):** A part of a program which allows control to be transferred to one of a number of alternatives (see, for example, *case statement*).

**SWITCHED LINE:** A communications link which is not permanently established (cf. *leased line*) but which is set up when required by dialling.

**SWITCHED NETWORK:** Used as a synonym for the *Public Switched Telephone Network*.

**SWUNET:** An acronym for *South West Universities Network*, a packet-switching computer network in the south-west of England. It is a *star network* with a central switching computer and was originally homogeneous, using ICL computers.

**SYMBOL (1):** A character or set of characters which represent some item.

**SYMBOL (2):** An experimental computer system designed to execute high-level languages directly, rather than their having to be compiled into *machine code*.

**SYMBOL TABLE:** A table consisting of all *symbols* used in a particular operation. For example, all the identifiers used in a high-level language program.

**SYMBOLIC:** Pertaining to the use of *symbols*.

**SYMBOLIC ADDRESS:** An *address* expressed as a *symbol* which is meaningful to the programmer rather than the *absolute address* (to which it must be converted before execution).

**SYMBOLIC CODING:** The writing of programs using *symbols* rather than in *absolute code*.

**SYMBOLIC LANGUAGE:** Any programming language which permits the use of *symbols*.

**SYN:** An abbreviation for *synchronous idle*. A control character usually used to maintain synchronism between the ends of a communication line. In ASCII, its value is binary 0010110 (control-V).

**SYNCHRONOUS:** Occurring in step, particularly used in the context of two (or more) processes which are controlled by a single timing mechanism (*clock*).

**SYNCHRONOUS NETWORK:** A computer network in which all the communication channels are synchronised to a common clock.

**SYNCHRONOUS TRANSMISSION:** Transmission of data in which the sender and receiver are operating in step, controlled by the exchange of special synchronisation characters (*SYN*). Compare with *asynchronous*.

**SYNTAX:** The formal rules governing the grammar and structure of a language, particularly *high-level* computer languages. There are a number of ways of defining formally the syntax of such languages, such as *BNF*. See also "semantics".

**SYNTAX CHECKER:** A program (or part of a *compiler*) which examines *source code* for deviations from a specified *syntax*.

**SYNTHESIS:** The combination of parts into a larger whole. The opposite is *analysis*.

**SYSGEN:** An abbreviation for *system generation*, referring to the process of constructing an operating system from a (usually large) number of modules, many of which can be modified by the use of suitable parameters to optimise for the particular situation.

**SYSTEM:** Any organised grouping but more often used as an abbreviation for a computer system.

**SYSTEM DISK:** The *disk* on which are stored the *operating system*, various system *utilities*, *job queues* etc.

**SYSTEM GENERATION:** See *sysgen*.

**SYSTEM QUEUE AREA:** An area of main storage (or, sometimes, backing storage) which is reserved for the system queues and their associated control blocks.

**SYSTEM X:** A name for the electronic exchanges which British Telecom are starting to install in the UK.

**SYSTEMS ANALYSIS:** The examination of an activity (usually a business activity) to determine how best the same activity could be carried out with the help of a computer.

**SYSTEMS ANALYST:** A person who specialises in *systems analysis*.

**SYSTEMS IMPLEMENTATION LANGUAGE:** A generic term applied to various high-level languages which either produce very efficient code or have other specific features enabling them to be used conveniently for writing systems programs. In general, they retain the efficiency required for this purpose given by assembly language while at the same time enabling the requisite algorithms to be clearly coded.

**SYSTEMS NETWORK ARCHITECTURE:** An architecture for distributed systems announced by IBM in 1974. It provides facilities for distributed computation and allows many devices to be connected by means of a variety of ways (e.g. dial-up lines). SNA has a number of levels and one major concept is that of "peer-level communication" in which any level conceptually communicates only with the corresponding level in another machine. The system runs under the control of a *NCP*, usually resident in the 3705. Various enhancements to the system have been announced at intervals.

**SYSTEMS PROGRAM:** Specific programs which can be considered to be part of a computer system, such as *compilers* and *utilities*.

**SYSTEMS RESOURCE:** Any *resource* of a computer system which is under the control of the *operating system*.

# T

**TAB:** An abbreviation for *tabulate* or *tabulation character*.

**TABLE:** A set of data, ordered in some way such as a two-dimensional matrix.

**TABLE LOOK-UP:** The procedure of searching a *table* in order to find one element.

**TABULAR:** Laid out in the form of a *table*.

**TABULATE:** To carry out the process of *tabulation*.

**TABULATION (1):** The process of laying out data in the form of a *table* (and, usually, to include totals of each column or row in the table).

**TABULATION (2):** The moving of a printing mechanism (or *cursor* in the case of non-printing devices) to a specified position, usually by means of a *tabulation character*.

**TABULATION CHARACTER:** A control character used to effect the process of *tabulation*, either in a horizontal or a vertical direction (see *horizontal tab* and *vertical tab*).

**TAG:** One or more bits which might be attached to a data item or an instruction in order to convey additional information. For example, a *tag* might be used in the case of a data item to define its type.

**TANDY:** A UK retailer, best known for the *TRS-80* personal computer. The company is known as Radio Shack in the USA.

**TAPE:** See *magnetic tape* or *paper tape*.

**TAPE DECK:** Usually used as a synonym for *tape drive*.

**TAPE DRIVE:** A device which consists of read/write heads, a transport mechanism and, usually, an associated controller which is used for the storage of data on *magnetic tape*.

**TAPE LABEL:** Usually used to refer to a *record* placed at the beginning of a *magnetic tape* which defines information about the tape, such as its *volume* number. The term is also used as a general term synonymously with *header label* and *trailer label*. It is also sometimes used for the paper label attached to a *tape reel* which identifies the tape to an *operator*.

**TAPE MARK:** A character used to indicate the end of a magnetic tape.

**TAPE SERIAL NUMBER:** A unique identifier (not always numeric) for a *magnetic tape* which is usually recorded in the *tape label*.

**TAPE SORT:** The procedure of *sorting* data contained on *magnetic tape(s)*.

**TAPE TRANSPORT:** Usually used as a synonym for *tape drive*.

**TARGET COMPUTER:** The computer on which a program is to be run, to be contrasted with that on which the program is compiled. It is used as a synonym for *object computer*.

**TARGET LANGUAGE:** A synonym for *object language*.

**TARGET PROGRAM:** A synonym for *object program*.

**TASI:** An acronym for *time assignment speech interpolaton*.

**TASK:** A basic unit of work for a computer. In the context of a *multi-programming* system, the word is often used synonymously with *job* but this is a rather restricted viewpoint.

**TASK MANAGEMENT:** The management of *tasks* within a computer system or the set of routines (in the *operating system*) which performs this management.

**TCAM:** An acronym for *telecommunications access method*.

**TCB:** An abbreviation for *task control block*. A *control block* required by *task management* routines.

**TCP:** An abbreviation for *transmission control program*, a *network control program* which implements inter-network protocols.

**TDM:** An abbreviation for *time division multiplexing*.

**TDMA:** An abbreviation for *time division multiple access*.

**TELE-:** A prefix indicating *at or over a distance*.

**TELECOMMUNICATIONS:** The branch of science concerned with the transfer of data over distances by means of communications links.

**TELECONFERENCING:** The techniques associated with conducting a conference over communications links, usually by means of fairly complex programs which facilitate the required functions. Of the programs available for this purpose, perhaps FORUM and EMISARI are the best known.

**TELEMATICS:** A fairly recently coined word to indicate the synthesis of a number of disciplines including telecommunications, information processing and office technology. It is also used, more or less synonymously with the terms *informatics* and *information technology*, as well as the French term Télématique.

**TELENET:** A *packet-switching* network in the USA based on *ARPANET* technology but using X.25 protocols.

**TELEPRINTER:** An input/output device used for transmitting data over low grade lines. Usually only a restricted set of characters are available (especially since a 5-bit code is usually used).

**TELEPROCESSING:** The use of communications lines to transmit data from its source to a remote location where it is processed then returned whence it came.

**TELETEX:** A generic name applied to the interconnection of systems such as Telex and *word processors* into a network which performs similar functions to the present Telex network, but operating at far higher bandwidths than the current 75 bps.

**TELETEXT:** A technique for transmitting information in the blanking lines of a television transmission. This data may be decoded by suitable hardware and shown as pictures (frames of information). A maximum of 800 or so frames may be transmitted when two lines are used (as in the case of the systems developed by the BBC and IBA, *Ceefax* and *Oracle*, where the data is transmitted at the same time as the ordinary television transmission). In practice, a lesser number of frames is transmitted in order to retain an acceptable response time – one hundred giving a mean response time of twelve seconds.

**TELETYPE:** A trademark of the Teletype Corporation but now often used to mean a low-speed (usually 10 cps) asynchronous, upper case, hard-copy ASCII terminal. Models of Teletype include the 33 (upper-case only) and the newer 43 which is a 10 or 30 cps, upper or lower case terminal.

**TELEX:** An acronym for *Teletypewriter Exchange Service* of Western Union but now used more generally to signify a low bandwidth network (operating at 75 bps) interconnecting *teleprinters*.

**TELIDON:** The Canadian *videotex* service. It differs in a number of respects from the UK *Prestel* service, particularly in that the data is transmitted in the form of "picture description instructions" rather than as a serial character stream. As these PDIs occupy more than one byte each, it might be thought that it is a less efficient method of transmitting data but this is, in fact, dependent on the data being transmitted. The graphics displayed are very much higher resolution than those possible in an alpha-mosaic system such as Prestel.

**TEMPORARY DATA SET:** A *file* which is created during the processing of a *job* for the storage of intermediate results (usually because the volume of data is higher than that which can be stored in primary memory) and which is deleted at the termination of job execution. Often the user does not need to specify the name of the file, the *system* generating the unique name including the date and time of day.

**TEMPORARY STORAGE:** Storage which is used for the retention of intermediate results. Also known as *working storage*.

**TERA-:** A prefix indicating one million million ($10^{12}$, a billion).

**TERABIT MEMORY:** A general term applied to storage devices whose capacity is of the order of $10^{12}$ bits. Such devices include the IBM *data cell*, the Unicon laser memory and the Ampex videotape memory.

**TERMINAL:** A device which is capable of receiving and/or sending data.

**TERMINAL USER:** A person who accesses an interactive system by means of a *terminal*.

**TERNARY:** Pertaining to the base three (cf. *binary*).

**TERTIARY STORAGE:** Storage such as *punched cards* or *paper tape* which has the attributes of being slow, bulky and cheap for relatively small amounts of data (although expensive on a per bit basis). To be compared with *secondary storage* (e.g. *disks*, *tape*) and *primary storage* (e.g. *core*).

**TEST:** To examine some item to determine whether it satisfies a given criterion.

**TEST DATA:** Data which is prepared in order to test the functioning of a specified program.

**TEST PROGRAM:** A program which is specifically designed to test specific aspects of a computer system.

**TEST RUN:** Either the execution of a *test program* or the execution of a program with its *test data*.

**TEXT:** The information content of a message, usually contained between the "start of text" and "end of text" control characters. The term is also used more generally to indicate any set of *alphanumeric* characters which convey information.

**THIRD GENERATION:** Pertaining to computer technology based on solid state components.

**THREE ADDRESS:** Pertaining to instructions in which three addresses are specified.

**THROUGHPUT:** The amount of work performed by a computer system (or part of it) per unit time. Also used to indicate the amount of data transmitted per unit time over telecommunications links.

**TIME DIVISION MULTIPLEXING:** A technique of data transmission whereby the time domain is split, each interaction occupying a separate time slot.

**TIME OUT:** A time interval within which a specified event is expected to occur or the action occurring at the end of that interval. "Timeouts" are particularly useful in *real time systems* where errors are likely to occur. For example, timeouts are heavily used in computer networks.

**TIMESHARING:** The technique of using a computer system (often on an interactive basis) whereby each user is allocated a proportion of processor time. If this is calculated correctly, it may appear that the user has sole use of the system as the time required to service all other users is less than his response time.

**TIME SLICE:** The proportion of processor time allocated to each user in a *timesharing* environment.

**TIMER:** Used in general as a synonym for *clock* but sometimes with the additional meaning of a device which, after a certain number of time intervals, will generate some signal, usually an interrupt.

**TIP:** An acronym for *Terminal Interface Message Processor*. The node processor for *ARPANET (IMP)*, modified by the addition of a multi-line controller so that it can perform terminal handling functions.

**ToD:** An abbreviation for *time of day*.

**TOGGLE:** Either a device which has two stable states (see *bistable*) or the action of changing such a device from one state to the other (e.g. changing the value of a single bit in the computer's memory).

**TOP OF FORM:** Used in the context of printing on *continuous stationery*, the term indicates the position of the paper so that the current print position is at the top of a new sheet of paper.

**TORN-TAPE:** Refers to early *store and forward* networks in which output was received on a device which was able to punch tape, torn off and inserted in a similar device for onward transmission.

**TRACE:** To record the sequence of instructions in the execution of a program (or the actual record produced).

**TRACE PROGRAM:** A program which enables the user to *trace* execution of another program, usually in order to facilitate *debugging*.

**TRACK:** A subdivision of the storage on a device such as a *magnetic tape* or *magnetic disk*. In the latter case, the surface of the disk is divided up into a number of concentric tracks which are further subdivided into *sectors*.

**TRACTOR FEED:** A mechanism for feeding paper into a printer or similar device. The stationery is continuous with perforations along the edges and the tractor has sprockets to engage these holes, thus providing stable feeding with accurate registration.

**TRAILER:** A synonym for *trailer record.*

**TRAILER RECORD:** A *record* appended to a *file* which records information about that file. See also *header record.*

**TRAILING EDGE:** The edge of a *punched card* which enters the *card reader* last. Compare with *leading edge.*

**TRANSACTION:** A change in a data item within a data processing system.

**TRANSACTION FILE:** A synonym for *amendment file.*

**TRANSACTION RECORD:** A synonym for *amendment record.*

**TRANSFER:** To move data from one place to another (sometimes with the implication of destroying the original data rather than merely copying it).

**TRANSFER RATE:** The speed at which data is moved from one place to another, usually measured in bits per second.

**TRANSFORM:** To change from one form to another.

**TRANSIENT AREA:** An area in main storage into which routines are loaded when needed. The term is used in operating systems such as *CP/M.*

**TRANSIENT ERROR:** An error which occurs seemingly randomly (cf. *permanent error*).

**TRANSISTOR:** A semiconductor device, developed at Bell Laboratories, which formed the basis of *second generation* computer technology.

**TRANSITION:** The change from one state to another.

**TRANSLATE:** To convert from one language to another without changing the meaning. The term is sometimes used synonymously with *compile* but is more often used in a similar context when the *target language* is not *machine code.*

**TRANSLATOR:** A device or program which is able to *translate*. Sometimes used as a synonym for *compiler*.

**TRANSMISSION:** The sending of data from one location to another.

**TRANSMIT:** To send data from one location to another.

**TRANSPOSE:** To interchange two items of data.

**TRANSPUT:** A word used to mean input and/or output.

**TRAP:** Usually used as a verb in the context of "trapping an interrupt" (or other error condition) meaning to detect the occurrence of the condition and, instead of returning control to the operating system, to take suitable corrective action. This is usually achieved by notifying the operating system of a location to which control is to be transferred in such an event (the location also being known as a "trap").

**TREE:** A data structure which consists of a number of *nodes*. one node is designated the "root node" and the remaining nodes are divided into a number of disjoint sets, each of which is a "tree". There are many varieties of trees such as binary trees, AVL trees and B-trees.

**TRS-80:** A *home computer* made by Tandy Corporation (Radio Shack) based on the Z-80 processor.

**TRUNCATE:** To remove digits of a number, thus lessening accuracy. For example, the constant "e" (the base of natural logarithms) truncated to four decimal places is 2.7182 while rounded it is 2.7183 (the actual value is 2.718281828 . . . ).

**TSO:** An acronym for *Time Sharing Option*, an option available with many IBM operating systems enabling it to be used interactively by a number of users.

**TTL:** An abbreviation for *transistor-transistor logic*.

**TTY:** An abbreviation for *teletypewriter* or, more commonly, for *teletype*.

**TURNAROUND:** To reverse some process — for example, when using a *half-duplex* line, it has to be turned around for transmission to take place in the opposite direction.

**TURNAROUND TIME:** The time taken to *turnaround*, but more commonly used to mean the time between submitting a *job* to a computer system and receiving the output.

**TWO ADDRESS:** Pertaining to a computer instruction format in which two addresses are defined.

**TWOS COMPLEMENT:** A form of representing signed integers in binary arithmetic whereby a negative integer is formed by subtracting the modulus from binary zeros, using ordinary binary arithmetic and ignoring any borrow needed. This leads to a representation in which, with a wordlength of "n" bits, values from $-2^{n-1}$ to $+2^{n-1}-1$ can be represented (i.e. the range is unsymmetrical). The most significant bit is one if the number is negative.

**TWX:** An acronym for *Teletypewriter Exchange Service*.

**TYMNET:** An early *value added network*, owned by Tymshare Inc. which started operation in the USA in 1970. It now has a total of nearly 300 nodes and is available in 25 countries.

**TYPE FACE:** See *fount*.

# U

**UADS:** An abbreviation for *user attribute data set*, a file which contains information about the users of a computer system.

**UART:** An acronym for *Universal Asynchronous Receiver and Transmitter*. A single *chip* which provides control of asynchronous devices (e.g. Teletype) under program control. Now it is more common for the chip to handle synchronous as well as asynchronous devices and this is known as a *USART*.

**UC:** An abbreviation for *upper case* (letters whose value lie in the range 1000001 to 1011010 in ASCII character code). In ASCII, a lower case letter is obtained from the corresponding upper case one by adding 0100000 (which is the representation for the space character). In EBCDIC, the same transformation is achieved by subtracting hexadecimal 40 which is again the space character.

**UCS:** An abbreviation for *universal character set*, a feature of hard-copy devices enabling them to print a wide range of character sets (for example, by having interchangeable *print chains*).

**UNARY:** A synonym for *monadic*.

**UNBOUNDED:** Pertaining to a value which is not constrained in any way.

**UNBUNDLED:** Pertaining to the selling of the software of a computer system separately from its hardware. The software is known as *unbundled*.

**UNCONDITIONAL BRANCH:** A transfer of control which occurs irrespective of any conditions which occur. In many high-level languages, this is denoted by "GOTO".

**UNCONDITIONAL TRANSFER OF CONTROL:** A synonym for *unconditional branch*.

**UNDEFINED:** Pertaining to an item which cannot be assumed to have any specific value, for example, variables prior to initialisation.

**UNDERFLOW:** The condition of a value being calculated which is smaller than can be represented in the computer. In some systems, this gives rise to an *interrupt*; in others, the value is replaced by zero.

**UNDERLINE:** The character (or the function of using the character) which consists of a horizontal line which is placed under text for emphasis. In ASCII, its value is 1011111.

**UNIBUS:** A *bus* used in the PDP-11 series of computers.

**UNIPUNCH:** A device which enables users to punch single holes in punched tape, usually in order to correct minor errors.

**UNIT:** A device which has a specified function, such as the *arithmetic/ logical unit*.

**UNIT ADDRESS:** A unique address assigned to I/O devices (*units*) on a system.

**UNIT SEPARATOR:** See *US*.

**UNIVAC:** A US computer manufacturer who produced the first American commercial computer (the Univac I) in 1949.

**UNIVERSAL LANGUAGE:** A term used to indicate a language which is available over a wide range of computers, such as FORTRAN or COBOL. They are also known as *machine independent languages*.

**UNIX:** A trademark of Bell Laboratories used for a general-purpose, multi-user interactive operating system, available on PDP-11 and Inter- data 8/32 computers. It is now available at about a thousand installations and provides many advanced features. In addition, it has available a large amount of system software, perhaps the best known of which is the *C* programming language. UNIX is itself written in C.

  1. Ritchie, D.M. and Thompson, K., "The Unix Time-Sharing System", Bell Syst. Tech. J., **57**, 1905–1929, 1978.

**UNPACK:** To separate items of data which previously have been *packed*.

**UNRECOVERABLE:** Pertaining to a class of errors from which it is not possible to perform recovery functions.

**UNSET:** To change the value of a bit (or a group of bits) to binary zero.

**UP-ARROW:** A character which is used to denote exponentiation (raising to a power). In ASCII, its value is 1011110 and it is sometimes printed as the arrow-head alone (i.e. a circumflex accent).

**UPDATE:** To modify a file in accordance with events that have taken place. It is used in particular to indicate the changing of a *master file* according to transactions which have occurred since it was last updated.

**UPTIME:** The time when some equipment (usually a complete computer system) is working, although it may not necessarily be performing useful work (see *idle time*). The term is also used to mean the length of time in the current session for which the equipment has been working.

**UPWARDS COMPATIBLE:** A term used to indicate that programs which work on one member of a range of computers will work without change on larger members of that range, although not necessarily on smaller ones. Often this general statement is qualified in various ways, for example, with regard to time dependent features.

**US:** An abbreviation for *unit separator*, a control character which, in the ASCII character set has the value binary 0011111.

**USART:** An acronym for *Universal Synchronous/Asynchronous Receiver and Transmitter*. A single *chip* occurring in many microprocessor systems which provides control of both synchronous and asynchronous devices under program control.

**USASCII:** A synonym for *ASCII*.

**USER:** A person who makes use of the facilities of a computer system.

**USER FRIENDLY:** A term used to indicate that the interface to the computer or program appears simple to use to the uninitiated user and provides many facilities to help, such as clear error messages (often in a hierarchical system so that a brief message is given initially but more detailed information can be accessed if required) and menu selection of options.

**USER GROUP:** A group of users of one particular computer (or range of computers) who share knowledge by means of meetings and publications. See, for example, *DECUS*.

**USER ORIENTED LANGUAGE:** A language which is oriented towards the needs of its users rather than towards the computer on which programs written in the language will be run. See also *problem-oriented language*.

**UTILITY:** A routine or set of routines which perform common tasks in a computer system (such as making copies of disks, printing tapes etc.) and which are provided for the use of any system user.

**UTILITY ROUTINE:** See *utility*.

**UUO:** An abbreviation for *unimplemented user operation*, terminology used on the DECsystem-10 for a *supervisor call*.

# V

**V SERIES:** A series of recommendations from CCITT concerned with data transmission over telephone and telex lines.

**V.24:** Perhaps the best known of the V series recommendations defining asynchronous connections, most often implemented as the 25-pin "D-type" connector.

**VALIDATE:** To perform the process of *validation*.

**VALIDATION:** The process of checking data to ensure that it fulfils certain specified criteria. For example, a set of people's ages might be validated by checking that the values lie between 0 and, say, 100.

**VALUE ADDED NETWORK:** A network which does not offer computer services but merely acts as a transmission medium, taking the telephone lines from the supplier and "adding value", by reducing error rates (by means of error checking and retransmission) and similar facilities. "Value added networks" are illegal in many European countries.

**VALUE ADDED SERVICE:** A name applied to services which are provided on a network to add services, such as *electronic mail* facilities.

**VAN:** An acronym for *value added network*.

**VARIABLE:** An item which may take any of a range of values (cf. *constant*).

**VARIABLE FIELD:** A descriptor applied to data layout in which the *fields* may occupy different lengths.

**VARIABLE LENGTH:** A descriptor most commonly applied to data storage which permits records to be of different lengths within a block, or blocks to be of different lengths.

**VARIABLE LENGTH BLOCK:** A *block* whose size is not fixed.

**VARIABLE LENGTH RECORD:** A *record* whose length is not fixed. For example, within a *block*, records are usually fixed length but in some applications, it is more convenient to permit records to be of variable length and, of course, it is necessary to include (usually with each record) an indication of the record lengths.

**VARIABLE WORD LENGTH:** Pertaining to a system in which the machine word may be a variable number of bits.

**VDL:** An acronym for *Vienna Definition Language*, a language for defining the semantics of programming languages.

**VDU:** An acronym for *visual (or video) display unit*.

**VECTOR:** A set of data items which have the same attributes (e.g. integer) and which are stored in contiguous locations. As a result, individual items may be accessed by means of an *index*. Vectors are also known as one-dimensional *arrays*.

**VECTOR MACHINE:** A term used to describe computers which have hardware so that they are able to perform operations on entire *vectors*, usually at extremely high speeds. Two well known *vector machines* are the CDC STAR-100 and the TI ASC.

**VENN DIAGRAM:** A pictorial repesentation of the relationship between sets.

**VERIFICATION:** The process of checking the accuracy of data, most commonly applied to the checking of punched cards for errors by means of a *verifier*.

**VERIFIER:** A device similar in appearance to a *card punch* (and often combined with one) which is used to verify that the data punched onto a deck of cards is correct. The cards are "repunched" by a second operator and, if the data typed the second time does not match the holes punched on any card, an error is signalled, enabling the card to be correctly punched.

**VERIFY:** To carry out the procedure of *verification*.

**VERTICAL REDUNDANCY CHECK:** A form of error checking in which the bits forming one character are checked. The most common form of vertical redundancy check is *parity*. It is usually abbreviated as *VRC*.

**VERTICAL TAB:** A control character (in ASCII, it is binary 0001011) which moves the paper (or other output medium) a fixed amount vertically. The amount is determined, in the case of many printing devices, by means of a *carriage control tape*.

**VIDEODISK:** A system for recording video information on a disk, similar to a long-playing record, which enables them to be replayed. However such a system can also be used to record digital data and such disks can hold very large amounts of information, although the data can only be writen once and, in order to amend data, it has to be rewritten to a blank part of the disk.

**VIDEOTEX:** The international name for the system originally designated *viewdata*, but also often taken to mean the broadcast services, generically known as *Teletext*, in addition. Sometimes, the term "broadcast videotex" is used for Teletext.

**VIEWDATA:** This is the generic name for a publicly available information dissemination system developed by the British Post Office in the early 1970s and now known by the trade name of Prestel. The name *videotex* is now being used internationally for the same system.

The hardware system is a conventional television set, modified by the addition of a modem and some storage and control circuitry, connected via a telephone line to a remote computer which allows access to a database. The database is essentially a tree, although various cross-linkages are allowed. One major design criterion for the system is that the protocol for accessing data should be as simple as possible. On obtaining access to the viewdata computer, the user is presented with the first "routing page" which gives a choice of up to ten options. One is selected by pressing the appropriate digit on the keypad (which also contains # and * for control purposes) and so on until the required information is reached on an "end page". In addition to traversing the tree to obtain the required information, it is possible to obtain pages directly if these numbers are known by the user.

The system is based on an extended ISO7 character set allowing the use of colour (red, green, yellow, blue, cyan, magenta and white) and a relatively simple form of graphics.

The British Post Office undertook a Pilot Trial followed by a restricted Test Service in 1978. The full Public Service started in late 1979 based on a number of GEC 4082 minicomputers. The users access "Retrieval Centres", connected via 2400 bps leased lines to a single "Update

Centre". The organisations providing the data (the *Information Providers*) edit that information on the Update Centre computer whence it is transmitted to each Retrieval Centre within a few minutes. At the beginning of the Public Service, the entire database was replicated in each centre but it is proposed that each centre should contain a local database in addition to the national one.

The system can also be used to transmit messages between users and a facility has already been implemented specifically to allow deaf people to communicate over telephone lines using viewdata.

Associated with and compatible with viewdata (which is an interactive service) are the broadcast Teletext services. In an ordinary television transmission, there is a period to allow field flyback in receivers and some of the lines transmitted in this period (which do not appear on the television screen) are already used for such purposes as testing. Teletext uses two such lines for transmitting data and about 100 separate frames can be transmitted. Wide-band services are also being developed where all the lines of the transmission are used for digital data.

The frames in Teletext are transmitted cyclically. Because it is not interactive, it is insensitive to its load factor, whereas this can be critical in non-broadcast systems.

Other related systems are being developed. In particular, the Canadian PTT is developing a system (*Telidon*) which does not transmit the graphical data as a sequence of characters (*alpha-mosaic*) but rather as a description of the picture to be transmitted.

To give an example of the use of viewdata, consider a user who wishes to known the composition of the House of Commons. The user finds (probably by means of a hard-copy index, although it is possible to traverse the tree from the root) that frame 500 contains information on Government. On keying *500 # he obtains a frame which invites him to key in choices:

    0.  Parliament
    1.  Guide to Government Services
    2.  Central Film Library
    3.  Legal Aid and Advice

The choice is obviously zero and, on keying this, another routing page (50000) is obtained. He then continues down the tree by keying 2 then 1, finally obtaining the "end page" 500021 which contains the required information.

Viewdata is not an information retrieval database system but should perhaps best be regarded as a new publishing medium with the significant advantage over conventional media of immediacy of information.

1. Fedida, S., "Viewdata: An Interactive Information Service for the General Public", *Proc.* EUROCOMP, 262–282, 1975.
2. Stokes, A.V., "Viewdata: A Public Information Utility" (2nd edition), Input Two-Nine Ltd., 1980.

**VIRTUAL ADDRESS:** An *address* in *virtual memory*.

**VIRTUAL MEMORY:** A technique for managing computer memory whereby a user writes his program using *virtual addresses*, within a given (usually large) range and these are then mapped by the hardware into real addresses. An immediate extension of this concept is the *one level store* whereby the backing storage is considered part of the virtual address space and, whenever a location is referenced which is on backing store, data is swapped between backing storage and main storage. The data is split up into units which are often known as *pages*, although, when these may be of different sizes, the word *segment* is often used.

**VIRTUAL STORAGE:** A synonym for *virtual memory*.

**VISICALC:** A package, available on the Apple computer, which enables the user to tabulate data and perform calculations on the various entries.

**VISUAL DISPLAY UNIT:** An I/O device consisting of a *keyboard* and a screen (there are many technologies used for the screen, but the most common is a cathode ray tube). It has the same facilities as a Teletype or similar terminal with the added advantages that it is quieter and, depending n the computer on which it is used, faster – quite often, operating at speeds of 960 characters per second. It has the obvious disadvantage that it does not produce *hard-copy* output, although a number of VDUs do include a small unit which allows a copy to be taken of the current screen contents. More sophisticated VDUs include such features as *cursor addressing* and, by the provision of storage within the terminal, local editing facilities.

**VLSI:** An acronym for *very large scale integration*.

**VM:** An acronym for *virtual memory*.

**VME:** An acronym for *Virtual Memory Environment*, an operating system produced by ICL for use on its 2900 series of computers.

**VOICE FREQUENCY:** A frequency which falls in the range generated by the human voice, about 300 to 3000 Hz.

**VOICE GRADE:** Applied to any transmission medium, particularly telephone lines, it refers to those which are capable of transmitting voice signals.

**VOICE OUTPUT:** The technique of producing computer output in the form similar to that of a human voice, particularly useful in some factory environments, when responses have to be transmitted over a telephone.

**VOICE RECOGNITION:** The techniques associated with voice input to a computer, whereby the computer recognises what is being said. This is very simple when a small range (say, 16 or 32) of words is used and *boards* can be bought for many *home computers* allowing this restricted form of voice recognition. However, the recognition of a large vocabulary and sentences is extremely complex.

**VOLATILE:** An adjective applied to memory which loses its data when power is no longer supplied. Current semiconductor memory is volatile and, if it is vital that data be maintained in the event of a power failure, back-up power supplies such as batteries must be supplied.

**VOLUME:** A physical unit of storage accessible to a read/write mechanism, such as a disk pack or a magnetic tape.

**VON NEUMANN MACHINE:** A computer based on concepts expounded by John von Neumann, in particular, the program is stored within the machine and executed under the control of a sequence register (contrast with *data flow machines*).

**VRC:** An acronym for *vertical redundancy check*.

**VS:** An abbreviation for *virtual system*.

**VTOC:** An acronym for *volume table of contents*, a listing of the contents of a (disk) directory.

# W

**WAIT:** To halt temporarily until the occurrence of a specified event.

**WAIT STATE:** The condition in which a process is temporarily halted pending the occurrence of a specified event.

**WAFER:** A thin disk of silicon onto which *integrated circuits* are etched, then the wafer is cut up into a number of individual ICs, then called "chips".

**WAN:** An abbreviation for *wide area network*.

**WARM START:** A restart of a computer system in which information about currently executing jobs (and those awaiting execution) is retained.

**WATFOR:** An acronym for *Waterloo FORTRAN*, a version of FORTRAN developed at the University of Waterloo (Ontario, Canada) which operates in *compile and go* mode and gives very high throughput.

**WATFIV:** A successor to *WATFOR*.

**WATS:** An acronym for *Wide Area Telephone Service*, a telephone service provided in the USA.

**WELL:** Storage (primary or secondary) reserved as input/output buffers.

**WHO-ARE-YOU:** A control character which requests a telecommunications device to identify itself (usually by means of an *answerback drum*) in order to provide security. It is usually abbreviated as *WRU*.

**WIDE AREA NETWORK:** A name fairly recently introduced (in order to distinguish such a network from a *local area network*) to describe a network which spans a large geographic area, such as an entire continent (e.g. *ARPANET*). Such a network is likely to use high-bandwidth (e.g. 50 Kbps) communication lines but these bandwidths are orders of magnitude lower than those available in local area networks; conversely, the distances spanned are orders of magnitude greater and Metcalfe made the interesting observation that the product of distance and bandwidth is constant irrespective of the type of network.

**WIDEBAND:** An adjective pertaining to communication lines which have a high capacity, for example, 50 Kbps.

**WIENER:** Norbert Wiener (1894–1964) was concerned with the theory of automata and founded the science of cybernetics.

**WINCHESTER:** Originally, IBM's code name for a series of *hard disk* products in the early 1970s. The term is now used generally to mean a high density non-removable *hard disk*, particularly the 8'' versions which started to come onto the market in 1979 and 5.25'' "mini-disks" which became available in 1981. These are used with microcomputers and occupy the same space as *floppy disk* drives.

**WORD:** A set of bits which are treated as a single unit and stored in one location. Often the basic address unit of the computer.

**WORD LENGTH:** The number of bits in a *word*.

**WORD ORIENTED:** Pertaining to a computer system where the basic address unit is a *word*.

**WORD PROCESSOR:** A computer system (usually consisting of a memory-mapped, or cursor-addressable, VDU, a microcomputer and a high-quality printer) which is used for generating documents and performing related functions. It differs from a standard microcomputer in that it is dedicated to the particular function of "word-processing" and that the keyboard has many extra keys to perform specific functions, such as deleting a paragraph.

**WORK AREA:** An area of storage (usually main memory), used for temporary results.

**WORK FILE:** A *file* used to contain temporary (intermediate) results and which is usually destroyed at the end of the *job* which created it.

**WORKING STORAGE:** A synonym for *work area*.

**WORKSPACE:** A synonym for *work area*.

**WRITE:** To transfer data to a storage device, for example, main memory or disk. If data is transferred to an output medium, this process is usually known as "printing".

**WRITE HEAD:** The part of a storage device which *writes* data onto a magnetic storage medium such as a disk.

**WRITE INHIBIT:** Either used as a verb denoting the action of preventing data being written to storage or to the state of that storage after the action has been taken.

**WRITE INHIBIT RING:** A ring (usually plastic) which is attached to a magnetic tape reel to prevent data being written to that tape.

**WRITE PERMIT:** Either used as a verb denoting the action of allowing data to be written to storage or the state of that storage after the action has been taken.

**WRITE PERMIT RING:** A ring (usually plastic) which is attached to a magnetic tape reel to allow data to be written to that tape.

**WRITE PROTECT:** A synonym for *write inhibit*.

**WRITE PROTECT RING:** A synonym for *write inhibit ring*.

**WRITE RING:** A synonym for *write permit ring*.

**WRITE TIME:** The time required to write data to some storage medium.

**WRU:** See *who-are-you*.

# X

**XENIX:** A commercially available version of *Unix*.

**XEROGRAPHY:** A means of copying images by means of electrostatic charges on a drum. The technique can be used for high-speed printers, often capable of printing a page at a time (*page printers*).

**X-OFF:** An abbreviation for *transmitter off*.

**X-ON:** An abbreviation for *transmitter on*.

**XOR:** An acronym for *exclusive or*.

**X-POSITION:** The second row of punch positions on a *punched card*, also known as the "eleven position".

**X-PUNCH:** A hole punched in the *X-position* of a punched card. If this hole is punched alone, it usually indicates the "−" character.

**X SERIES:** A series of CCITT recommendations concerned with data transmission over public data networks.

# Y

**Y-POSITION:** The top row of a *punched card*, also known as "row 12".

**Y-PUNCH:** A hole punched in the *Y-position* of a punched card. If punched alone, it usually denotes the character "+".

# Z

**Z-80:** A *cpu* developed by Zilog Corporation which forms the basis of many microcomputers, such as the *TRS-80*.

**Z-80 SOFTCARD:** See *softcard*.

**ZAP:** A semi-slang term used to denote a small amendment, often in a manner which ignores all software protection facilities. IBM have a system utility called "super-zap" (IMASPZAP) which allows the user to patch any location on disk or in memory. The term is also sometimes used to denote destructive overwriting of data.

**ZAP-SENSE MULTIPLE ACCESS:** A term coined by Kleinrock for the technique also known as "listen-while-talk" in systems (particularly packet-radio and local area networks) which employ contention. In order to reduce overheads, a station listens to the transmission medium while it is transmitting and, if it detects another station also transmitting, it immediately aborts transmission.

**ZERO:** Nothing. The term is used for the concept of zero, the numeral representing zero or the respresentation of it within a binary computer. In *ones complement* representation, there are two values of zero, one using all binary zeros (known as "plus zero") and one using all binary ones ("minus zero").

**ZERO ADDRESS:** A descriptor applied to instruction formats which do not require an operand address, either because the instruction requires no operands or because the address is implicit (for example, in instructions which operate on a *stack*).

**ZERO FILL:** To place a repesentation of zero in the specified locations, usually in order to extend a field to a given boundary.

**ZERO FLAG:** A *flip-flop* which takes the value 1 if the result of the given operation is zero. This is used in comparison operations particularly.

**ZERO ROW:** The third row from the top on a *punched card*. If this position alone is punched, it represents zero.

**ZERO SUPPRESSION:** The inhibition of *leading zeros* during a printing operation (and, often, their replacement by leading spaces).

**ZONE:** The area on a punched card consisting of the first, second or third rows. By derivation, it is also used to mean the four high-order bits in a byte when *zoned decimal* representation is used.

**ZONE BITS:** See *zone*.

**ZONE PUNCH:** A hole punched in the *zone* positions of a punched card, i.e. the first, second or third rows.

**ZONED DECIMAL:** A means of representing decimal numbers in a binary computer (particularly in the IBM System/370 series). Each byte contains a single decimal digit, occupying the low-order four bits, the upper four bits being the *zone*, except in the case of the rightmost byte of the field, in which case, the upper four bits represent the sign.

# Appendix A:
# Acronyms and Abbreviations

| | |
|---|---|
| **AAAS** | American Association for the Advancement of Science |
| **ABC** | Atansoff-Berry Computer |
| **ABEND** | Abnormal End |
| **ABL** | Atlas Basic Language |
| **ACARD** | Advisory Council for Applied Research and Development |
| **ACC** | Accumulator |
| **ACE** | Automatic Computing Engine |
| **ACK** | Acknowledgement |
| **ACM** | Association for Computing Machinery |
| **ACTP** | Advanced Computer Technology Project |
| **ACU** | Automatic Call Unit |
| **A/D** | Analogue to Digital |
| **ADC** | Analogue-to-Digital Converter |
| **ADCCP** | Advanced Data Communication Control Procedure |
| **ADP** | Automatic Data Processing |
| **AEC** | Atomic Energy Commission |
| **AFIPS** | American Federation of Information Processing Societies |
| **AFNOR** | Association Française de Normalisation |
| **AGRIS** | Agricultural Information System |
| **ALGOL** | Algorithmic Language |
| **ALU** | Arithmetic/Logical Unit |
| **AM** | Amplitude Modulation |
| **AMA** | American Management Association |
| **ANSI** | American National Standards Institute |
| **ANTIOPE** | l'Acquisition Numérique et Télévisualisation d'Images Organisée en Pages d'Écriture |
| **APL** | A Programming Language |
| **APSE** | Ada Programming Support Environment |
| **ART** | Automatic Programming Tool |
| **ARPA** | Advanced Research Projects Agency (of US Department of Defense) |
| **ARQ** | Automatic Request for Repetition |
| **ASA** | American Standards Association (now ANSI) |
| **ASCC** | Automatic Sequence Controlled Calculator |
| **ASCII** | American Standard Code for Information Interchange |

| ASLIB | Association of Special Libraries and Information Bureaux |
| ASR | Automatic Send/Receive (terminal) |
| ASSASSIN | A System for Storage And Subsequent Selection of Information |
| ATDM | Asynchronous Time Division Multiplexing |
| ATS | Administrative Terminal System |
| AUTODIN | AUTOmatic DIgital Network (US Department of Defense) |
| AVL | Adelson-Velskii Landis |
| | |
| BAL | Basic Assembler Language |
| BASIC | Beginners' All-Purpose Symbolic Instruction Code |
| BASIS | British Airways' Staff Information System |
| BATS | Basic Additional Teleprocessing Support |
| BCC | Block Control Character |
| BCD | Binary Coded Decimal |
| BCPL | Basic CPL |
| BCS | British Computer Society |
| BDAM | Basic Data Access Method |
| BDOS | Basic Disk Operating System |
| BETA | Business Equipment Trade Association |
| BIM | British Institute of Management |
| BINAC | Binary Automatic Computer |
| BIOS | Basic Input-Output System |
| BISAM | Basic Indexed Sequential Access Method |
| Bit | Binary Digit |
| BJT | Bipolar Junction Transistor |
| BLAISE | British Library Automated Information Service |
| BLISS | Basic Language for Implementing Systems Software |
| BNF | (1) Backus-Naur Form |
| | (2) Backus Normal Form |
| BOMP | Bill of Material and Requirement Planning |
| BOSS | Burroughs Operational System Simulator |
| BPAM | Basic Partitioned Access Method |
| bpi | Bits per inch (magnetic tape density) |
| BPO | British Post Office |
| bps | Bits per second |
| BS | (1) British Standard |
| | (2) Backspace |
| BSAM | Basic Sequential Access Method |
| BSC | Binary Synchronous Communication |
| BSI | British Standards Institution |

| | |
|---|---|
| **BSN** | Back-end Storage Network |
| **BT** | British Telecom |
| **BTAM** | Basic Telecommunications Access Method |
| **CAD** | Computer Aided Design |
| **CADC** | Computer Aided Design Centre (UK) |
| **CAFS** | Content Addressable File Store |
| **CAI** | Computer Aided Instruction |
| **CAL** | Computer Aided Learning |
| **CAM** | (1) Computer Aided Manufacturing |
| | (2) Content Addressable Memory |
| **CAMAC** | Computer Automated Measurement and Control |
| **CAN** | Cancel |
| **CAPTAINS** | Character and Pattern Telephone Access Information System |
| **CAR** | Channel Address Register |
| **CAW** | Channel Address Word |
| **CBI** | Confederation of British Industry |
| **CBIOS** | Customised BIOS |
| **CBL** | Computer Based Learning |
| **CBX** | Computer-Controlled Branch Exchange |
| **CCA** | (1) Computer Corporation of America |
| | (2) Central Computer Agency (UK) |
| **CCB** | Channel Control Block |
| **CCD** | Charge Coupled Device |
| **CCETT** | Centre Commun d'Études de Télévision et Télécommunications |
| **CCITT** | Comité Consultatif Internationale Télégraphique et Téléphonique |
| **CCP** | Console Command Processor |
| **CCW** | Channel Command Word |
| **CDC** | Control Data Corporation |
| **CE** | Customer Engineering |
| **CEPT** | Conférence Européenne des Administration des Postes et de Télécommunications |
| **CERN** | Centre Européenne pour la Recherche Nucléaire |
| **CHILL** | CCITT High-Level Language |
| **CHKPT** | Checkpoint |
| **CICS** | Customer Information Control System |
| **CIDST** | Committee for Information and Documentation on Science and Technology |
| **CII** | Compagnie Internationale pour l'Informatique |
| **CIU** | Computer Interface Unit |

| | |
|---|---|
| **CLK** | Clock |
| **CMI** | Computer Managed Instruction |
| **CMOS** | Complementary Metal Oxide Semiconductor |
| **CMS** | (1)  Cambridge Monitor System |
| | (2)  Conversational Monitor System |
| **COBOL** | Common Business Oriented Language |
| **CODASYL** | Conference on Data Systems Languages |
| **COGO** | Co-ordinate Geometry |
| **COM** | Computer Output to Microfilm |
| **COMSAT** | Communications Satellite |
| **COSBA** | Computer Services and Bureaux Association |
| **CPL** | Combined Programming Language |
| **CP/M** | Control Program for Microprocessors |
| **cps** | (1)  Characters per Second |
| | (2)  Cycles per second |
| **cpu** | Central Processor Unit |
| **CR** | Carriage Return |
| **CRAM** | Card Random Access Method |
| **CRC** | Cyclic Redundancy Check |
| **CRJE** | Conversational Remote Job Entry |
| **CRO** | Cathode Ray Oscilloscope |
| **CRT** | Cathode Ray Tube |
| **CSECT** | Control Section |
| **CSIRO** | Commonwealth Scientific and Industrial Research Organisation |
| **CSMA** | Carrier-Sense Multiple Access |
| **CSMA-CD** | Carrier-Sense Multiple Access – Collision Detection |
| **CSMP** | Continuous System Modelling Program |
| **CSW** | Channel Status Word |
| **CTNE** | Compania Telefonica Nacional de España (Spanish PTT) |
| **CTS** | Clear to send |
| **CUG** | Closed User Group |
| | |
| **D/A** | Digital to Analogue |
| **DAC** | Digital-to-Analog(ue) Converter |
| **DAIR** | Dynamic Allocation Interface Routine |
| **DAP** | Distributed Array Processor |
| **DASD** | Direct Access Storage Device |
| **dB** | Decibel |
| **DBMS** | Data Base Management System |
| **DC** | Device Control |
| **DCA** | Defense Communications Agency (USA) |

| | |
|---|---|
| **DCB** | Data Control Block |
| **DCD** | Data Carrier Detect |
| **DCE** | Data-Circuit Terminating Equipment |
| **DD** | Data Definition |
| **DDA** | Digital Differential Analyser |
| **DDC** | Direct Digital Control |
| **DDCMP** | Digital Data Communication Message Protocol |
| **DDD** | Direct Distance Dialling |
| **DDL** | Data Description Language |
| **DDT** | Dynamic Debugging Tool |
| **DEB** | Data Extension Block |
| **DEC** | Digital Equipment Corporation |
| **DECUS** | Digital Equipment Corporation Users' Society |
| **DEL** | Delete |
| **DEUCE** | Digital Electronic Universal Calculating Engine |
| **DIANE** | Direct Information Access Network – Europe |
| **DIL** | Dual-in-Line |
| **DIP** | Dual-in-Line Package |
| **DLE** | Data Link Escape |
| **DMA** | Direct Memory Access |
| **DMS** | Data Management System |
| **DNA** | Digital Network Architecture |
| **DNC** | Direct Numerical Control |
| **DOS** | Disk Operating System |
| **DPM** | Data Processing Manager |
| **DPMA** | Data Processing Management Association |
| **DPS** | Data Processing Standards |
| **DSE** | Data Switching Exchange |
| **DSECT** | Dummy Section |
| **DSM** | Digital Standard MUMPS |
| **DSN** | Data Set Name |
| **DTE** | Data Terminal Equipment |
| **DTL** | Diode Transistor Logic |
| **DTMF** | Dual Tone Multifrequency |
| **DTSS** | Dartmouth Time Sharing System |
| | |
| **EAM** | Electronic Accounting Machine |
| **EAN** | European Article Number |
| **EAPROM** | Electrically-Alterable Programmable Read-Only Memory |
| **EAROM** | Electrically-Alterable Read Only Memory |
| **EBCDIC** | Extended Binary Coded Decimal Interchange Code |
| **ECAP** | Electronic Circuit Analysis Program |

| | |
|---|---|
| **ECB** | Event Control Block |
| **ECE** | Economic Commission for Europe (UN) |
| **ECL** | Emitter coupled logic |
| **ECMA** | European Computer Manufacturers' Association |
| **EDP** | Electronic Data Processing |
| **EDS** | Exchangeable Disk Store |
| **EDSAC** | Electronic Delayed-Storage Automatic Computer |
| **EDUCOM** | Educational Communications (USA) |
| **EDVAC** | Electronic Discrete Variable Automatic Computer |
| **EEC** | European Economic Community |
| **EEPROM** | Electrically Erasable Programmable Read-Only Memory |
| **EFTS** | Eletronic Funds Transfer Service |
| **EIA** | Electronic Industries Association |
| **EIN** | European Informatics Network |
| **EM** | End of Medium |
| **ENIAC** | Electronic Numerical Integrator and Calculator |
| **ENQ** | Enquiry |
| **EOB** | End Of Block |
| **EOF** | End Of File |
| **EOJ** | End Of Job |
| **EOM** | End Of Message |
| **EOR** | End Of Record |
| **EOT** | (1) End Of Transmission |
| | (2) End Of Tape |
| **EOV** | End Of Volume |
| **EPROM** | Erasable Programmable Read Only Memory |
| **EPSS** | Experimental Packet Switched Network (BPO) |
| **EQ** | Equal to |
| **ESC** | Escape |
| **ETB** | End of Transmission Block |
| **ETX** | End of text |
| **EXTRN** | External (reference) |
| | |
| **FAMOS** | Floating Gate Avalanche Injection MOS |
| **FAX** | Facsimile |
| **FCB** | File Control Block |
| **FCC** | Federal Communications Commission |
| **FD(X)** | Full Duplex |
| **FDM** | Frequency Division Multiplexing |
| **FEP** | Front End Processor |
| **FET** | Field Effect Transistor |
| **FF** | Form Feed |

| | |
|---|---|
| **FFT** | Fast Fourier Transform |
| **FIFO** | First-in, first-out |
| **FJCC** | Fall Joint Computer Conference (AFIPS) |
| **FLUB** | First Language Under Bootstrap |
| **FM** | (1) Frequency Modulation |
| | (2) Functional Memory |
| **FORMAC** | Formula Manipulation Compiler |
| **FORTRAN** | FORmula TRANslator |
| **FPLA** | Field Programmable Logic Array |
| **FRED** | Frantically Rapid Electronic Device |
| **FS** | File Separator |
| **FSK** | Frequency Shift Keying |
| **FTP** | File Transfer Protocol |
| | |
| **GE** | (1) General Electric (USA) |
| | (2) Greater than or equal to |
| **GEC** | General Electric Company (UK) |
| **GECOS** | General Electric Comprehensive Operating System |
| **GEIS** | General Electric Information Service |
| **GENESYS** | General Engineering System |
| **GEORGE** | General Organisational Environment |
| **GIGO** | Garbage In, Garbage Out |
| **GPSS** | General Purpose Systems Simulator |
| **GS** | Group Separator |
| **GSC** | Group Switching Exchange |
| **GT** | Greater than |
| **GUTS** | Gothenberg University Terminal System |
| | |
| **HASP** | Houston Automatic Spooling Priority system |
| **HD(X)** | Half Duplex |
| **HDLC** | High-Level Data Link Control |
| **HIS** | Honeywell Information Systems |
| **HMOS** | High-speed Metal-Oxide Semiconductor |
| **HPIB** | Hewlett-Packard Interface Bus |
| **HT** | Horizontal Tabulation |
| **Hz** | Hertz (cycles/second) |
| | |
| **IAn** | International Alphabet n |
| **IAL** | International Algebraic Language |
| **IBM** | International Business Machines |
| **IC** | Integrated Circuit |
| **ICE** | In-Circuit Emulator |
| **ICES** | Integrated Civil Engineering System |

| | |
|---|---|
| **ICL** | International Computers Ltd. (UK) |
| **IDP** | Integrated Data Processing |
| **IDPM** | Institute of Data Processing Management (UK) |
| **IEE** | Institution of Electrical Engineers (UK) |
| **IEEE** | Institute of Electrical and Electronics Engineers (USA) |
| **IFIP** | International Federation for Information Processing |
| **IGFET** | Insulated Gate Field Effect Transistor |
| **IIL** | Isoplanar Injection Logic |
| **ILLIAC** | Illinois Automatic Computer |
| **IMIS** | Integrated Management Information System |
| **IMP** | Interface Message Processor (ARPANET) |
| **IMS** | Information Management System |
| **INRIA** | Institut National de Recherche en Informatique et en Automatique |
| **INWG** | International Network Working Group |
| **IO (I/O)** | Input-Output |
| **IOCS** | Input-Output Control System |
| **IOR** | Inclusive OR |
| **IP** | Information Provider |
| **IPL** | (1) Information Processing Language |
| | (2) Initial Program Load |
| **ips** | Inches per second |
| **IPSS** | International Packet Switched Service |
| **IR** | Information Retrieval |
| **IRG** | Inter-Record Gap |
| **IRIA** | Institut de Récherche d'Informatique et d'Automatique |
| **ISAM** | Indexed Sequential Access Method |
| **ISO** | International Standards Organisation |
| **ISR** | Information Storage and Retrieval |
| **IT** | Information Technology |
| **ITT** | International Telephone and Telegraphs |
| **ITU** | International Telecommunications Union |
| | |
| **JCL** | Job Control Language |
| **JDL** | Job Description Language |
| **JFCB** | Job File Control Block |
| **JFET** | Junction Field Effect Transistor |
| **JOHNNIAC** | John (von Neumann's) Integrator and Automatic Computer |
| **JOSS** | Johnniac Open-Shop System |
| **JOVIAL** | Jules' Own Version of IAL |

| | |
|---|---|
| **K** | Kilo- (one thousand) |
| **KB** | (1) Keyboard |
| | (2) Kilobits |
| | (3) Kilobytes |
| **KSR** | Keyboard Send/Receive |
| **KWIC** | Keyword in Context |
| **KWIT** | Keyword in Title |
| **KWOC** | Keyword out of Context |
| | |
| **LACES** | London Airport Cargo EDP System |
| **LAMSAC** | Local Authorities Management Services and Computer Committee |
| **LAN** | Local Area Network |
| **LAP** | Link Access Protocol |
| **LC** | Lower Case |
| **LCD** | Liquid Crystal Display |
| **LCN** | Local Computer Network |
| **LCS** | Large Capacity Store |
| **LE** | Less than or equal to |
| **LED** | Light Emitting Diode |
| **LEO** | Lyons' Electronic Office (UK) |
| **LF** | Line Feed |
| **LIFO** | Last-In, First-Out |
| **LISP** | List Processing (language) |
| **LPM** | Lines per minute |
| **LRC** | Longitudinal Redundancy Check |
| **LSB** | Least Significant Bit |
| **LSI** | Large-scale Integration |
| **LSQA** | Local System Queue Area |
| **LT** | Less than or equal |
| | |
| **M** | Mega- (one million) |
| **MAC** | (1) Machine Aided Cognition |
| | (2) Multi-Access Computer |
| **MANIAC** | Mechanical And Numerical Integrator and Computer |
| **MAP** | Microprocessor Applications Project |
| **MAR** | Memory Address Register |
| **MARC** | Machine Readable Catalogue |
| **MCAR** | Machine Check Analysis and Recording |
| **MCH** | Machine Check Handler |
| **MCP** | Master Control Program |
| **MDS** | Mohawk Data Systems |
| **MEDLARS** | Medical Literature Analysis and Retrieval System |

| | |
|---|---|
| **MEDLINE** | MEDLARS On-Line System |
| **MFT** | Multiprogramming with a Fixed Number of Tasks |
| **MHz** | Megahertz |
| **MICR** | Magnetic Ink Character Recognition |
| **Mil** | One thousandth of an inch |
| **MIMD** | Multiple Instruction, Multiple Data stream |
| **MIMR** | Magnetic Ink Mark Recognition |
| **MIS** | Management Information System |
| **MIT** | Massachusetts Institute of Technology |
| **MLC** | Multi-Line Controller |
| **MNOS** | Metal Nitride Oxide Semiconductor |
| **MODEM** | Modulator-Demodulator |
| **MOL** | Machine-Oriented Language |
| **MOP** | Multiple On-Line Programming |
| **MOS** | Metal Oxide Semiconductor |
| **MOSFET** | Metal Oxide Semiconductor Field Effect Transistor |
| **MPX** | Multiplex |
| **msec** | Millisecond |
| **MSB** | Most Significant Bit |
| **MSI** | Medium Scale Integration |
| **MT** | Magnetic Tape |
| **MTBF** | Mean Time Between Failure |
| **MTS** | Michigan Terminal System |
| **MTTF** | Mean Time To Failure |
| **MTTR** | Mean Time To Repair |
| **MULTICS** | Multiplexed Information and Computing Service |
| **MUMPS** | Massachusetts General Hospital Utility Multiprogramming System |
| **MUX** | Multiplex(or) |
| **MVT** | Multiprogramming with a Variable Number of Tasks |
| | |
| **NAG** | Numerical Algorithms Group |
| **NAK** | Negative Acknowledgement |
| **NAM** | Network Access Machine |
| **NBS** | National Bureau of Standards (USA) |
| **NCC** | (1) Network Control Centre |
| | (2) National Computing Centre (UK) |
| | (3) National Computing Conference (AFIPS) |
| **NCP** | Network Control Program |
| **NCR** | National Cash Register Company |
| **NE** | Not equal to |
| **NEAT** | NCR Electronic Autocoding Technique |
| **NEL** | National Engineering Laboratory |

| | |
|---|---|
| **NIH** | National Institutes of Health (USA) |
| **NL** | Newline |
| **NLM** | National Library of Medicine (USA) |
| **NMC** | Network Measurement Centre |
| **NMM** | Network Measurement Machine |
| **NOS** | Network Operating System |
| **NOVRAM** | Non-Volatile RAM |
| **NPL** | National Physical Laboratory (UK) |
| **NRZ** | Non-return to zero |
| **NRZ-C** | Non-return to zero change |
| **NRZ-I** | Non-return to zero inverted |
| **NRZ-M** | Non-return to zero mark |
| **NSA** | National Security Agency (USA) |
| **NSW** | National Software Works |
| **NTU** | Network Termination Unit |
| **NUI** | Network User Identification |
| **NUL** | Null |
| | |
| **OCR** | (1) Optical Character Recognition |
| | (2) Optical Character Reader |
| **OEM** | Original Equipment Manufacturer |
| **OLRT** | On-Line Real Time |
| **OLTEP** | On-Line Test Executive Program |
| **OLTS** | On-Line Test System |
| **OMR** | Optical Mark Recognition |
| **ONR** | Office of Naval Research (USA) |
| **ORACLE** | Optional Reception of Announcements by Coded Line Electronics |
| **OS** | Operating System |
| **OSI** | Open Systems Interconnection |
| **OSTI** | Office for Scientific and Technical Information |
| | |
| **PABX** | Private Automatic Branch Exchange |
| **PAD** | Packet Assembly/Disassembly |
| **PAM** | Pulse Amplitude Modulation |
| **PC** | Program Counter |
| **PCB** | Printed Circuit Board |
| **PCM** | (1) Pulse Code Modulation |
| | (2) Plug Compatible Manufacturer |
| **PCP** | Primary Control Program |
| **PDM** | Pulse Duration Modulation |
| **PDP** | Programmed Data Processor |
| **PDS** | Partitioned Data Set |

| | |
|---|---|
| **PEPE** | Parallel Elements of Processing Ensemble |
| **PERT** | Program Evaluation and Review Technique |
| **PET** | Personal Electronic Transactor |
| **PI** | Program(med) Interrupt |
| **PIO** | Programmed Input/Output |
| **PIP** | Peripheral Interchange Program |
| **PLA** | Programmable Logic Array |
| **PL/1** | Programming Language 1 |
| **PLATO** | Programmed Logic for Automatic Teaching Operations |
| **PM** | (1) Preventive Maintenance |
| | (2) Phase Modulation |
| | (3) Post Mortem |
| **PMOS** | P-Channel Metal Oxide Semiconductor |
| **PoS** | Point of Sale |
| **PP** | Peripheral Processor |
| **PPM** | Pulse Position Modulation |
| **PROM** | Programmable Read Only Memory |
| **pS** | Picosecond |
| **PSE** | Packet Switching Exchange |
| **PSN** | Public Switched Network |
| **PSS** | Packet Switching Service (UK) |
| **PSTN** | Public Switched Telephone Network |
| **PSW** | Program Status Word |
| **PT** | Paper tape |
| **PTT** | Post, Telegraph and Telephone Administration |
| **PUFFT** | Purdue University Fast FORTRAN |
| **PWM** | Pulse Width Modulation |
| | |
| **QCB** | Queue Control Block |
| **QED** | Quick Editor |
| **QISAM** | Queued Indexed Sequential Access Method |
| **QSAM** | Queued Sequential Access Method |
| **QTAM** | Queued Telecommunications Access Method |
| | |
| **RAM** | Random Access Memory |
| **RBE** | Remote Batch Entry |
| **RCA** | Radio Corporation of America |
| **RFC** | (1) Request for Comments (ARPANET) |
| | (2) Request for Connection (ARPANET) |
| **RITA** | Rand Intelligent Terminal Agent |
| **RJE** | Remote Job Entry |
| **RO** | Read Only |
| **ROM** | Read Only Memory |

| | |
|---|---|
| **RPG** | Report Program Generator |
| **RRE** | Royal Radar Establishment |
| **RS** | Record Separator |
| **RSEXEC** | Resource Sharing Executive |
| **RTOS** | Real Time Operating System |
| **RTS** | Request to Send |
| **RTT** | Régie des Télégraphs et des Téléphones (Belgian PTT) |
| **R/W** | Read/Write |
| **RWM** | Read-Write Memory |
| | |
| **SBS** | Satellite Business Systems |
| **SCICON** | Scientific Control Systems |
| **SCR** | (1)  Sequence Control Register |
| | (2)  Silicon Controlled Rectifier |
| **SDI** | Selective Dissemination of Information |
| **SDLC** | Synchronous Data Link Control |
| **SDM** | Space Division Multiplexing |
| **SEAC** | Standards Eastern Automatic Computer |
| **SERC** | Science and Engineering Research Council |
| **SI** | Shift In |
| **SID** | Symbolic Instruction Debugger |
| **SIG** | Special Interest Group |
| **SIL** | Systems Implementation Language |
| **SIR** | Selective Information Retrieval |
| **SIMD** | Single Instruction stream, Multiple Data stream |
| **SISD** | Single Instruction stream, Single Data stream |
| **SITA** | Société Internationale de Télécommunications Aéronautiques |
| **SJCC** | Spring Joint Computer Conference (AFIPS) |
| **SLANG** | Systems Language |
| **SMALL** | Small Machine Algol-Like Language |
| **SMF** | System Management Facilities |
| **SNA** | Systems Network Architecture |
| **SO** | Shift Out |
| **SOH** | Start of Header |
| **SOM** | Start of Message |
| **SOS** | (1)  Son of Stopgap |
| | (2)  Silicon on Sapphire |
| **SP** | Space |
| **SRC** | Science Research Council |
| **SRI** | Stanford Research Institute |
| **STC** | Standard Telephone and Cables |
| **STD** | Subscriber Trunk Dialling |

| | |
|---|---|
| **STEP** | Supervisory Tape Executive Program |
| **STX** | Start of Text |
| **SUB** | Substitute |
| **SVC** | Supervisor Call |
| **SWIFT** | Society for Worldwide Interbank Financial Telecommunication |
| **SWUNET** | South West Universities Network (UK) |
| **SYN** | Synchronous Idle |
| | |
| **TASI** | Time Assignment Speech Interpolation |
| **TCAM** | Telecommunications Access Method |
| **TCB** | Task Control Block |
| **TCP** | Transmission Control Program |
| **TDM** | Time Division Multiplexing |
| **TDMA** | Time Division Multiple Access |
| **TIP** | Terminal Interface Message Processor (ARPANET) |
| **ToD** | Time of Day |
| **TPA** | Transient Program Area |
| **TSO** | Time Sharing Option |
| **TTL** | Transistor-Transistor Logic |
| **TTY** | Teletypewriter |
| **TWX** | Teletypewriter Exchange Service |
| | |
| **UADS** | User Attribute Data Set |
| **UART** | Universal Asynchronous Receiver and Transmitter |
| **UC** | Upper Case |
| **UCLA** | University of California at Los Angeles |
| **UCS** | Universal Character Set |
| **UJT** | UniJunction Transistor |
| **ULA** | Uncommitted Logic Array |
| **UNIVAC** | Universal Automatic Computer |
| **US** | Unit Separator |
| **USART** | Universal Synchronous/Asynchronous Receiver and Transmitter |
| **UUO** | Unimplemented User Operation |
| | |
| **VAN** | Value Added Network |
| **VDL** | Vienna Definition Language |
| **VDU** | (1) Visual Display Unit |
| | (2) Video Display Unit |
| **VLSI** | Very Large Scale Integration |
| **VM** | Virtual Memory |
| **VME** | Virtual Machine Environment |

| | |
|---|---|
| **VRC** | (1) Visible Record Computer |
| | (2) Vertical Redundancy Check |
| **VS** | Virtual Storage |
| **VSAM** | Virtual Sequential Access Method |
| **VSS** | Virtual Storage System |
| **VT** | Vertical Tabulation |
| **VTAM** | Virtual Telecommunications Access Method |
| **VTOC** | Volume Table of Contents |
| **VTP** | Virtual Terminal Protocol |
| | |
| **WAN** | Wide-Area Network |
| **WATFOR** | (University of) Waterloo FORTRAN |
| **WATS** | Wide Area Telephone Service |
| **WRU** | Who are you (character) |
| **WXTRN** | Weak External Reference |
| | |
| **X-OFF** | Transmitter Off |
| **X-ON** | Transmitter On |
| **XDS** | Xerox Data Systems |
| **XMT** | Transmit |
| **XOR** | Exclusive OR |
| | |
| **ZIF** | Zero Insertion Force |

# Appendix B:
# ASCII Character Set

|    | 0   | 1   | 2   | 3   | 4   | 5   | 6   | 7   |
|----|-----|-----|-----|-----|-----|-----|-----|-----|
| 0  | NUL | SOH | STX | ETX | EOT | ENQ | ACK | BEL |
| 1  | BS  | HT  | LF  | VT  | FF  | CR  | SO  | SI  |
| 2  | DLE | DC1 | DC2 | DC3 | DC4 | NAK | SYN | ETB |
| 3  | CAN | EM  | SUB | ESC | FS  | GS  | RS  | US  |
| 4  | SP  | !   | ''  | #   | $   | %   | &   | '   |
| 5  | (   | )   | *   | +   | ,   | −   | .   | /   |
| 6  | 0   | 1   | 2   | 3   | 4   | 5   | 6   | 7   |
| 7  | 8   | 9   | :   | ;   | <   | =   | >   | ?   |
| 10 | @   | A   | B   | C   | D   | E   | F   | G   |
| 11 | H   | I   | J   | K   | L   | M   | N   | O   |
| 12 | P   | Q   | R   | S   | T   | U   | V   | W   |
| 13 | X   | Y   | Z   | [   | \   | ]   | ^   | ___ |
| 14 | `   | a   | b   | c   | d   | e   | f   | g   |
| 15 | h   | i   | j   | k   | l   | m   | n   | o   |
| 16 | p   | q   | r   | s   | t   | u   | v   | w   |
| 17 | x   | y   | z   | {   | \|  | }   | ~   | DEL |

# Appendix C:
# EBCDIC Character Set

|   | 0 | 1 | 2 | 3 | 4 | 5 | 6 | 7 | 8 | 9 | A | B | C | D | E | F |
|---|---|---|---|---|---|---|---|---|---|---|---|---|---|---|---|---|
| 0 | NUL | SOH | STX | ETX | PF | HT | LC | DEL | | | SMM | VT | FF | CR | SO | SI |
| 1 | DLE | DC1 | DC2 | TM | RES | NL | BS | IL | CAN | EM | CC | CU1 | IFS | IGS | IRS | IUS |
| 2 | DS | SOS | FS | | BYP | LF | ETB | ESC | | | SM | CU2 | | ENQ | ACK | BEL |
| 3 | | | SYN | | PN | RS | UC | EOT | | | | CU3 | DC4 | NAK | | SUB |
| 4 | SP | | | | | | | | | | ¢ | . | < | ( | + | \| |
| 5 | & | | | | | | | | | | ! | $ | * | ) | ; | ¬ |
| 6 | - | / | | | | | | | | | \| | , | % | _ | > | ? |
| 7 | | | | | | | | | | | ` | : | # | @ | ' | = | " |
| 8 | | a | b | c | d | e | f | g | h | i | | | | | | |
| 9 | | j | k | l | m | n | o | p | q | r | | | | | | |
| A | | ~ | s | t | u | v | w | x | y | z | | | | | | |
| B | | | | | | | | | | | | | | | | |
| C | { | A | B | C | D | E | F | G | H | I | | | | | | |
| D | } | J | K | L | M | N | O | P | Q | R | | | | | | |
| E | \ | | S | T | U | V | W | X | Y | Z | | | | | | |
| F | 0 | 1 | 2 | 3 | 4 | 5 | 6 | 7 | 8 | 9 | | | | | | |